"I often tell guests, or curious visitors, at our monastery that one of the things a monastery is good for is that it puts on display, as an evangelizing word, the ingredients of any serious Christian life. Peters's book affirms this in systematic detail, linking key texts from the tradition of monastic life with an invitation to contemporary Christians to let those insights mark them. It crosses denominational divides as it does so. This book meets the contemporary interest in monasticism, an ancient tradition still very much alive."

—**Jeremy Driscoll, OSB**, Abbot of Mount Angel Abbey

"This is essential reading for anyone interested in the roots of monasticism and why monastic life still matters today. *The Monkhood of All Believers* could not be more timely, since for the first time in history there are now more lay associates of monasteries—men and women, Catholic and Protestant, married and single, working and retired—than there are monks and sisters living within monastery walls. They are among the growing number of believers Peters identifies as interior monks. Just as Martin Luther spoke of the priesthood of all believers, Peters sees the definition of 'monk' and 'monastic' expanding and adapting into the monkhood of all believers, reflecting the spiritual reality of the twenty-first century."

—**Judith Valente**, author of *How to Live: What the Rule of St. Benedict Teaches Us about Happiness, Meaning, and Community* and *The Art of Pausing: Meditations for the Overworked and Overwhelmed*

"This reader-friendly book is an exploration on the meaning of monk from various early and medieval sources. A monk is simply one who is single-mindedly devoted to God despite being associated with institutional forms. By drawing upon medieval sources such as Robert de Sorbon's sermon on marriage and *The Abbey of the Holy Ghost*, and the more recent Russian Orthodox writer Paul Evdokimov, as well as Luther's and Calvin's critiques of the institutions of monasticism of their day, Peters presents an 'ecumenical theology of monasticism.' His work, which makes room for Protestants to live out an interior monasticism of the heart, adds an important theological dimension to the explorations of monastic spirituality today across the Christian and Orthodox spec╆   "

—**Mary Form**

f Saint Benedict and
:sota; prioress of the
Cottonwood, Idaho

THE **MONKHOOD** OF **ALL BELIEVERS**

THE MONASTIC FOUNDATION OF CHRISTIAN SPIRITUALITY

GREG PETERS

Baker Academic
a division of Baker Publishing Group
Grand Rapids, Michigan

Published by Baker Academic
a division of Baker Publishing Group
PO Box 6287, Grand Rapids, MI 49516-6287
www.bakeracademic.com

Printed in the United States of America

Library of Congress Cataloging-in-Publication Data
Names: Peters, Greg, 1971– author.
Title: The monkhood of all believers : the monastic foundation of Christian spirituality / Greg
   Peters.
Description: Grand Rapids : Baker Publishing Group, 2018. | Includes bibliographical references
   and index.
Identifiers: LCCN 2018005065 | ISBN 9780801098055 (pbk. : alk. paper)
Subjects: LCSH: Monasticism and religious orders.
Classification: LCC BX2432.3 .P478 2018 | DDC 271—dc23
LC record available at https://lccn.loc.gov/2018005065

18   19   20   21   22   23   24   7   6   5   4   3   2   1

To those who have taught me the most about monasticism:

Fr. Abbot Denis Farkasfalvy, OCist
Fr. Columba Stewart, OSB
Prioress Mary Forman, OSB
Fr. Michael Cusato, OFM
Fr. T. Allan Smith, CSB
Fr. Luke Dysinger, OSB
Fr. Luigi Gioia, OSB

Though they might not agree with everything written in
this book, I owe most of what I know about Christian
monasticism to their teaching and scholarship.

CONTENTS

FOREWORD

Virginia Woolf once wrote that there is a spot the size of a shilling at the back of one's head, and that "one of the good offices" that men and women can perform for one another is to describe that spot. There are, she suggests, things about us that we just cannot see for ourselves.[1]

Suppose it is the same in the church. Suppose that there are things about each ecclesial body that it cannot see for itself. Suppose, then, that Lutherans can know themselves better when Roman Catholics describe them, that Copts can learn about themselves by listening to Methodists.

If that is the case, we ought not to be surprised to find a cradle Baptist seeing something in the history of monasticism that has often been overlooked. Though he is now an Anglican, Greg Peters retains the Protestant attention to personal devotion, centrality of the laity to the life of the church, and suspicion of any two-tiered account of holiness.

What Peters finds—and here is where he will surely ruffle some feathers—is that the church of Jesus Christ is "composed exclusively of monks." By virtue of our baptism into the life of Christ, every believer is called to love God with an undivided heart, is called to an "interior monasticism." *All* believers are monks. Further vows do not intensify this primary calling; they only specify its location. "I Surrender All" is a song for all believers, not just those behind the cloister wall.

This would be an easy argument to get wrong. Even if we grant the necessity of personal holiness, does not this obscure the witness of historic monasticism? It certainly might, but it might just as easily serve to highlight something often neglected: the common call to holiness in life together. As Peters points

---

1. Virginia Woolf, *A Room of One's Own* (New York: Harcourt, 1929), 90.

out, recognition of the common priesthood of all believers rarely leads to the elimination of church leaders; rather, it invites and empowers the laity to take responsibility for the work of the church. Similarly, universal monasticism need not signal the end of the cloister; it might instead awaken believers to the uncomfortable reality that monks and nuns are not surrogates, that even engineers and teachers are called by Christ to be entirely devoted to God. Peters himself insists that he is no iconoclast. In arguing that all Christians are monks, he does not suggest that we are in a postmonasticism moment. No, God continues to call women and men into monastic institutions, not least to exemplify the call that all Christians receive in baptism to be single-minded toward God.

Furthermore—and this is salient to Peters's argument—his is not a particularly Protestant argument. The monastic life has always been about the "interior singleness of heart"—rather than, say, celibacy, perpetual vows, or religious orders—and Peters argues (mostly from non-Protestant sources) that this best accounts for the diversity of expressions and self-understandings of monks. This is not merely a critical corrective, but an "ecumenical theology of monasticism."

Matt Jenson
Biola University

ACKNOWLEDGMENTS

I have had the welcome opportunity of writing several books over the past few years, and I have come to learn something about the task of writing; or at least I have learned something about writing nonfiction, academic books—they start and end with great enthusiasm, but there is the *longue durée* in the middle. During this season I have often wondered, what have I gotten myself into here? Or, why did I think this was a good idea when I first proposed the book? Or, more simply, will I ever finish? This has been my experience several times now, and I have come to realize that getting through this *longue durée* takes a large dose of good, old-fashioned self-discipline. But it also takes people, and the assistance they provide, which is sometimes obvious but more often less apparent than we realize. During the writing of this book I was assisted by a number of people, who were often just being themselves but who, in the long run, made this book possible.

I would like to thank my colleagues and students at Biola University and, especially, those in the Torrey Honors Institute. Release time was provided through a research and development grant from Biola University and from a generous course release provided by Jamie Campbell Whittaker, dean of the School of Humanities and Social Sciences. Nadia Poli and Rebecca Collins, my research assistants, were valuable in their support. I would like to offer a special word of thanks to Matt Jenson for writing the foreword and to the Torrey Honors Institute office staff past and present (Jessamy Delling, Ellie Martin, Chad Glazener, Juliana Semione, David Walton, and Megan Johnson) for many great conversations and distractions during arduous days of research and writing. The students of the Torrey Honors Institute continue to ask insightful questions that help refine my thinking. I am grateful for their thoughtfulness and relentless pursuit of the truth. My former colleague

Robert Thomas Llizo and his students at Houston Baptist University helped with the translation of Robert de Sorbon's sermon on marriage, for which I am grateful.

I would also like to thank Bob Hosack, my editor at Baker Academic, for seeing something in this project and for shepherding it to completion. A number of years ago Bob assured me that there was something in the Christian monastic tradition that Christian believers needed to hear today, so he has given me not only one but two opportunities to make that case. I deeply appreciate his support and friendship. Steve Ayers, also of Baker Publishing, not only has become a good friend but also is a constant supporter of my work. Conversations with Steve remind me that books are life-giving, and I hope this modest contribution does indeed bring life to the Christian church.

The parishioners of Anglican Church of the Epiphany, La Mirada, California, continue to remain some of my most enthusiastic supporters. They have tolerated long absences while I researched far from home, and continue to allow me to talk about monasticism whenever I get the chance. I could not imagine a better group of believers to worship with and to walk alongside. I am privileged to be their pastor.

No matter how monotonous research and writing becomes, I also get the chance to come home every night to a wonderful family who knows how to laugh and tolerate a husband and father who has monks and nuns on his mind all the time. My wife, Christina, literally makes it possible for me to do what I do, and a mere "thank you" will never be enough to repay her or show her how thankful I am for her. Without my sons, Brendan and Nathanael, life would be boring. I am grateful for their presence in my life.

Last, I am thankful for the women and men who have taught me so much about monasticism over the years, both formally and informally. I have had the opportunity to visit many monasteries and to have countless conversations over a refectory table or in a monastic church after prayer. These folks shared with me not only their "book knowledge" of monasticism but also their personal experiences. I am thankful for every one of these providential moments, too many to recall, but particularly to the students of my Monastic Spiritual Theology course at St. John's School of Theology in summer 2015 who listened and discussed with me many of the ideas presented in this book. I dedicate this book to those few who have been my primary teachers about all things monastic. I am grateful for each of them and for their assistance along the way.

ABBREVIATIONS

ACW	Ancient Christian Writers
FC	Fathers of the Church
LW	*Luther's Works*. Philadelphia: Fortress; St. Louis: Concordia, 1958–86, 2008–.
NPNF¹	*A Select Library of Nicene and Post-Nicene Fathers of the Christian Church*. 1st series. Edited by Philip Schaff. 14 vols. New York: Christian Literature, 1886–89. Reprint, Peabody, MA: Hendrickson, 1994.
NPNF²	*A Select Library of Nicene and Post-Nicene Fathers of the Christian Church*. 2nd series. Edited by Philip Schaff and Henry Wace. 14 vols. New York: Christian Literature, 1890–1900. Reprint, Peabody, MA: Hendrickson, 1994.
PG	Patrologia Graeca. Edited by Jacques-Paul Migne. 162 vols. Paris, 1857–86.
PL	Patrologia Latina. Edited by Jacques-Paul Migne. 217 vols. Paris, 1844–64.
RB	Benedict of Nursia, *Regula*
WA	*D. Martin Luthers Werke* [Weimar Ausgabe]. 136 vols. Weimar: Böhlau, 1883–2009.

INTRODUCTION

Sometime during 1971–72 a bronze bas-relief titled *Monaco* (*Monk*) was made from the Italian painter and sculptor Lucio Fontana's (d. 1968) plaster original, which had been submitted in a design contest for Door V of the Duomo in Milan in 1951–52. Though Fontana and another sculptor named Luciano Minguzzi (d. 2004) won the contest, the production of the door was ultimately entrusted to Minguzzi alone. In 1973 the Fabbrica del Duomo di Milano donated *Monaco* to the Vatican Museum. In its own description of the work, the Vatican Museum notes that the whole composition turns around an imaginary diagonal line that runs from the head of the monk to his feet. This highlights that the monk is kneeling on a bench while writing or copying a manuscript on a desk-like shelf in front of him. The monk's habit is clearly visible, for he has pulled his hood over his head. Above the desk hangs a cross, though the monk's gaze is intently focused on the work at hand.[1] This bas-relief, though somewhat straightforward in its composition and simple in its elegance, communicates a lot about monasticism. First, monastics are called to an expression of the Christian life that is unique, symbolized in the relief by the monk's habit. The habit does not make the monk, of course, but the presence of a habit always identifies the monk. Second, his kneeling posture is indicative of a monk, as one who prays and one who reads and studies for spiritual growth and edification for the good of the church. Monastic life is a life of mind and heart. Third, his posture and the presence of a stylus in his hand suggest that he is copying a manuscript, highlighting that monks not only pray but also work: *ora et labora*. Finally, the cross on the wall indicates

---

1. For an image, see "Lucio Fontana, *Monaco*," Musei Vaticani, http://www.museivaticani .va/content/museivaticani/en/collezioni/musei/collezione-d_arte-contemporanea/sala-3--milano -e-litalia-settentrionale/lucio-fontana--monaco--ii-grado-.html (accessed June 15, 2017).

both the source of the monk's life (the death, burial, and resurrection of Jesus Christ) and the *telos* (end) of his life (death to self in full conformity with the Son of God through the taking up of his cross daily). With these four aspects before us, this introduction will show why monasticism is important and relevant to all believers. I will then provide a highly selective historical overview of Christian monasticism, focusing on the fact that it has always been present in the Christian church and is a lived reality in all major branches of Christianity: Roman Catholic, Orthodox, and Protestant.

The Importance of Monasticism

No exact date, no day or time, marks the beginning of Christian monasticism.[2] In the words of monastic historian Claude Peifer, "The origins of monasticism are shrouded in obscurity."[3] There is no person who bears the title "Christianity's First Monk."[4] In one sense the institution of monasticism has always been part of the Christian church. Over the centuries a certain historiography about monasticism has come into being and often gets repeated, though its historical accuracy is easily disproven. For example, there is a tradition that claims that Anthony of Egypt (d. 356) and his followers were the first monks, exemplified in statements such as "The first monks were those of St. Anthony, who, toward the close of the fourth century, formed them into a regular body, engaged them to live in society with each other, and prescribed to them fixed rules for the direction of their conduct";[5] or monasticism "began with St. Anthony of Egypt."[6] More accurately, there has been some form of monastic presence in the Christian church since the first century.[7]

But it is not the details of its origin that make monasticism an important Christian institution. Rather, it is the nature and end of the monastic life that justifies its existence and, as I will argue later in this book, a robust theology of vocation that demands monasticism's existence. For now, using Fontana's

2. A nuanced definition of *monasticism* will be offered in chap. 1, but for now the following will suffice: monasticism either signifies men and women who live alone, in a solitary manner, or refers to a group of men and women who live together in community according to a particular form of life. See Peters, "Monasticism" (2011).

3. Peifer, *Monastic Spirituality*, 31.

4. The English word *monk* comes from the Latin word *monachus*, which is a transliteration of the Greek word *monachos*. The original meaning of *monachos* was likely equivalent to the English word *solitary* and was not meant to refer to male monastics. Thus, it is appropriate to refer to men *and* women as "monks."

5. Watson, *Biblical and Theological Dictionary*, 666.

6. Sorg, *Holy Work*, 25.

7. See Peters, *Story of Monasticism*, 1–20; and Peters, "Monasticism" (2014).

Monaco as a guide, I will isolate three other areas that commend monasticism to the Christian church: first, prayer; second, work, a kind of which is accomplished particularly well by monastics; and third, self-denial, as found in Jesus's command to take up our cross.

Prayer

That Christians ought to pray is to state the obvious because it is commanded and expected by God in the Scriptures: "pray without ceasing" (1 Thess. 5:17); "*when* you pray" (Matt. 6:5, 6, 7); "we will devote ourselves to prayer" (Acts 6:4); "be constant in prayer" (Rom. 12:12); "praying at all times in the Spirit" (Eph. 6:18); "continue steadfastly in prayer" (Col. 4:2); and "I remember you constantly in my prayers night and day" (2 Tim. 1:3). Prayer has always been God's chosen method of communication and God's answer to the difficulties and challenges of daily life. When I am in trouble, I should pray. When I am doing fine, I should pray. When we gather together as the church, we should pray. "First of all, then, I urge that supplications, prayers, intercessions, and thanksgivings be made for all people . . . [and] I desire then that in every place [people] should pray," writes the apostle Paul (1 Tim. 2:1, 8). Prayer is a *sine qua non* of the church and for all Christian believers. Yet from the start monastics have been characterized in particular by their commitment to pray.

For example, the cenobitic communities that came into existence in the third century in the deserts of Egypt, under the initial leadership of Pachomius, made prayer the central act of the community.[8] In fact, "no one shall find pretexts for himself for not going to the *synaxis*, the psalmody, and the prayer. One shall not neglect the times of prayer and psalmody, whether he is on a boat, in the monastery, in the fields, or on a journey, or fulfilling any service whatever."[9] The *Regulations of Horsiesius*, one of Pachomius's successors, describes in detail the liturgical horarium (schedule) of the community: (1) the signal is given for prayer; (2) another signal is given to kneel; (3) the monks make the sign of the cross before kneeling; (4) while lying prostrate the monks weep in their hearts for their sins; (5) all rise and make the sign of the cross again; (6) all say the Prayer of the Gospel; (7) all say, "Lord, instill your fear into our hearts that we may labor for eternal life and hold you in fear"; (8) each monk, in his heart, says prayers for purification; (9) a signal

8. Monks who live in community are known historically as "cenobites," with their form of life termed "cenobitic." *Cenobitic* has its roots in the Greek words κοινός (common) and βίος (life); hence, "life in common." Cf. Peters, "Coenobitism."

9. Pachomius, *Precepts* 141–42, in Veilleux, *Pachomian Koinonia*, 2:166. For a full study of Pachomian prayer practices, see Veilleux, *La liturgie*.

is given to be seated; (10) the monks sign themselves on the forehead with the sign of the cross; (11) all sit; (12) the Scriptures are recited; (13) all are dismissed, reciting additional Scriptures to themselves until they reach their cells.[10] Prayer continued, of course, in the cell and even when the monks were not praying together in community.

A more curious example of monastic commitment to prayer is the Constantinopolitan "Sleepless Ones" (ἀκοίμητοι).[11] This monastic community, purportedly founded by Alexander the Akoimetos (i.e., the Sleepless One) between 405 and 425, was "pledged to perpetual praise of God; their offices . . . were continuous and uninterrupted, performed by three choirs in succession, each doing one eight-hour shift per day," which "was actually a mitigation of Alexander's original ideal of perpetual prayer" in which "he had imposed an unending cycle of 24 offices, one per hour, with a minimum of time permitted for unavoidable bodily needs."[12] Many years earlier Alexander had settled along the Euphrates River, where he was joined, we are told, by four hundred monks. So "Alexander divided these disciples into fifty-man choirs and marshaled them according to a schedule of prayer that conformed to that of the apostles. Later . . . he scrupulously devised a more ambitious cycle of genuflection, hymn-singing, and doxology, performed in liturgical shifts that never ceased."[13] Next, Alexander selected a number of his followers to walk up and down the Euphrates, endlessly singing psalms, and then went to Antioch to start a community but was driven out by the local bishop with help from the resident military commander. Finally, he made his way to Constantinople, after an absence of fifty years, organizing the "Sleepless Ones."

By the mid-fifth century the Constantinopolitan monastery of the ἀκοίμητοι was thriving under the direction of Markellos the Akoimetos, whose *vita* says that monks joined the monastery "because they believed that they were bringing back not only the exactness of ascesis, but they were also [returning] a certain holiness (*hagiasmon*) to the houses and men devoted to God."[14] Though all monastic communities followed a demanding horarium, a schedule of the daily recitation of the psalms, the ἀκοίμητοι did so in a more rigorous manner. According to Peter Hatlie, for the ἀκοίμητοι "the unceasing chanting of the Psalms and the fulfillment of their other liturgical obligations were

10. Horsiesius, *Regulations of Horsiesius* 8–10, in Veilleux, *Pachomian Koinonia*, 2:199–200.

11. Stoop, "Vie d'Alexandre l'Acémète," 700–701: "τὸ ἐπιλεγόμενον τῶν ἀκοιμήτων διὰ τὴν ἀκατάπαυστον αὐτῶν καὶ πάντη ἄϋπνον δοξολογίαν." (That which is said about those who are sleepless on account of their unceasing and never-resting praise.)

12. Talbot and Taft, "Akoimetoi, Monastery of," 46.

13. Caner, *Wandering, Begging Monks*, 131. See Stoop, "Vie d'Alexandre l'Acémète," 677–78.

14. *Vita of Markellos of Akoimetai* 13, quoted in Hatlie, *Monks and Monasteries*, 103. Greek text in Dagron, "La Vie ancienne," 298.

themselves considered a monk's proper form of ascesis and single most important activity."[15] So much so they ensured that members of the community were praying at all times; and not just in private but corporately. For them this was the only way to fulfill the apostle Paul's injunction to "pray without ceasing." Whereas for many monastic communities each monk would pray the "standard" seven (sometimes eight) canonical offices, the ἀκοίμητοι opted for a much more ascetic approach to monastic prayer.

Now, given that prayer is such an essential element of the Christian life and the Christian church, and that it is enjoined upon all believers, it needs to be done. And if it is commanded by God, then it seems reasonable to assume that there will be some believers who perceive that they have a vocation to intentional prayer. This, of course, does not necessitate the existence of monasteries, but perhaps it is only reasonable to assume that if some are called to intentional prayer, then there should be intentional communities of prayer to pursue this vocation. The church is *the* primary community for this activity, but monasteries are merely extensions of the church (sometimes referred to in Christian history as *ecclesiola in ecclesia*), so they too should be communities of prayer.[16] If Christians are to pray, and if God calls some women and men to a life of prayer, then monasteries would be meeting an essential need, fulfilling a divine command, and thereby should be viewed as gifts of God to the church. To be clear, this alone is not an *unmitigated* reason for monasteries to exist, but it is a *sufficient* reason.

Work

Since the monks needed to eat, work (i.e., manual labor) also became a standard fixture of Christian monastic life. This work was not meant to compete with a life of prayer but to complement it. In the words of the *Regulations of Horsiesius*: "Even if we are laboring at perishable things in order to sustain the body—which is necessary—let us be watchful not to render our soul . . . a stranger to eternal life under the pretext of a necessity which will disappear. . . . Let us fulfill the canons of the prayer; those of the *synaxis* and those of the Six Sections at their fixed hours in accord with the precept."[17] Manual labor was practiced by monks living alone as solitaries and by those living in communities. Anthony of Egypt, we are told, taught that a monk was to be doing three things in her cell: working with her hands, meditating

15. Hatlie, *Monks and Monasteries*, 103.
16. *Ecclesiola in ecclesia*: "little church within the church." See Driscoll, "Monastic Community," 211–24.
17. Horsiesius, *Regulations of Horsiesius* 37–38, in Veilleux, *Pachomian Koinonia*, 2:210.

on the Psalms, and praying.[18] Anthony's biographer, Athanasius of Alexandria (d. 373), records that Anthony followed his own advice: "He worked with his hands, though, having heard that he who is idle, *let him not eat*. And he spent what he made partly for bread, and partly on those in need. He prayed constantly."[19] Another desert monk, Pambo, is quoted as saying, "From the time that I came into the place of solitude and built my cell, and dwelt in it, I do not call to mind that I have eaten bread save what my hands have toiled for."[20]

For those living in community, both the Pachomian foundations in Egypt and the Basilian foundations in Asia Minor prescribed manual labor. Jerome's preface to the rules of Pachomius says that "Brothers of the same craft are gathered together into one house under one master," implying that the monks were active in different forms of manual labor (e.g., as linen weavers, tailors, and shoemakers).[21] Basil of Caesarea (d. 379) in his so-called *Long Rules* writes, "The Apostle bids us labor and work with our own hands the things which are good. . . . It is, therefore, immediately obvious that we must toil with diligence and not think that our goal of piety offers an escape from work or a pretext for idleness." Basil goes on to postulate that manual labor is beneficial for two reasons: "bringing the body into subjection" and "showing charity to our neighbor."[22] Added to that, of course, is the need for monks to be self-supporting. In fact, John Cassian (d. mid-430s) goes so far as to say that monks *alone* are truly self-supporting: "The whole human race relies on the charitable compassion of others, with the sole exception of the race of monks which, in accordance with the Apostle's precept, lives by the daily toil of its hands."[23] Whether Cassian is correct in this assessment is secondary to the point that monks *must* be self-supporting to be true monks.

But beyond being self-supporting, what kind of work might monastics engage in that makes their work *monastic*, if you will? Like life in general, monastics were engaged in a lot of necessary but ordinary work: growing and harvesting food, making clothes for members of the community, and so on. Yet one type of work that was exceptionally suited to a monastic rhythm and ethos was the making of books and thereby preserving and disseminating literary culture. Jerome (d. 420) was perhaps the most learned and productive of all the monastics of the early Christian church. Though he moved around frequently in his lifetime, he remained at heart a hermit, and he knew that as

18. Sorg, *Holy Work*, 25.
19. Athanasius, *Life of Antony* 3 (Gregg, 32, italics original), quoting from 2 Thess. 3:10.
20. Waddell, *Desert Fathers*, 63.
21. Veilleux, *Pachomian Koinonia*, 2:143.
22. Basil of Caesarea, *Long Rules* 37 (FC 9:306).
23. Cassian, *Conferences* 24.12.2 (ACW 57:834).

a monastic he was to be engaged in manual labor. Yet Jerome's scholarship, consisting primarily of translating the Bible into Latin (the Latin Vulgate), was not always viewed by others as manual labor, as work appropriate to a monastic. If this were truly the case, then Jerome would not have been self-supporting but would have been freeloading off the generosity of others. On occasion Jerome was forced to defend his scholarly activity as being not only properly monastic and theologically orthodox but also as fulfilling the apostle's admonition that those who do not work should not eat: "I have taken nothing from anyone. I accept nothing as an idler. It is by the sweat of our brow that we daily seek our food."[24] He goes even further in his preface to his translation of Job, in which he equates his scholarly work with the monastic basket weavers of Egypt:

> If I were to weave a basket from rushes or to plait palm leaves, so that I might eat my bread in the sweat of my brow and work to fill my belly with a troubled mind, no-one would criticize me, no-one would reproach me. But now, since according to the word of the Savior I wish to store up food that does not perish, and to purge the ancient track of the divine volumes from brambles and brushwood, I who have made authenticity my cause, I, a corrector of vice, am called a forger, and it is said that I do not remove errors, but sow them. . . . So, therefore, Paula and Eustochium . . . in place of the straw mat and the little rush baskets, the small presents of the monks, receive these spiritual and enduring gifts.[25]

What is at stake here in Jerome's defense of his literary activity is captured well by Megan Williams:

> The goals of the monastic life, and its underlying worldview, were deeply at odds with the literary culture that was Jerome's real qualification as a writer. The central values of monasticism were humility, poverty, and obedience. . . . Monastic *askesis* aimed at subduing, even at eradicating, self-seeking impulses. . . . Humble, even degrading manual labor played a central role in the monastic program of radical self-transformation. . . . To equate literary production with the characteristic labor of the monk was implicitly to represent it as a way of destroying, rather than maintaining, those carefully cultivated dispositions.[26]

In the end Jerome was fully justified in his defense of literary activity as a true form of monastic manual labor; and in the decades ahead not only

---

24. Jerome, *Letter* 17.4 (ACW 33:77).
25. Quoted in M. Williams, *Monk and the Book*, 167 (Latin text in 167n1).
26. M. Williams, *Monk and the Book*, 168 (italics original).

would thousands of monks take up literary activity as their chosen form of work (writing, copying, and illustrating books), but they would do so to such an extent that the monks have even been credited with saving much of early literary culture.[27] Such vital work seems to speak well of the institution of monasticism, so much so that it perhaps justifies its very existence. The making of books is now so quintessentially monastic that Fontana can simply place his monk in that posture without qualification.

Self-Denial

In Matthew 16:24 Jesus told his disciples that if they wanted to follow him, they would need to deny themselves, take up their cross, and follow him, for it is in losing one's life that one truly finds life. Thus, self-denial is not life-taking but life-giving. It is the primary way in which one becomes a true disciple, a loyal follower of the Christ, and it is the proper way in which to live the Christian life. And it is Jesus's own *via crucis* that is both the source and summit of the Christian's life and, in definitive ways, the monk's life. Monks, of course, are called to the same ascetical and spiritual standards as nonmonastic believers. Yet monks frame their very existence around a number of ascetical-spiritual practices and with an intensity and particularity that is often not characteristic in nonmonastic settings. There is also, unfortunately, an excessive mortification that accompanies some expressions of Christian monasticism. These aberrant practices aside, monasticism is known for its ascetical balance and example.

Perhaps no one in early monasticism was as vocal about the ascetical life as Basil of Caesarea. In a series of short treatises Basil laid out his vision for monastic asceticism: "Set before yourself a life without house, homeland, or possessions. Be free and at liberty from all worldly cares, lest desire of a wife or anxiety for child fetter you."[28] "[God] calls us to Himself, inviting us . . . to make haste to embrace the cross-bearing life of the monks by ridding ourselves through confession and good works of the load of sins contracted by our use of worldly goods."[29] As in most ascetical treatises from early Christianity, a tension exists between the spiritual and the worldly in Basil's thought. There is a sense that the world holds one back from being as spiritual as one can be, angelic even.[30] In particular, by necessity most people will

27. See, e.g., Cahill, *How the Irish Saved Civilization*.
28. Basil of Caesarea, *An Introduction to the Ascetical Life* 1 (FC 9:10; PG 31:620).
29. Basil of Caesarea, *An Ascetical Discourse and Exhortation* 1 (FC 9:15; PG 31:625).
30. Basil of Caesarea, *Ascetical Discourse and Exhortation* 2 (FC 9:18): "an active participant in the angelical life" (καὶ τῆς ἀγγελικῆς διαγωγῆς πραγματευτής) (PG 31:629). See also Basil of Caesarea, *An Ascetical Discourse* 2.

marry and reproduce, and although these married Christians can receive the same counsels regarding renunciation of the world and observe Christ's precepts, those who aspire to something higher must "betake [themselves] to the company of the monks."[31] And what does it look like to join the company of monks? Basil's *Discourse on Ascetical Discipline* goes into great detail, but two points in particular are worth noting. "First and foremost," writes Basil, "the monk should own nothing in this world," and "before all else, also, the monk must abstain from the society of women and wine-bibbing."[32] The dangers of owning possessions and keeping company with women are commonplace monastic tropes, though Basil's ascetical theology cannot be reduced to just these two concerns.

Basil believes that humans were made in the image and likeness of God but that sin has marred this image, making us prone to passionate desires (τὰς ἐμπαθεῖς ἐπιθυμίας).[33] When we lost this likeness to God, we lost our ability to participate in the true life of God; thus "separated and estranged from God . . . it is impossible for [humankind] to enjoy the blessedness of the divine life." Through the gift of God's grace, however, humanity is able to return (ἐπανέλθωμεν) to the beauty of God's image by the "quieting of our passions" (διὰ τῆς ἀπαθείας).[34] In a beautiful and moving passage Basil writes, "He who, to the best of his ability, copies within himself the tranquility of the divine nature attains to a likeness with the very soul of God; and, being made like to God in the manner aforesaid, he also achieves in full a semblance to the divine life and abides continually in unending blessedness."[35] Monks make this return to God and attain again this divine likeness when they aspire to the life of virginity,[36] quell their passions, steady their emotions, regulate their dependence on material goods according to need, and live well together in community, under obedience. Though most of these ascetical practices should be observed by nonmonastics as well, it is with particular devotion that monks do so, not because they are better or more worthy than nonmonastics, but in order to return to the true life, which is the divine life. Such a return is especially monastic, commending the institution's existence.

31. Basil of Caesarea, *Ascetical Discourse and Exhortation* 2 (FC 9:18).
32. Basil of Caesarea, *A Discourse on Ascetical Discipline* 1 and 2 (FC 9:33, 35; PG 31:648–49).
33. Basil of Caesarea, *Ascetical Discourse* 1 (FC 9:207; PG 31:869).
34. Basil of Caesarea, *Ascetical Discourse* 1 (FC 9:207; PG 31:869, 872).
35. Basil of Caesarea, *Ascetical Discourse* 1 (FC 9:207; PG 31:872).
36. In this use of "virginity" Basil does not mean only the procreation of children but that "our whole life, conduct and moral character should be virginal, illustrating in every action the integrity required of the virgin." *Ascetical Discourse* 1 (FC 9:208).

The History of Monasticism

Though it did not flourish and become a cultural phenomenon until the middle of the fourth century, monasticism is as old as the church itself.[37] The seeds for monastic life were sown throughout the biblical era but did not rise above ground until the first century, ultimately blooming in the fourth century and beyond. In many ways the history of monasticism is an unlikely story inasmuch as there is no explicit biblical command to "go, therefore, and become monks and nuns." Benedictine monk Columba Stewart writes, "Understanding the differences between the real history [of monasticism] and the received version, why parts of the story have been privileged and others left out entirely, is a pressing issue for those of us interested not only in the past, but also in how monasticism may yet develop."[38] Nonetheless, the genesis of monasticism may be found in Jesus's commandment to "love the Lord your God with all your heart and with all your soul and with all your mind. This is the great and first commandment. And a second is like it: You shall love your neighbor as yourself" (Matt. 22:37–39). Though Jesus's words come from Leviticus and Deuteronomy, he uses them to establish the so-called new covenant—the covenant that becomes the spiritual and moral norm for all believers following Jesus's advent. This covenant is binding for all Christian believers, whereas the old (Mosaic) covenant was binding only for the people of Israel. The new covenant is universal in ways that the old covenant was not. When Jesus establishes this foundation he is providing the *telos* of the church, the spiritual ground upon which believers are to live obediently. Within this context, some men and women chose to obey this covenant as monastics. Thus, not just Israel but all followers of the Messiah are invited to partake of the divine life, the divine love existing between the Father and the Son. And this divine life of inter-trinitarian communion became the model for how all humans were to love one another. "[I ask] that they may all be one, just as you, Father, are in me, and I in you, that they also may be in us," prayed Jesus (John 17:21). Though the earliest Christians adopted a posture of eager anticipation for the return of Christ, when that did not happen, their desire to be united with God, along with commands, for example, to "be holy in all your conduct" (1 Pet. 1:15), led them to create institutions to support their common life together (e.g., the enrolled widows of 1 Tim. 5:9–12). Monasticism grew out of this ethos of expectation and obedience to God's commands.

37. Peters, *Story of Monasticism*, 23–36.
38. Stewart, "Origins and Fate of Monasticism," 258.

Early Monasticism

According to Timothy Barnes, "The Christian monasticism of the later Roman Empire appears to derive ultimately from first-century Judaism, whose traditions of asceticism, preserved in Mesopotamia, may have been reintroduced to Syria, Palestine, and Egypt by Manichean missionaries."[39] Though this monastic genealogy is debatable, it supports the church historian Eusebius of Caesarea's (d. 339) own observation regarding the Therapeutae.[40] Philo of Alexandria (d. 50) in his *De vita contemplativa* records the existence of an ascetic community living near Alexandria that he called the Therapeutae ("healers"), who are at times equated with the Essenes of Qumran.[41] Philo, while discussing the ritual associated with a banquet held among the Therapeutae every seven weeks, describes the virtue of charity as extolled by the ascetic sect:

> The women, too, take part in the feast; most of them are aged virgins who have maintained their purity not under constraint . . . but voluntarily through their zealous desire for wisdom. Eager to enjoy intimacy with [wisdom], [the aged virgins] have been unconcerned with the pleasures of the body, desiring a progeny not mortal but immortal, which only the soul that loves God is capable of engendering unaided, since the Father has sown in her intelligible rays whereby she can behold the teachings of wisdom.[42]

Thus, the Therapeutae are men and women who practice lifelong virginity. Philo also tells us that they "each live apart in seclusion," although they are able to hear one another, and that they engage in prayer and study.[43] Therefore, the Therapeutae provide proof that there was a group of men and women who lived together, although physically separated, observing lifelong virginity, engaged in intentional prayer and study in the early first century. Further, Philo tells us that these individuals "lay down self-control [ἐγκράτειαν] as a sort of foundation of the soul and on this build the other virtues."[44]

In the hands of Eusebius, the Therapeutae become Christians, in particular because of their emphasis on self-control: "We think that these words of Philo are clear and indisputably refer to our communion" (that is, the church), for these practices "cannot be found among any, save only in the worship of

---

39. Barnes, *Constantine and Eusebius*, 195.
40. Daniel Caner goes so far as to say that "Christian monasticism was a late antique invention" and that it was not "until the late fourth and early fifth centuries" that monastic history began "to be written or, rather, invented." Caner, "'Not of This World,'" 588.
41. See Vermes, *Post-Biblical Jewish Studies*, 8–36; and Schürer, *Jewish People*, 2:591–97.
42. Philo, *Contemplative Life* 8.68 (Winston, 53). Greek text in *Philo*, 9:112–69.
43. Philo, *Contemplative Life* 3.30 (Winston, 46–47).
44. Philo, *Contemplative Life* 4.34 (Winston, 47).

Christians according to the Gospel."[45] This means that there were *Christian* ascetics living in the early first century. Furthermore, Eusebius compares the Therapeutae to other Christian ascetics, which shows that he was aware of a group of Christian ascetics with whom he could compare the Therapeutae: Philo's "very accurate description of the life of *our* ascetics."[46] Moreover, Philo uses language that became standard in later Christian monastic vocabulary. For example, "In each house there is a sacred chamber, which is called a sanctuary or closet [μοναστήριον]."[47] "Closet" is more appropriately translated as "monastery"[48] and is, in fact, the first ever use of the word.[49] In the end Eusebius, writing a history of the church, identifies monasticism as existing as early as the first century.

By the second century the Christian church placed great emphasis on the practice of asceticism, and this manifested itself frequently and consistently in monastic communities, especially in Syria.[50] The communities in Persia, Mesopotamia, and Syria were fundamentally ascetic and seem to have developed completely independently of the monastic movement in Egypt.[51] Moreover, up until the time of Clement of Alexandria (d. 215), the martyr was the quintessential image of a faithful Christian. Beginning with Clement, however, this began to change. Clement understood a martyr as (1) someone who by her death confesses her Christian faith and fidelity to her baptism; (2) someone who through death bears witness to the doctrine of Christ; and (3) someone who "bears witness to the 'truth of preaching' by the Church."[52] Clement understood that not all Christians were called to die as martyrs, so he "proposed a new ideal of Christian perfection which he called gnostic martyrdom."[53] Clement writes, "If therefore confession before God is martyrdom, every soul that has lived purely in the knowledge of God, that is, that has obeyed his commandments is, in whatsoever manner it be released from its body, a martyr both in life and word pouring out its faith like blood, throughout its whole life even to the end."[54] By the time of the legalization of Christianity in the early fourth century, this concept

45. Eusebius, *Ecclesiastical History* 2.17.18 (Lake, 1:153).
46. Eusebius, *Ecclesiastical History* 2.17.2 (Lake, 1:145, italics added).
47. Philo, *Contemplative Life* 3.25 (Winston, 46).
48. See Lake, *Eusebius*, 149.
49. Winston, *Philo of Alexandria*, 317n15.
50. Vööbus, *History of Asceticism*.
51. Vööbus, "Monasticism in Mesopotamia."
52. Malone, *Monk and the Martyr*, 7.
53. Malone, *Monk and the Martyr*, 8.
54. Clement of Alexandria, *Stromata* 4.4, quoted in Malone, *Monk and the Martyr*, 8, with Greek text.

of the monk as the successor of the martyr was a commonplace in monastic theology and literature.[55]

By the fourth century there were, if we can trust the reports, thousands of monks and nuns living in every corner of the Roman Empire, but no corner was more populated than the deserts of Egypt, Palestine, and the Holy Land. For example, John Cassian writes that there were five thousand monks in one Pachomian monastery in Egypt, and Palladius of Galatia (d. ca. 420s), in his *Lausiac History*, reports two thousand monks in the hills of Lower Egypt.[56] The aforementioned *Life of Anthony* reports that

> when, entering the Lord's house once more, [Anthony] heard in the Gospel the Lord saying, *Do not be anxious about tomorrow*, he could not remain any longer, but going out he gave those remaining possessions also to the needy. Placing his sister in the charge of respected and trusted virgins, and giving her over to the convent [παρθενῶνα] for rearing, he devoted himself from then on to the discipline [i.e., monastic life] rather than the household. . . . There were not yet many monasteries in Egypt, and no monk knew at all the great desert, but each of those wishing to give attention to his life disciplined himself in isolation, not far from his own village. Now at that time in the neighboring village there was an old man who had practiced from his youth the solitary life [τὸν μονήρη βίον]. When Antony [*sic*] saw him, he emulated him in goodness.[57]

Of significance is that Anthony's sister was able to be placed in a monastic community and that he himself was able to be tutored under a solitary, evidence that monasticism was alive and well not only in the Egyptian desert but in urban Egypt too. Similar patterns were beginning to manifest themselves in other parts of the late antique world. Cenobitic monasteries and solitary monks emerged everywhere, with monasteries located in cities (Rome, Jerusalem, and Constantinople), in towns (Bethlehem), in deserts (Egypt and Sinai), on islands (Lérins), in caves (St. Sabas in Palestine), and even on pillars (Syria). It was a golden age of monasticism.

Moreover, during the fourth and fifth centuries monasticism began to spread to such an extent that it became a "global" phenomenon. In particular monasticism took hold in Gaul (what is now France).[58] One of the most well-known, if not *the* most well-known, early monastic centers was on the island of Lérins,

---

55. See chap. 5 of this volume for a twentieth-century take on this line of thinking in the thought of Paul Evdokimov.

56. Cassian, *Institutes* 4.1 (ACW 58:79); and Palladius, *Lausiac History* 7.1–2 (Meyer, 40).

57. Athanasius, *Life of Antony* 3 (Gregg, 31–32, italics original), quoting from Matt. 6:34.

58. It appears that the first monastery founded in Gaul was Marmoutier, established by Martin of Tours on the outskirts of Tours ca. 372.

just off the southern coast of France from Cannes. In the early fifth century Honoratus, Caprasius, and Eucherius settled on a neighboring island, which by the early 430s had become the gathering place for a number of individuals seeking the monastic life, perhaps as "a refuge from political perils."[59] Many of these early monks became bishops throughout Gaul, but monastic life on Lérins continued to flourish, resulting in a number of early monastic rules that exercised an influence beyond their original context.[60] These rules tend to give the abbot, prior, and elder monks a great deal of authority and place great emphasis on prayer: "nothing may be put ahead of the [Divine] Office."[61]

As the influence of these Lérinian rules spread, so too did other forms of monasticism. Some monasteries began in houses and villas. Marilyn Dunn writes, "Many minor monasteries were created throughout Gaul and Italy throughout the fifth century, as the result of personal devotion or asceticism, small and informal communities where no rule would have been required. House and villa 'monasteries' sprang up as aristocrats or the prosperous took to a life of religion and turned their own homes into religious retreats for family and friends."[62] Monasteries were also founded at this time in places that held important saints' relics (e.g., Nola in southern Italy) and at principal basilicas (e.g., St. Sebastian on the Appian Way outside Rome).[63]

The fifth and sixth centuries saw the rise of many communities for women and the appearance of rules written especially for women, perhaps none more significant than that associated with the Lérinian monk Caesarius of Arles (d. 542).[64] Caesarius's first attempt at founding a community of women failed in 508 because of the so-called Barbarian Invasion, but a new monastery, located within the city walls, was consecrated in 512.[65] Setting the community on a stable financial footing, Caesarius then composed a rule for the nuns. Dunn summarizes:

> His *Rule for Virgins* divides into five sections. The first sets down regulations for admission and practice based on Cassian and those of Lérins. . . . A second section is partly based on the *Rules* ascribed to St Augustine of Hippo . . . [that]

59. Dunn, *Emergence of Monasticism*, 82.
60. E.g., *The Rule of the Four Fathers* and *The Second Rule of the Fathers*. See Kardong, *Pillars of Community*, 191–241.
61. *Second Rule of the Fathers* 6.31, in Kardong, *Pillars of Community*, 228.
62. Dunn, *Emergence of Monasticism*, 90. See also Percival, "Villas and Monasteries."
63. Dunn, *Emergence of Monasticism*, 90–93.
64. E.g., see *The Life of the Jura Fathers* 25: "Romanus and Lupicinus with paternal love installed an abbess for virgins and handed over to her the governance of that religious community; there she ruled one hundred fifty female monastics." Vivian, Vivian, and Russell, *Jura Fathers*, 113.
65. See the *Life of Caesarius* 28 and 35.

lay down the spiritual basis of the community's life. . . . The third section of the rule contains Caesarius' own ideas; a fourth is the so-called *Recapitulation* in which he goes over and confirms or revises what he has set down already, while the fifth consists of regulations for fasting and liturgy based on those of Lérins.[66]

Caesarius's rule for nuns came to exercise great influence in Gaul, which had the good benefit of bequeathing to Latin monasticism continuity with earlier forms of monastic life since *The Rule for Virgins* was dependent on earlier texts. Largely, there is a continuity of monastic tradition from the East to the West (by way of Cassian and Caesarius, for example), a progressive developmental arc as opposed to a series of parallel movements, so much so that monastic history can be viewed as a garment made from numerous threads, many of which are related historically or textually to one another. Subsequent monastic history continues this story and enlarges the thread count.

Eastern Monasticism

Early Christian monasticism in Asia Minor and Greece gave birth to a thriving monastic culture during the Byzantine Empire, exemplified by Mount Athos.[67] Before cenobitic monasticism was recorded on the peninsula in the tenth century, there is textual evidence of hermits on Athos from at least the mid-ninth century. According to Joseph Genesius (ca. tenth century), Mount Athos was a major monastic center by 843. In 883 the Byzantine emperor Basil I issued a document protecting the Athonite monks and their lands, suggesting that a number of monks on the peninsula were organized in some manner. The permanence of cenobitism was given a boost by the arrival of a monk named Athanasius (d. 1000) in 957/58. He had entered the monastic life around 952 on Mount Olympus, drawing the favor of the future emperor Nicephorus II Phocas, who came frequently to Mount Olympus because his nephew Michael was Athanasius's abbot. Athanasius allegedly came to Mount Athos to avoid the fame that he was receiving for his holiness on Mount Olympus, initially settling for a year in a hermitage with the Athonite monk Zygos and then moving to a cell in 959. Yet it was Nicephorus who implored Athanasius to establish a lavra.

The Greek word λαύρα ("lane" or "alley") originally referred to the paths that connected individual monastic cells to a central church but later came to designate a monastic complex where the monks spent the week praying,

---

66. Dunn, *Emergence of Monasticism*, 100.
67. Mount Athos, or the Holy Mountain, is the name given to the northernmost projection of land on the Chalkidiki peninsula of Greece.

working, and eating in their individual cells and coming together once a week for a common liturgy.[68] Because Athanasius was not convinced that Nicephorus's idea was worth pursuing, he spent the year 960 living in solitude on the tip of the Athonite peninsula. Nicephorus returned to Constantinople, becoming emperor for six years before his assassination in 969. As emperor, Nicephorus sent the monk Methodius to Athanasius with a letter and financial assistance. In time Methodius prevailed on Athanasius to have a lavra built with financial support from Nicephorus and other donors. In 963 Athanasius wrote the monastery's rule (dedicated to Mary the Mother of God but known as the "Great Lavra"), which borrowed heavily from a previous rule written in the ninth century by Theodore Studites (d. 826) for the monastery of St. John Stoudios in Constantinople.

By the close of the tenth century many monasteries had been built on Mount Athos, and by 1001 there were forty-six monasteries on the peninsula. Vatopedi (its first historical attestation is from 985) was most likely a restoration of an earlier, ruined monastery undertaken by three disciples of Athanasius. The Iviron monastery was built by Georgian monks, and Esphigmenou is first mentioned in 998, becoming the home of many Chalcedonian Armenian monks. Hilandar was likely established in the late tenth century, but by 1015 it was deserted while under the oversight of the Kastamonitou monastery, then rebuilt by Serbian monks in the twelfth century. Finally, the Panteleimon monastery originally consisted of two monasteries that merged in the twelfth century to become home to Slavic-speaking monks from medieval Russia.

Monasticism had arrived (again?) in medieval Rus' at nearly the same time as the (re)introduction of the Christian faith. According to the *Russian Primary Chronicle*, Christianity was first brought to ancient Russia when the apostle Andrew crossed the mouth of the Dnieper River, passed over the hills on which Kiev was later founded, and went as far north as the ancient city of Novgorod.[69] More realistically, however, Christianity was known in ancient Rus' from at least the middle of the tenth century. Prince Vladimir I's grandmother Olga had been a Christian, and a Christian church was operative in 944. Yet it was only in 988 that the country "officially" adopted Christianity.[70] The earliest material for monasticism in Russia is also found in the *Russian*

68. Thus, lavriotic monasticism had three primary characteristics: (1) a combination of both an eremitical, solitary monastic lifestyle and coenobitic, communal aspects; (2) monks spent time in private and communal prayer and in eating individual and communal meals each week; and (3) monks performed manual labor that benefited the whole community.

69. Zenkovsky, *Medieval Russia*, 47.

70. An account of the Christianization of Rus' is found in the *Russian Primary Chronicle*. See Zenkovsky, *Medieval Russia*, 67–71.

Primary Chronicle and comprises notices and sections on the origin and early history of Kievan monasteries, in particular the Monastery of the Caves.[71] From this source we learn that a priest named Hilarion walked a hill near the Dnieper River to say his prayers in private, digging a cave in the side of the hill to use as his oratory.[72] He later became metropolitan (i.e., archbishop) of Kiev, so his cave lay unused until Anthony, a layman, became attracted to the monastic life, made a pilgrimage to Mount Athos, and was professed monk around 1051. He was instructed in an Athonite monastery and sent back to Russia to spread monastic life. In Rus' he found the Kievan monasteries inadequate until coming upon the empty cave of Hilarion, settling there as a hermit. He enlarged the cave and was visited by pious laypeople and supplied with food by faithful Christians. Soon his name spread throughout Rus', and he was joined by others called to the same manner of life. In time Anthony was the head of a monastery, though this ran counter to his desire for a solitary life. He therefore appointed another superior, leaving to dig a new cave, where he lived for another forty years. The community increased, so a monastery was built on the site of the first cave. With this "the superior and brethren founded there a great church and fenced in the monastery with a palisade. They constructed many cells, completed the church and adorned it with icons."[73] From these humble beginnings monasticism grew and spread across Russia, where it continues to thrive today.[74]

Western Monasticism

As the institution of monasticism grew beyond its place(s) of birth, it eventually took root in every area of the world that boasted a Christian presence. In short, where there was Christianity there was monasticism, even if these local manifestations, in time, ceased to exist. Moreover, it was often the religious orders that were the vanguard of Christian missionary activity.[75] The sixteenth-century Reformation proved a bit of an exception to this general pattern in ecclesiastical history. For various reasons, not all of which are fully understood today (and likely will never be fully understood), King Henry VIII of England (d. 1547) began in 1536 to dissolve all the monasteries in his lands. Though he was likely motivated by financial or political reasons

71. These are found in the entries under the years 1051, 1072–75, 1089, 1091, 1096, and 1107–10.
72. See R. Casey, "Early Russian Monasticism"; and Heppell, *The "Paterik."*
73. Zenkovsky, *Medieval Russia*, 108.
74. See, e.g., Kenworthy, *Heart of Russia.*
75. See, e.g., Smither, *Missionary Monks*; Addison, *Medieval Missionary*, 75–105; and Dawson, *Mission to Asia.*

over theological convictions, the result was the same. By the end of the 1540s all the monasteries in England no longer existed, and the newly reformed Church of England lacked a monastic presence, a situation that lasted until June 6, 1841, when the Anglican Marion Hughes (d. 1912) took the traditional monastic vows of poverty, chastity, and obedience before Edward Pusey (d. 1882). Because I have discussed this reintroduction of monasticism into Anglicanism elsewhere, it is unnecessary to belabor the point.[76] Further, not only has the Church of England seen the reestablishment of monasticism, but so have other Protestant traditions (e.g., Lutheran) and sometimes in the most surprising of places.[77]

Initially trained in monasticism at Glasnevin near Dublin, the monk Columba (also known as Columcille; d. 597) moved to the islands west of present-day Scotland in order to spread monasticism and Christianity. In 563 he and his companions landed on a small island (known in Gaelic as *Ì* and now in English as Iona) that was soon to become an important center of monastic activity, leading to the founding of other such important monasteries as Lindisfarne, Whitby, and Melrose. Iona's importance is attested to by the church historian the Venerable Bede (d. 735), who writes that the "monastery [of Iona] was for a long time the principal monastery of nearly all the northern Scots and all the Picts and exercised a widespread authority."[78] Despite its early history of influence and artistic triumph (e.g., the Book of Kells was made there ca. 800), the island was plundered and the monks murdered by Vikings in 806 and again in 986. In 1203 the monastery became Benedictine, but monastic life ceased in the 1500s as a result of the Reformation and Henry VIII's dissolution of the monasteries. The medieval buildings gradually fell into disrepair, and the island's influence in the church became a memory, captured well by William Wordsworth's poem "Iona" from 1833:

> How sad a welcome! To each voyager
> Some ragged child holds up for sale a store
> Of wave-worn pebbles, pleading on the shore
> Where once came monk and nun with gentle stir,
> Blessings to give, news ask, or suit prefer.
> Yet is yon neat, trim church a grateful speck
> Of novelty amid the sacred wreck
> Strewn far and wide. Think, proud philosopher!
> Fallen though she be, this glory of the west,

76. See Peters, *Reforming the Monastery*, 53–90.
77. See Peters, *Story of Monasticism*, 224–42.
78. Bede, *History of the English Church and People* 3.3 (Sherley-Price, 145).

> Still on her sons the beams of mercy shine;
> And hopes, perhaps more heavenly bright than thine,
> A grace by thee unsought and unpossest,
> A faith more fixed, a rapture more divine,
> Shall gild their passage to eternal rest.[79]

Wordsworth is able to understand the former glory of the island and also, amid the ruins, to sense the spiritual importance of the island. He was not alone in his assessment.

In 1899 the sacred buildings and sites were given to the Iona Cathedral Trust after some preliminary restoration work, but it was the Church of Scotland minister George MacLeod (d. 1991) who restored monastic observance to the island. MacLeod, a Presbyterian minister, had pastored a church since 1930 in Govan, Scotland, and before then in Edinburgh. But over the course of his eight years in Govan, MacLeod felt that the church was not doing enough to reach the large numbers of working-class people. He became convinced that only new patterns of Christian living would reach the masses. "What MacLeod envisioned was a company of pioneers who would be willing to live under economic and devotional disciplines but in the midst of modern industrial society. He saw the necessity for a training center in Christian living that would be more or less removed from the pressures of modern culture." Thus, he "grasped the opportunity that was then open to him to rebuild the ancient abbey of Iona."[80] When the Duke of Argyll entrusted the island to the Iona Cathedral Trust, he included in his bequest that Christian groups be allowed to worship in the abbey. Thus, in 1938 when MacLeod began the Iona Community, he was in one sense simply fulfilling the duke's request.

To begin his community MacLeod gathered together ministers, laypeople, and craftspersons to restore the abbey's building. They spent every summer working and praying on the island, completing the restorations in 1965. Since that time the community, which now consists of a number of members who live on the island year-round as well as members scattered around the world, has run retreats and youth camps alongside welcoming thousands of visitors each year who come to see the restored ancient monastic site and join the community for daily prayer. From its start the Iona Community has sought to maintain a balance between prayerful contemplation and social relevance. What the Iona Community represents well, however, is the fact that monasticism is part of the Protestant tradition again, demonstrating

---

79. William Wordsworth, "Iona," part 2, "Upon Landing," lines 15–28, http://www.bartleby.com/270/3/216.html (accessed June 27, 2016).

80. Bloesch, *Centers of Christian Renewal*, 101.

that the institution of monasticism is a fixture of the Christian church *in toto*: Roman Catholic, Eastern Orthodox, and Protestant. Therefore, given its presence in the historical and present Christian church, it is necessary to understand monasticism and to articulate a theology of monasticism that is not sectarian but relevant to the whole church of God. This book attempts to offer such a theology.

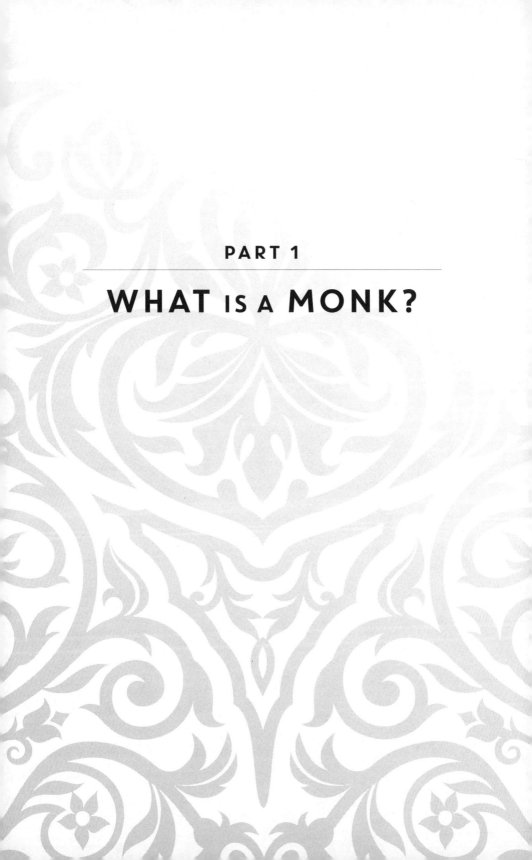

PART 1

WHAT IS A MONK?

One

....

Defining the Monk

When some people are asked, "What do you think of when you hear the word *monk*?" they may imagine a dour-looking individual dressed in black with head bowed while he quickly scurries from one place to the next, anxious to avoid any unnecessary conversation in order to keep himself unspotted from the world. Such an erroneous conception of a monk even became a stereotype, for example, in the satirical cartoons of *Punch* magazine in nineteenth-century England, when the Church of England was undergoing a revival of monasticism that was unfairly characterized and demonized as "Roman Catholic" (a slur).[1] Others may imagine an overly scrupulous masochist, wearing a hair shirt and flagellating himself regularly in order to discipline his unruly body. This image of the monk, unfortunately, is put forward by popular fiction writer Dan Brown's *The Da Vinci Code*, for example. Of course, anyone who has spent time at a monastery (certainly in the past forty years) knows that the above caricatures are exactly that—caricatures. Sure, monks like those described above may have existed at some monasteries in the past (and may even endure in some houses today), but there is no doubt that these images are unfair (mis)representations of the monastic life, which is more often characterized by joyfulness than somberness and by other-centeredness than excessive introspection. In fact, it is not only (nor primarily) what is on the outside that makes the monk (i.e., a habit or living in a monastery) but what is on the inside; that is, the inner life of the monk, not its outward, visible manifestations, is what truly makes one a monk,

1. Kollar, "'Punch' and the Nuns."

though the two are related. Thus, this chapter will strive to answer the question, What is a monk? To that end, an etymological study will be followed by examples from the patristic and early medieval Christian tradition that talk about what characterizes the monastic person.

"Monk"

In his groundbreaking *Der Ursprung des Mönchtums*, Karl Heussi writes that though there is a Christian ascetic impulse going back to the New Testament, the "constituent element" of earliest Christian monasticism is found in withdrawal from the world.[2] This conclusion is called into question by Christoph Joest when he says that Heussi's conclusion "is a projection onto a movement that at the time was more fluid and diverse."[3] Though the beginnings of the institution of monasticism cannot be traced to one moment of inspiration,[4] it is clear that the origin of the Christian monastic impulse is found in the Scriptures.[5] However, though the impulse is found in the Christian Scriptures, they did *not* give to the Christian tradition a word by which to identify those whom we now refer to as monks. The terminology was worked out later by those living what we now understand as the monastic life.[6]

The earliest evidence for the use of the word μοναχός in reference to the institution of monasticism comes from texts dated to 323 and 324 CE.[7] The first is a papyrus contract recording the sale of a house to a monk (μ[ονα]χῷ), and it can only be assumed that this "house" would be for the purpose of a monastic community.[8] The latter papyrus records a petition made to the *Praepositus* Dioscorus Caeso by Isidorus, who had been badly beaten by two men, Pamounis and Harpalus, and might have been killed had it not been for the monk Isaac (Ἰςὰκ μοναχοῦ) and the deacon Antoninus (Ἀντωνίνου διάκονος) walking by

2. Heussi, *Der Ursprung des Mönchtums*, 53: "Der Unterschied beruht vielmehr darauf, daß in der älteren Askese ein Moment fehlt, das für das Mönchtum gerade das eigentlich Konstitutive ist: die Schaffung einer Sonderwelt durch das Leben in der Einsiedlerzelle, der Einsiedlerkolonie oder dem Kloster." (The difference is more due to the fact that the older asceticism lacks a moment; that is, an actually constitutive moment for monasticism: the creation of a separate world through life in a hermit cell, a hermit colony, or the monastery.)

3. Joest, "Once Again," 161.

4. See Goehring, *Ascetics*, 13–35.

5. See Peters, *Story of Monasticism*, 1–36; and Peters, "Monasticism" (2014).

6. For a general overview see "Monastic Terminology: Monk, Cenobite, Nun," in Fry, *RB 1980*, 301–21.

7. For consideration of other early Christian monastic terminology, such as ἀναχωρητής and ἀποτακτικός, see Goehring, *Ascetics*, 53–72; and Choat, "Terms for 'Monk.'"

8. On the dating of this papyrus (P. Coll. Youtie 77), see Worp, "Marginalia on Published Documents," 135.

and breaking up the brawl.[9] Since Isaac's title is used with such casualness, it must have been a title known by the authorities, suggesting that it was somewhat common among fourth-century Egyptians. Joest suggests that "this term and the way of life it describes must have become familiar and accepted some time *before* the incident. This would take us back to at least the end of the third century."[10] Furthermore, that Isaac was even walking by Isidorus's property suggests that he was not a hermit who lived far beyond society and, according to E. A. Judge, also that he was "not a monk from a cenobitic monastery."[11] Not much more can be said about this passing reference to the monk Isaac. What is important to notice, however, is that by the first quarter of the fourth century the word μοναχός was known well enough that it did not require an additional word of explanation. Further, monks seem to have lived in such a way that they had (at least on occasion) interaction with others. In the century ahead the word μοναχός took on overt theological connotations.[12]

Eusebius of Caesarea

The use and history of the Greek word μοναχός is well known and well documented.[13] Eusebius of Caesarea (d. ca. 340) is likely the first ecclesiastical author to use it.[14] In his commentary on Psalm 68:6 ("God settles the solitary in a home"), written circa 330, Eusebius compares the five Greek versions of the text found in the Hexapla.[15] Among these Greek versions, four different words are used for "solitary":

9. Original Greek text and translation of the papyrus in Judge, "Earliest Use of *Monachos*," 73. *Praepositus* is a term used "during the Roman Imperial Period and in Late Antiquity to refer to leadership functions in a variety of areas of public service." Tinnefeld, "Praepositus."
10. Joest, "Once Again," 161 (italics original).
11. Judge, "Earliest Use of *Monachos*," 74. Judge's reasoning must be that since Isaac is out in the countryside, he does not live in a community that would have required him to remain at the monastery. Yet Pachomian monks, for example, were allowed to travel outside the monastery (e.g., to visit a sick relative), so Isaac's presence in the countryside is perhaps not completely unwarranted. In fact, Pachomius legislates that a monk who leaves the monastery must travel with another monk. Perhaps Antoninus is Isaac's monastic travel partner. See Veilleux, *Pachomian Koinonia*, 2:155.
12. Joest ("Once Again," 162) refers to the "*theological* use of *monachós*" (italics original).
13. E.g., see Sheridan, "Early Egyptian Monasticism."
14. Martin Tetz has argued that the Pseudo-Athanasian *De patientia* was written in 311–13, and it employs the term μοναχός. If Tetz is correct, then this would be the first Christian use of μοναχός. In *De patientia* 7 (PG 26:1305A-C) the μοναχοὶ τέλειοι are a part of the Christian community alongside the πρεσβύτεροι (elders/presbyters), διάκονοι (deacons), ἀναγνῶσται (readers), παρθένοι (virgins), and χῆραι (widows). See Tetz, "Eine asketische Ermunterung."
15. For a detailed description of the Hexapla, see Brock, "De Übersetzungen des Alten Testaments." Interestingly, there are only seven uses of the word μοναχός and its variants in the Septuagint and other early Greek translations of the Old Testament.

Septuagint   μονοτρόπους
Aquila   μονογενεῖς
Quinta   μονοζώνους
Theodotion   μοναχοὺς
Symmachus   μοναχοῖς

Noting these variants, Eusebius concludes:

> And this (giving the *monachói* a home) was his (God's) first and greatest provision for [hu]mankind, because they are the front rank of those advancing in Christ. However, they are rare. This explains why Aquila calls them *monogeneís*, likening them to the only-begotten Son of God. According to the Septuagint translation they are *monotrópoi* (living in one way) and *polutrópoi* (living in many ways), who do not shift and change, but hold to the one way that leads to the pinnacle of virtue. The *Quinta* called them *monodzonói* because they live alone and gird themselves. . . . All of them live their lives in solitude and chastity, they, the precursors of whom were the disciples of our Saviour. To them he [Jesus] had said: "Take no gold, nor silver in your girdle."[16]

These μοναχοί are few and far between, but they are at the forefront of spiritual advancement, following the narrow road to virtue by way of living alone and girding themselves (i.e., living sexually chaste lives). Thus, by the mid-fourth century Eusebius knows enough about the μοναχοί to describe their lifestyle, suggesting that though rare they are common enough to be known by a bishop in Caesarea. Moreover, he knows that there are organized bodies of monks (τάγμα) akin to the orders of widows and orphans in the fourth-century church.[17]

Eusebius's main description of the μοναχοί is that they live alone and are sexually chaste.[18] Regarding the question of chastity, Françoise Morard

16. Translation from Joest, "Once Again," 162–63. Parenthetical notes are Joest's. Greek text in PG 23:689B:

> Καὶ τοῦτ' ἦν τὸ πρῶτον αὐτοῦ κατόρθωμα ὃ δὴ καὶ μέγιστον τῶν αὐτοῦ κατορθωμάτων τῷ τῶν ἀνθρώπων δεδώρηται γένει. Τὸ γοῦν πρῶτον τάγμα τῶν ἐν Χριστῷ προκοπτόντων τὸ τῶν μοναχῶν τυγχάνει. Σπάνιοι δέ εἰσιν οὗτοι διὸ κατὰ τὸν Ἀκύλαν μονογενεῖς ὠνομάσθησαν ἀφωμοιωμένοι τῷ μονογενεῖ Υἱῷ τοῦ Θεοῦ. Κατὰ δὲ τοὺς Ἑβδομήκοντα μονότροποι τυγχάνουσιν, ἀλλ' οὐ πολύτροποι, οὐδὲ ἄλλοτε ἄλλως τὸν ἑαυτῶν μεταβάλλοντες τρόπον, ἕνα δὲ μόνον κατορθοῦντες, τὸν εἰς ἄκρον ἥκοντα ἀρετῆς. Μονοζώνους δὲ αὐτοὺς ἡ πέμπτη ἔκδοσις ὠνόμασεν, ὡς ἂν μονήρεις καὶ καθ' ἑαυτοὺς ἀνεζωσμένους. Τοιοῦτοι δὲ πάντες εἰσὶν οἱ τὸν μονήρη καὶ ἁγνὸν κατορθοῦντες βίον, ὧν πρῶτοι γεγόνασιν οἱ τοῦ Σωτῆρος ἡμῶν μαθηταί, οἷς εἴρητο "Μὴ κτήσησθε χρυσὸν, μηδὲ ἄργυρον εἰς τὰς ζώνας ὑμῶν. . . ."

17. Judge, "Earliest Use of *Monachos*," 75.

18. See also Clement of Alexandria, *Stromata* 3.9.67.

writes that "Μονόζωνος, μονήρης, ἁγνός here are synonymous terms and refer quite explicitly to the state of the chaste life and celibacy."[19] Yet as Judge notices, "Eusebius makes no attempt to draw out celibacy as the guiding principle of monasticism. He is concerned to use the various renderings to show that μοναχοί are 'single-minded' in a general moral sense (which includes chastity)."[20] And it is this insight that sets the stage for later discussions of what it means to be a monk. Yes, chastity may be an aspect of it, but it is not necessarily the *central* aspect.[21] Rather, monks in the mid-fourth century were primarily a group of men (akin to female virgins and widows, who were recognized as unique ranks in the first century CE)[22] who shared a common vision of the Christian life. They were not just celibates but shared a common mind.[23] In the words of Joest, "These *monachói* are not simply 'alone' in the sense of being unmarried, but they were people who have turned their hearts completely to God. They have oriented themselves unwaveringly toward one single cause." He continues, "We can see that during the first centuries Christians considered someone called *monachós* to be a person who was focused exclusively on God with his innermost heart and life, who lived unmarried by himself and essentially renounced personal property."[24] It is this singular focus on God from the heart that continues to receive attention in subsequent literature.

Augustine of Hippo

Between 392 and approximately 418, Augustine of Hippo (d. 430) preached through the entire Psalter, offering a verse-by-verse explication of all 150 psalms. The nature of the work is summed up well by the title given to it in the sixteenth century by Erasmus of Rotterdam (d. 1536)—*Enarrationes in*

19. Morard, "Monachos, Moine," 381: "Μονόζωνος, μονήρης, ἁγνός sont ici des termes synonymes et désignent assez explicitement l'état de vie chaste et célibataire."

20. Judge, "Earliest Use of *Monachos*," 76.

21. Though this statement may seem controversial, I hope to show below that it is accurate. Though μοναχός and some of its earliest antecedents and synonyms (e.g., *iḥîdāyā*) contain connotations of celibacy, they are not mere equivalents of the words *chaste* or *celibate*. That is, μοναχός means more than just unmarried or celibate.

22. See, e.g., 1 Tim. 4:9–10.

23. This usage is more consistent with Greek papyrological evidence from Egypt—which uses the adjective μοναχός not strictly to mean "singular" (i.e., alone) but to carry a range of meaning (simple, uncomplicated, unique, a single part of a whole, or, especially, undivided)—than it is with the "monk" of the late third century and early fourth century. See Morard, "Monachos, Moine," 346 and 353–54.

24. Joest, "Once Again," 164. See also Guillaumont, *Monachisme chrétien*, 62–66 and 220–22.

Psalmos. Throughout history, up to Erasmus, manuscripts of the work refer to it as an *expositio*, *sermo*, *tractatus* (treatise), *commentum*, and *explanatio*. *Enarrationes*, which means "running explanations," however, captures well the nature of the work: "Augustine's focus was not the historical, literal sense of the Psalms as expressions of Israel's worship; rather, in close continuity with the New Testament, they were prophecies that find ongoing fulfillment in Christianity."[25] Learned and long, the *Enarrationes* were an influential commentary in subsequent Christian history.

Augustine's exposition of Psalm 132 (now 133) becomes in the African bishop's hand a masterful treatise on the monastic life.[26] For Augustine the text reads,

> See how good and how pleasant it is
> > for brothers to dwell together in unity!
> Like a fragrant oil upon the head,
> > flowing down upon the beard,
> Aaron's beard,
> > the oil that flowed down to the border of his tunic.
> Like the dew of Hermon,
> > which flows down to the mountains of Zion.
> For there has the Lord ordained blessing:
> > life for ever.

After noting the beauty and the brevity of the psalm, Augustine asks, "Are the ones who dwell in unity certain particular individuals, who have reached maturity and enjoy a blessing granted to them but not to all, even though it does distil from them to the rest?"[27] Augustine immediately picks up on the top-to-bottom movement in the psalm and wonders who these "brothers" are at the top who will become a source of blessing (and, as will be seen, a source of spiritual nourishment) to those below them. Without hesitation he says that these are the church's monks and even goes so far as to say that this psalm "has given birth to monasteries." "Brothers and sisters who longed to live as one [*habitare in unum*] were awakened by the song; this verse roused them like a trumpet," writes Augustine.[28] In essence, what Augustine is doing is taking the whole of salvation history and making it a story of monastic history.

25. Cameron, "*Enarrationes in Psalmos*," 290.

26. Verheijen, "*L'Enarratio in Psalmum* 132."

27. Augustine, *Enarrationes in Psalmos* 132.1, in *Expositions of the Psalms 121–150*, 175. Latin text in Gori, *Augustinus*.

28. Augustine, *Enarrationes in Psalmos* 132.2, in *Expositions of the Psalms 121–150*, 175.

The bishop of Hippo's argument is as follows: (1) God's salvific call "rang all around the world"; (2) yet this call was "not heard in Judea" because they "were deaf to the sound of it"; (3) but others heard the call and responded (e.g., the prophets, the apostles, the five hundred who witnessed Jesus's resurrection,[29] and the 120 gathered in the upper room[30]), giving birth to the Christian church at Pentecost. And why did the Holy Spirit descend on these believers at Pentecost? Augustine believes, it appears, that it was because they were gathered "together in one place" (*in uno loco constitutis*). Thus, those who longed to live as *one* gathered together in *one* place and, we are then told, began to live together as *one*. They did not just live together; they lived together "in unity" (*in unum*) by selling "all their possessions" and laying "the proceeds at the feet of the disciples."[31] Augustine is, of course, referencing a combination of Acts 2:45 and 4:32, in which these early believers in Jesus Christ form themselves into a community, holding all things in common (*omnia communia*).[32] Moreover, this group of believers is not just unified around common possessions but also unified by having "one mind and one heart" (*anima una et cor unum*).[33] It is these believers united in mind, heart, and possessions who "hear effectively the psalm's words, *See how good and how pleasant it is for brothers to dwell together in unity.*"[34] Desirous to move the history lesson further, Augustine reminds his readers that these Acts 2 and 4 believers were the first but not the only ones who responded to God's call. In short, every subsequent monastic was responding to the same summons to dwell together in unity: "The intense joy of charity came upon their descendants too, and with it the practice of vowing to God."[35] Psalm 132/133, therefore, is a call to the monastic life that has been heeded by vowed religious.

Augustine's use of texts from Acts 2 and 4 as biblical support for those who dwell together in unity (i.e., monastics) is consistent with his use of these texts in the so-called *Rule of Augustine* (RA).[36] Completed around 397 (that

29. See 1 Cor. 15:6.
30. See Acts 1:15.
31. Augustine, *Enarrationes in Psalmos* 132.2, in *Expositions of the Psalms 121–150*, 176.
32. Verheijen, *Saint Augustine's Monasticism*.
33. See Acts 4:32.
34. Augustine, *Enarrationes in Psalmos* 132.2, in *Expositions of the Psalms 121–150*, 176 (italics original).
35. Augustine, *Enarrationes in Psalmos* 132.2, in *Expositions of the Psalms 121–150*, 176. Augustine follows this comment with a brief discussion on vows, in which he says that it is better not to make a vow than to break it and disavows his readers of thinking that they could keep a vow in their own strength. It suggests that Augustine sees vows as a necessary element of monastic life.
36. See Lawless, *Augustine of Hippo*, for the intricate and detailed literary development of the *Rule*. I follow Lawless in viewing that portion of the RA known as the *Praeceptum* as the original *regula* of Augustine.

is, about five years into his work on the Psalms), the RA became an important monastic text in the Middle Ages despite the fact that the first reference to a *regula* written by Augustine only comes from the *Rule* of Eugippius a century after Augustine's death.[37] Nonetheless, the various texts that ultimately came to be the RA represent a fairly consistent vision of the monastic life, with Acts 2 and 4 forming a central pillar.[38] In the portion of the RA known as the *Praeceptum*, Augustine writes that the "chief motivation for your sharing life together is to live harmoniously in the house [*domo*] and to have one heart and one soul [*anima una et cor unum*] seeking God."[39] Further, the monk was not to call anything his own but to possess everything in common (*omnia communia*).[40] Even the work of the monastery was for the common purpose of the community (*in commune fiant*) and not for private purpose.[41] In the end it is clear that the monastic life, for Augustine, must involve holding all things in common, but even more so it must be built on oneness of heart and soul for the purpose of seeking God.

It is generally understood that Augustine read little Greek, and rarely does he appeal to the Greek text of the Bible. Instead, he cites an Old Latin version (or versions) of the biblical text (i.e., the *Vetus Latina*). Since these Old Latin Bibles are only extant by way of early Christian quotation, it is impossible to know whether Augustine added the phrase *in deum* to Acts 4:32 in both the commentary on Psalm 132 and the *Praeceptum* or whether he was quoting from an Old Latin Bible. The received Greek text reads, Τοῦ δὲ πλήθους τῶν πιστευσάντων ἦν καρδία καὶ ψυχὴ μία ("Now the full number of those who believed were of one heart and soul"), but Augustine follows "one heart and mind" (*anima una et cor unum*) with *in deum*.[42] Boulding translates this as "intent on God," and Lawless as "seeking God."[43] The end, then, for being of one heart and mind is not just to meet the financial needs of those having all things in common but to be in relationship with God.[44] Thus, for Augustine, to be a μόνος is to be of "one heart and mind" for the purpose of "seeking God." Again, Psalm 132's "dwell together in unity" becomes a call to monastic life. And this is further emphasized in Augustine's remarks in his psalm commentary on the Circumcellions.

37. Lawless, *Augustine of Hippo*, 65. The influence of Augustine's rule in the Middle Ages is evidenced, for example, in its adoption by the Dominicans in 1216.
38. See Kardong, *Pillars of Community*, 170–78.
39. Augustine, *Praeceptum* 1.2, in Lawless, *Augustine of Hippo*, 81. See Acts 4:32.
40. See Acts 4:32.
41. Augustine, *Praeceptum* 5.2, in Lawless, *Augustine of Hippo*, 95.
42. See Verheijen, *Saint Augustine's Monasticism*, 15–16.
43. Augustine, *Expositions of the Psalms 121–150*, 176; and Lawless, *Augustine of Hippo*, 81.
44. Kardong, *Pillars of Community*, 180.

Though commenting on Psalm 132, albeit in the form of a theology of monasticism, Augustine does not hesitate to address a contemporary issue, that of the Circumcellions. Though there is ongoing debate about the exact nature of the Circumcellions, it is clear that they were ascetics associated with the schismatic Donatist church in North Africa.[45] What is less clear is whether they were monks, and it is to this end that Augustine addresses his comments. W. H. C. Frend says without qualification that the "Circumcellions were not, however, monks, and the Donatists repudiated the term [monk],"[46] and this conclusion is accurate in light of Augustine's comments on Psalm 132. Augustine begins by reasserting that monks derive their name from this psalm and that the Circumcellions, instead of being monks themselves, simply hurl insults at those who are truly monks. In short, the Circumcellions are not monks, because they do not "dwell together in unity" but instead roam around storehouses and martyrs' shrines.[47] The Circumcellions are, in fact, false monks (*monachi falsi*).[48] Yet how does Augustine derive from *habitare fratres in unum* ("brothers to dwell together in unity") the concept of monk (μόνος)? He writes, "Μόνος means 'one,' but not any kind of 'one.' One person may be present in a crowd; he is 'one,' but one with many others. He can be called 'one' but not μόνος, because μόνος means 'one alone.' But where people live together in such unity that they form a single individual, where it is true of them, as scripture says, that they have but *one mind and one heart* (Acts 4:32)—many bodies but not many minds, many bodies but not many hearts—then they are rightly called μόνος, 'one alone.'"[49]

In essence Augustine is simply saying that a monk is not a man who is alone (i.e., in the sense of being completely separated from others). Nor is a monk a man who is alone in spite of being in the midst of others (i.e., a lone shopper in a busy market). Rather, a monk is a man who is alone in the midst of a community that is already characterized by its oneness in mind and heart.[50] There are two important things to notice here: (1) like Eusebius, Augustine

45. For a concise summary of Donatism, see Markus, "Donatus, Donatism."

46. Frend, "Circumcellions and Monks," 546.

47. See Frend, "Circumcellions and Monks"; and Frend, "*Cellae*." Isidore of Seville also sees the Circumcellions as pseudo-monks in *De Officiis Ecclesiasticis* 2.15.

48. Augustine, *Enarrationes in Psalmos* 132.4, in *Expositions of the Psalms 121–150*, 177.

49. Augustine, *Enarrationes in Psalmos* 132.6, in *Expositions of the Psalms 121–150*, 181 (italics original). The Latin text reads: "Μόνος enim unus dicitur: et non unus quomodocumque; nam et in turba est unus, sed una cum multis unus dici potest, μόνος non potest, id est, solus: μόνος enim unus solus est. Qui ergo sic vivunt in unum, ut unum hominem faciant, ut sit illis vere quod scriptum est, *una anima et unum cor*; multa corpora, sed non multae animae; multa corpora, sed non multa corda; recte dicitur μόνος, id est unus solus" (PL 37:1732–33).

50. This seems consistent, contra Kardong, with one of the earliest meanings of μοναχός (i.e., as a single part of a whole; see note 23 above). See Kardong, *Pillars of Community*, 176.

does not understand "monk" to mean alone, as in solitary, but a "monk" is a man who turns his heart (and mind) completely to God; and (2) one can only be a monk in the midst of a community and not just any community but one that is united (*in unum*) in mind and heart.[51] As Terrence Kardong comments, "Augustine has become convinced that the real meaning of *monos* is unity with another person."[52] Yet this unity with another person is not just with other monks (or even other Christians) but ultimately with God: "For Saint Augustine the unity of souls and hearts is ecclesial fraternity, first on the long way to God, and then in its definitive accomplishment in the total risen Christ."[53] The role of the heart (i.e., the inner self) as the main instrument of unity, therefore, becomes crucial.[54]

John Cassian

Contemporary with Augustine, John Cassian (d. mid-430s) is the monastic bridge between the deserts of Egypt, Syria, and Sinai and the Latin West. As a resident of the Egyptian desert (along with his friend Germanus) for about fifteen years (from approximately the mid-380s to 399/400), Cassian imbibed the monastic theology that thrived there. Forced to leave Egypt, Cassian made his way to Constantinople, where he was ordained deacon by John Chrysostom (d. 407). Yet because of political troubles in the capital city, Cassian (and Germanus) was tasked by John Chrysostom to deliver a note to the bishop of Rome, Pope Innocent I, arriving in Rome in the autumn of 404.[55] The next decade of Cassian's life is shrouded in uncertainty, but it appears that he arrived in Gaul, at modern-day Marseilles, in the middle of the 410s.[56] Within the next ten years Cassian wrote two of the most influential treatises of Christian monastic history: the *Institutes* and the *Conferences*.[57]

51. See Otten, "Augustine on Marriage," 403: "Augustine considers the community rather than the individual soul the perfect locus for attaining a life of charity guided by unity of heart."
52. Kardong, *Pillars of Community*, 176.
53. Verheijen, *Saint Augustine's Monasticism*, 97.
54. On biblical conceptions of "heart," see McCreesh, "Heart."
55. See Palladius, *Dialogue on the Life of John Chrysostom 3*, in *Palladius: Dialogue on the Life of St. John Chrysostom*, 24–29.
56. For theories on Cassian's whereabouts between late 404 and ca. 415 and the dating of his arrival in Marseilles, see Stewart, *Cassian the Monk*, 14–16. Richard J. Goodrich questions Cassian's connection to Marseilles in *Contextualizing Cassian*, 211–34.
57. The *Institutes* are directed toward assisting monks in overcoming the eight principal vices and consist of twelve books. The first four books discuss monastic clothing, the canonical hours of prayer, and the virtues. The remaining eight books each discuss one of the principal vices (gluttony, fornication, avarice, anger, sadness, acedia, vainglory, and pride). The *Conferences* comprise twenty-four books, detailing the monastic theology of fifteen Egyptian monks.

Cassian himself says that the *Institutes* were written for the benefit of the cenobitic monk (i.e., the monk who lives in community)[58] whereas the *Conferences* were written for anchorites (i.e., those monks who live alone).[59] More important, however, is Cassian's distinction between the outer and the inner person, which he maps onto the cenobitic and anchoritic life. The *Institutes*, which Cassian wrote first, begins, perhaps somewhat oddly, with a book on "The Garb of the Monks." Though Cassian is aware that the clothing does not make the monk, starting here allows him to establish the outer-inner dynamic that he will then highlight throughout his monastic theology. He writes, "Having exposed their outward appearance to view [i.e., the monk's clothing] we shall then be able to discuss, in logical sequence, their inner worship."[60] But Cassian does not think of this inner-outer dynamic only in terms of clothing, for in the next book, on the proper method of praying at nighttime, Cassian writes that in the *Institutes* he will sketch "the activity of the outer man" and lay "a foundation for prayer," but in the *Conferences* he will "discuss the condition of the inner man" reaching "the pinnacle of his prayer."[61] What Cassian appears to be describing is the fact that book 2 of the *Institutes* is mostly about the mechanics of prayer (the number of prayers, the manner of praying, etc.), whereas *Conferences* 9 and 10 are a theology of prayer. Thus, for Cassian, the "outer" is about what is on the surface (e.g., monastic clothing), but the "inner" has to do with the monk's heart.

With great conviction Cassian believes that the anchoritic life is superior to the cenobitic life and leads ultimately to contemplation of God: "The solitary life is greater and more sublime [*maior actuque sublimior est*] than that of the cenobia, and the contemplation of God . . . than the active life that is led in communities."[62] Cassian holds that the end (*finis/telos*) of the monastic life is the kingdom of God, whereas the goal (*scopos*; i.e., this-worldly end) of living monastically is "purity of heart" (*puritas cordis*).[63] For Cassian, all ascetic effort (e.g., fasts, vigils, labor, bodily deprivations, and readings) is in

58. On the *Institutes* being written for cenobites, see Cassian, *Conferences*, preface 5.

59. "Eremitical" is the most common designation of monks who live solitary lives or in loose-knit communities. They are also known as "anchorites" from the Greek ἀναχωρέω, meaning "to separate oneself, withdraw." "Eremitical" comes from the Greek word ἔρημος, meaning "desert," which is also the root of the English word *hermit*. On the *Conferences* being written for anchorites, see Cassian, *Conferences*, preface 2.

60. Cassian, *Institutes* 1.1.1 (ACW 58:21). The Latin text of the *Institutes* is found in Petschenig and Kreuz, *De Institutis Coenobiorum*, 3–231.

61. Cassian, *Institutes* 2.9.1 (ACW 58:42).

62. Cassian, *Conferences*, preface 4 (ACW 57:30). The Latin text of the *Conferences* is found in Petschenig and Kreuz, *Collationes XIIII*.

63. Cassian, *Conferences* 1.4.3 and 1.5.2. See Luckman and Kulzer, *Purity of Heart*, for discussions of "purity of heart" in biblical and early Christian texts.

service to the this-worldly end of contemplation, which is a foretaste in the present life of the vision of God that characterizes the life to come.[64] Cassian's "purity of heart" is equivalent to the ancient philosophical and monastic Christian conception of passionlessness (ἀπάθεια).[65] For Cassian, the phrase "purity of heart" is favored because it is biblical (see Matt. 5:8), but it is also a generic and inclusive concept for monastic perfection that "embraces Cassian's many other metaphors of perfection such as 'tranquility,' 'contemplation,' 'unceasing prayer,' 'chastity,' and 'spiritual knowledge.'"[66] It also includes within it the concept of single-mindedness, supported by Cassian's own use of the phrase "purity of heart" in the first *Conference*: "[In the world to come] everyone will pass over from this multiform [*multiplici*] or practical activity to the contemplation of divine things in perpetual purity of heart. Those whose concern it is to press on to knowledge and to the purification of their mind have chosen, even while living in the present world, to give themselves to this objective with all their power and strength."[67] Notice that the word "multiform" and the phrase "with all their power and strength" characterize the first stages of spiritual growth. Though human activity is "multiform" at first and not single-minded, it will not last forever. The monk moves beyond this multiplicity of activity and engages in contemplation of divine things. The "all" suggests single-mindedness, giving all for a particular *scopos*, which, in the case of Cassian, is purity of heart.

Even before moving to the inner person in the *Conferences*, Cassian has already hinted in the *Institutes* at the outward single-minded nature of monastic life when he describes the prayer life of the earliest Christians, which, he believed, was still practiced by the monks of the Egyptian desert. He writes, "And when all were seated, as is still the custom throughout Egypt, and had fixed the full attention of their hearts [*omni cordis intentione defixis*] upon the cantor's words, he sang eleven psalms."[68] This is echoed again in the same book of the *Institutes* when Cassian repeats that "they gave their heart's undivided attention [*omni cordis intentione dependeant*] to the cantor's voice."[69] To note: (1) as in Augustine, Cassian links the practices of monasticism with the earliest history of the Christian church as recorded in the Acts of the

64. For a summary of Cassian's theology of contemplation, see Stewart, *Cassian the Monk*, 47–61.

65. Though ἀπάθεια was originally a pagan Greek philosophical concept, it was baptized by Evagrius of Pontus (d. 399), Cassian's greatest influence. For a full discussion of ἀπάθεια, see Brady, "Apatheia."

66. Stewart, *Cassian the Monk*, 42.

67. Cassian, *Conferences* 1.10.5 (ACW 57:49).

68. Cassian, *Institutes* 2.5.5 (ACW 58:40).

69. Cassian, *Institutes* 2.12.1 (ACW 58:45).

Apostles; and (2) because the *Institutes* are concerned with the outer person and the *Conferences* with the inner person, we can assume that the proper single-minded focus at prayer outwardly leads to a proper single-minded focus and devotion inwardly. That is, the multiform practical activity of prayer leads to the single-minded contemplation of divine things in perpetual purity of heart. And this is what it means to be a monk.

Cassian begins the second book of the *Institutes* with the following line: "For in the early days of the faith few indeed—but they were very upright—were regarded as monks, and they had received that form of life from the evangelist Mark of blessed memory, who was the first to rule as bishop over the city of Alexandria."[70] Without mincing words, Columba Stewart concludes that Cassian's "account of the origins and evolution of monasticism . . . is historically worthless."[71] Yet Cassian's history is an interesting one and not at all idiosyncratic.[72] In his preface to the *Institutes* Cassian makes reference to the monasteries that were "founded by holy and spiritual fathers *at the time* when the apostles started preaching."[73] In brief, like Augustine, Cassian traces the institution of monasticism back to the apostolic preaching. Comparing this with book 2 of the *Institutes*, it is clear that Cassian means the form of life referenced in Acts 4, wherein the "multitude of believers had one heart and one soul" and possessed all things in common, practices that had resulted from the apostle's teaching, a fact that he makes explicit in the *Conferences*.[74] Though this had happened originally in Jerusalem, Cassian was quick to export it to Egypt by way of the evangelist Mark, saying more about Cassian's commitments to Egypt than an attempt to recount an accurate history.[75] Nonetheless, there were monks, says Cassian, and these monks were monks *because* they were of one heart and mind (*cor et anima una*) and had all things in common (*erant illis omnia communia*) and prayed with the full, undivided attention of their hearts. In short, they went from being multitudinous (*multitudinis*) to one (*una*), the same pattern that Cassian describes in *Conferences* 1.10.5 discussed above. Hence, to be a monk is to be single-minded toward God.

From this understanding Cassian enlarges the discussion by introducing four kinds (*genera*) of monks: cenobites, anchorites, sarabaites (*Sarabaitarum*), and

---

70. Cassian, *Institutes* 2.5.1 (ACW 58:39). The Latin text reads: "Nam cum in primordiis fidei pauci quidem sed probatissimi monachorum nomine censerentur, qui sicut a beatae memoriae euangelista Marco, qui primus Alexandriae urbi pontifex praefuit" (Petschenig and Kreuz, *De Institutis Coenobiorum*, 20).

71. Stewart, *Cassian the Monk*, 7.

72. See in general Vogüé, "Monachisme et Église."

73. Cassian, *Institutes*, preface 8 (ACW 58:14) (italics added).

74. Cassian, *Institutes* 2.5.1. See also Cassian, *Conferences* 18.5.1.

75. On Mark as the first bishop of Alexandria, see Eusebius, *Ecclesiastical History* 2.24.

the so-called anchorites.[76] This categorizing of monks also provides Cassian the opportunity to give a short account of monastic history. The cenobites came first, and they "live together in a community and are governed by the judgment of one elder."[77] It is this kind of monasticism, says Cassian, that arose with the disciples and is described in Acts 2 and 4. Interestingly, the whole church was cenobitic at first (i.e., they shared a common life), according to Cassian, but in his time there are few like that, for after the death of the apostles "the multitude of believers began to grow lukewarm" because either the apostles asked too little of them or the church became flooded with converted pagans who found it too difficult to give up some of their previous practices, such as "keeping their belongings and property."[78] This necessarily gave rise to cenobites proper, those who "were mindful of that earlier perfection" so they abandoned "their towns and the company of those who believed that the negligence of a more careless life was lawful" and moved to "rural and more secluded places" in order "to practice privately and individually [*priuatim ac peculiariter*] what they remembered had been taught by the apostles."[79] What happened next is significant: "As time went on they gradually separated themselves from the crowds of believers by reason of the fact that they abstained from marriage, cut themselves off from the company of their parents and from the life of this world, and were called monks [*monachi*] or μονάζοντες because of the strictness of their individual and solitary lives."[80] The source of Cassian's use of μονάζοντες for *monachi* (as opposed to other options, such as the straightforward μοναχός) is uncertain, but perhaps it is an echo of the Greek text of the *Quinta*. The significance, therefore, of this usage is that Cassian is *not* making a claim that monks are solitaries or even solitary celibates but rather that they live according to a unified way of life. As Antoine Guillaumont has noted, in the Septuagint's rendering of Psalm 68:6 (discussed above) the words μοναχός (used by Symmachus) and μονόζωνος (as used by the *Quinta*) are replaced by μονότροπος, signaling an equivalence of meaning in these terms. Using Eusebius as a guide, Guillaumont concludes that a "μονότροπος is one who, instead of acting now in one way, now in another, always has an identical behavior, one that is *unius*

---

76. The anchorites and the so-called anchorites constitute two groups in Cassian's list. Though Cassian says that these are four kinds of monks "in Egypt," it seems clear that he is also laying out a taxonomy for all Christian monasticism. Jerome lists three kinds of monks in *Epistola* 22.34–36, though all of his descriptions are concerned with the external life of monks (e.g., lifestyle and ascetical practices).

77. Cassian, *Conferences* 18.4.2 (ACW 57:637).

78. Cassian, *Conferences* 18.5.2 (ACW 57:638).

79. Cassian, *Conferences* 18.5.3 (ACW 57:638).

80. Cassian, *Conferences* 18.5.4 (ACW 57:638).

moris [a singular manner] as the Vulgate translates it; in other words, one whose entire activity is oriented towards a single end."[81] Guillaumont then concludes that μονότροπος only later came to be associated with celibacy by way of 1 Corinthians 7, which says that a married man's interests are divided (Gr. μεμέρισται / Lat. *divisus*).[82] Consequently, a nonmarried man's interests are not divided; they are μονότροπος. So when Cassian says these monks (μονάζοντες) are called such because of the "strictness of their individual and solitary lives," he means because of their singular mode of life; that is, their single-mindedness.

Cassian's second type of monk is the anchorite, who is so named because he goes apart (*secessores*), withdrawing to the desert in imitation of John the Baptist and the prophets Elijah and Elisha. The difference between Cassian's cenobite and anchorite seems to be primarily geographical—the former lives in a monastery with others, whereas the latter lives in the desert. Concerning Cassian's third type, the sarabaite, he is the first person to describe this kind of monk; therefore, all subsequent descriptions of this type depend on Cassian.[83] Just as the cenobites came to be in the earliest church, so too did the sarabaites. If Acts 4:32–37 describes the cenobites, then Acts 5:1–11 describes the sarabaites, who follow the pattern of Ananias and Sapphira. These sarabaites "withdrew themselves from the communities of the cenobia and as individuals [*singillatim*] cared for their own needs."[84] Furthermore, they do not long for the discipline of the cenobia, they do not place themselves under the judgment of other monastic elders, they are unformed in monastic living (*traditionibus institute*), they do not conquer their sinful willfulness, and they do not follow any rule of sound discretion (*discretionis regulam legitima*).[85] Rather, these so-called monks want to look like monks, so they go to some extent to do so, but ultimately, thinks Cassian, they fail because they become preoccupied with financial security and domestic affairs. In the end Cassian's main issue with the sarabaites is that they are living under a different economic model from the cenobites and the anchorites. Though Cassian's

81. Guillaumont, *Monachisme chrétien*, 51: "est *monotropos* celui qui, au lieu de se conduire tantôt d'une façon tantôt d'une autre, a un comportement toujours identique, celui qui est *unius moris*, comme traduit la Vulgate, en d'autres termes celui dont toute l'activité est orientée vers une seule fin."

82. Guillaumont, *Monachisme chrétien*, 51.

83. For example, Benedict of Nursia's description in his *regula* (1.6–9) is directly dependent on Cassian. It is possible, however, that Jerome's *remnuoth* are the same as Cassian's sarabaites (see Jerome, *Epistola* 22.34). Isidore of Seville thinks so in his *De ecclesiasticis officiis* 2.16.9–10.

84. Cassian, *Conferences* 18.7.2 (ACW 57:640).

85. This may suggest that Cassian thinks that all monastics are truly monastics only if they live under a prescribed (written?) rule.

main contention with the sarabaites is economic, it appears that they are also problematic because they are divided in the same way that the apostle Paul's married man is divided in 1 Corinthians 7:33–34. They want to be monks, but they are distracted by a need to care (perhaps even too much) for themselves, which is nearly the exact same situation presented by the apostle Paul. Again, from Cassian's discussion of the sarabaites we see him reinforcing his understanding that to be a monk is primarily about being single-minded and/ or being single-hearted.[86] It is more about one's inner disposition than about one's outer conduct, though the two are certainly connected. By the dawn of the Middle Ages such single-mindedness was the *sine qua non* of monasticism for some monastic authors, such as Pseudo-Dionysius the Areopagite.

Pseudo-Dionysius the Areopagite

Sometime after his conversion to the Christian faith, the apostle Paul preached a sermon on the rocky hillside, known as the Areopagus, next to the Parthenon in Athens. The Acts of the Apostles records that though many mocked Paul for his Christian teaching about the resurrection from the dead, some believed and joined him in the faith, including a man named Dionysius and a woman named Damaris.[87] Nearly five hundred years later, an unknown and still anonymous author, likely writing in Syria but greatly influenced by late Athenian Neoplatonism, produced a series of writings that claim to be from the hand of the apostle Paul's first-century convert Dionysius. Commonly known today as Pseudo-Dionysius, this anonymous author is first mentioned in Constantinople by the Monophysite supporters of Severus of Antioch in 532/33. In his *Ecclesiastical Hierarchy* he puts the singing of the Creed in the middle of the liturgy, something that was only introduced by Peter the Fuller at Antioch in 476.[88] Thus, Pseudo-Dionysius was writing at the turn of the sixth century. The subsequent history of the Dionysian corpus shows how important these texts became in both Eastern and Western theology despite their anonymity.[89]

---

86. Cf. Cassian, *Conferences* 24.6.1 (ACW 57:829): "For this reason a monk's whole attention should constantly be fixed on one thing [*monachi omnis intentio in unum semper est defigenda*], and the beginnings and the roundabout turns of all his thoughts should be strenuously called back to this very thing—that is, to the recollection of God."

87. See Acts 17:32–34.

88. Louth, *Denys the Areopagite*, 14. Dionysius (with a *u*) is the Latinization of the Greek Διονύσιος. In English his name is often translated as Dennis, though he is also referred to as Denis or Denys or even, in Italian, Dionigi.

89. On the influence of the Dionysian texts, see Coakley and Stang, *Re-Thinking Dionysius the Areopagite*.

Pseudo-Dionysius is the author of ten extant letters and four treatises: *Divine Names, Mystical Theology, Celestial Hierarchy,* and *Ecclesiastical Hierarchy.*[90] One of his guiding theological principles is hierarchy, which he understands as "a sacred order, a state of understanding and an activity approximating as closely as possible to the divine,"[91] or as "a certain perfect arrangement, an image of the beauty of God which sacredly works out the mysteries of its own enlightenment in the orders and levels of understanding of the hierarchy, and which is likened toward its own source as much as is permitted." The goal (σκοπός) of hierarchy "is to enable beings to be as like as possible to God and to be at one with him."[92] Hierarchy is the way in which reality is ordered so as to draw all things back to God himself, both the celestial realm (hence his *Celestial Hierarchy*) and the human realm (the ecclesiastical hierarchy and the "hierarchy according to the law" as per the *Ecclesiastical Hierarchy*).[93] Both realms are triadic in structure, representing the threefold movement back to God of purification, illumination, and perfection.[94] In the celestial realm there are three threefold groups (τρεῖς ἀφορίζει τριαδικάς): (1) seraphim, cherubim, and thrones (those who are forever around God and permanently united with him); (2) authorities, dominions, and powers; and (3) angels, archangels, and principalities. In the ecclesiastical realm there are also three threefold groups: (1) sacraments (consecration with oil [μύρον], synaxis/Communion/Eucharist, and baptism); (2) clergy (hierarch, priest, and deacon); and (3) laity (monks, communicants, and those being purified/catechumens).[95] Within the rank of the laity are the monks, those who hold "the most exalted order [τάξις]."[96]

Pseudo-Dionysius takes it for granted that there are monks in the church, just below those in sacred orders but above nonmonastic, baptized church members. But what is a monk? For Pseudo-Dionysius "monks" are so called "because of the purity of their duty and service to God and because their lives, far from being scattered [ἀμερίστου], are monopolized by their unifying [ἐνοποιούσης] and sacred recollection which excludes all distraction and enables them to achieve a singular mode of life conforming to God [τῶν

---

90. For an English translation of the whole *Corpus Areopagiticum*, see Pseudo-Dionysius, *Complete Works*. The Greek text is found in Suchla, *Corpus Dionysiacum*, vol. 1; and Heil and Ritter, *Corpus Dionysiacum*, vol. 2.

91. Pseudo-Dionysius, *Celestial Hierarchy* 3.1, in *Complete Works*, 153.

92. Pseudo-Dionysius, *Celestial Hierarchy* 3.2, in *Complete Works*, 154.

93. See Pseudo-Dionysius, *Ecclesiastical Hierarchy* 2.1 and 3.3.10.

94. See Pseudo-Dionysius, *Celestial Hierarchy* 7.3.

95. Rorem, *Pseudo-Dionysius*, 21. On the liturgical significance of Pseudo-Dionysius's hierarchies, see Rorem, *Pseudo-Dionysian Synthesis*.

96. Pseudo-Dionysius, *Ecclesiastical Hierarchy* 6.1.3, in *Complete Works*, 244.

διαιρετῶν ἱεραῖς συμπτύξεσιν εἰς θεοειδῆ μονάδα] and open to the perfection of God's love."[97] That God makes an individual whole is a common theme in the *Ecclesiastical Hierarchy*. For example, in the opening letter to Timothy, Pseudo-Dionysius says that God "pulls together all our many differences" (συμπτύσσει τάς πολλάς ἑτερότητας) and "makes our life, disposition, and activity something one [ἑνοειδῆ] and divine."[98] And when discussing the celebration of the Holy Eucharist he writes that "it is not possible to be gathered together toward the One and to partake of peaceful union with the One while divided [διῃρημένους] among ourselves."[99] Nonetheless, the oneness that characterizes monks is something more than this; otherwise the monks would not be a distinct order.

Alexander Golitzin believes that Pseudo-Dionysius is most helpfully read in light of his Syrian predecessors (who in turn were highly influenced by Jewish writers). Thus, he attributes Pseudo-Dionysius's emphasis on oneness to his dependence on the Syrian concept of *iḥîdāyā* (the "single one"),[100] which derives from the Syriac for "one" (*ḥad*). In the Syriac New Testament *iḥîdāyā* is used five times to describe Jesus as God's "single son" (Gr. μονογενής).[101] But as Robert Murray summarizes, the term carries with it three related elements: "(1) singleness by leaving family and not marrying; (2) single-mindedness . . . ; and (3) a special relationship to Christ, the Only-begotten Son (*Berâ Îḥîdāyâ*)."[102] Golitzin elaborates on this single-mindedness in Pseudo-Dionyius as "simple, i.e., uniquely and exclusively focused on Jesus and the things of God."[103] If Pseudo-Dionysius is dependent on the Syrian concept of *iḥîdāyā*, then he likely holds to a view that a monk is celibate, something that seems to be the case when he says that monks have "been purified of all stain,"[104] which may also explain why the monks are a different rank from other baptized and (most likely) married believers. However, inasmuch as Pseudo-Dionysius and the Syriac tradition see celibacy as constituent of monasticism, they also see

97. Pseudo-Dionysius, *Ecclesiastical Hierarchy* 6.1.3, in *Complete Works*, 245.

98. Pseudo-Dionysius, *Ecclesiastical Hierarchy* 1.1, in *Complete Works*, 196.

99. Pseudo-Dionysius, *Ecclesiastical Hierarchy* 3.3.8, in *Complete Works*, 218.

100. Other scholars have also made this connection between μοναχός and *iḥîdāyā*, such as Guillaumont, *Monachisme chrétien*, 48–50: "Le mot μοναχός . . . est . . . bien documentée pour son equivalent syriaque *iḥīdāyā* (49). (The word μοναχός . . . is . . . well documented for its equivalence to the Syriac *iḥīdāyā*.) Alfred Adam argues that μοναχός is the Greek translation of *iḥīdāyā*. See Adam, "Grundbegriffe des Mönchtums"; also Bumazhnov, "Some Further Observations," 22–23.

101. See Golitzin, *Mystagogy*, 330.

102. Murray, *Symbols of Church and Kingdom*, 14. See also Griffith, "Asceticism," 224–25.

103. Golitzin, *Mystagogy*, 330.

104. Pseudo-Dionysius, *Ecclesiastical Hierarchy* 6.1.3, in *Complete Works*, 244. This is Golitzin's understanding (*Mystagogy*, 331).

single-mindedness as an essential (and even a far more important) element.[105] Guillaumont concludes that if there was an early emphasis on celibacy in the Syriac tradition as a requirement to be a monk, that began to fade by the early fourth century in favor of other requirements, primarily single-mindedness (μονότροπος).[106] So "the term μονότροπος is the one that best expresses the essence of the monastic life."[107] Hence, single-mindedness is the essence of the monastic life. Consequently, Pseudo-Dionysius's unified monk is a single-minded monk pursuing a single-minded mode of life, which is consistent with the Greek tradition that precedes and comes after Pseudo-Dionysius.[108]

Other Examples

A select sampling demonstrates that other monastic theologians have also concluded that a "monk" is someone who is single-minded in their focus on God. Basil of Caesarea (d. 379) writes that the monastic life is "of only one kind [μονότροπος], having but one goal [σκοπόν]—the glory of God . . . [but the] life of those outside is of many kinds and very varied [πολύτροπος δὲ καὶ ποικίλος τῶν ἔξωθεν βίος], ever shifting this way and that in order to please any and everyone they meet."[109] In a homily attributed to Macarius the Egyptian (ca. 400), the author defines a monk as one who remains un-married, renouncing the world interiorly and exteriorly, and who is constant in prayer so that he purifies his mind from a multiplicity of reasoning that distracts him from focusing on God (τῶν πολλῶν καὶ χαλεπῶν λογισμῶν).[110] Cyril of Scythopolis (d. ca. 559), in his *Life of Sabas*, quotes (à la Eusebius) Psalm 68:6 as "the Lord gives the single-minded a home to dwell in" and ap-plies it to the small cenobium for novices founded by Sabas.[111] Thus, monks are the single-minded. This is made explicit again by Philoxenos of Mabbug (d. 523), a Monophysite theologian from Syria, who also quotes Psalm 68:6

---

105. See Aphrahat, *Demonstrations* 7.18: "And let the one who is building a house return to it, lest he call it to mind and not fight [with] full [attention]. It is the single ones who are ready for the struggle, since they set their faces toward what is before them and do not call to mind what is behind them." Lehto, *Demonstrations of Aphrahat*, 210–11.

106. Guillaumont, *Monachisme chrétien*, 52–53. See the discussion of μονότροπος as single-mindedness above in the section on John Cassian.

107. Guillaumont, *Monachisme chrétien*, 55: "Le terme μονότροπος est donc celui qui exprime le mieux l'essence de la vie monastique."

108. See Roques, "Éléments," 305–14.

109. Silvas, *Asketikon of St Basil the Great*, 217.

110. Marriott, *Macarii Anecdota*, 44. On Macarius see Moreschini and Norelli, *Greek and Latin Literature*, 2:64–67.

111. Cyril of Scythopolis, *Life of Sabas* 28 (*Lives of the Monks*, 122).

as support that a monk is only a monk if he is interiorly and exteriorly unified. Further, like Pseudo-Dionysius, Philoxenos makes an explicit connection
between μοναχός and *iḥîdāyā*.[112] Finally, Maximus the Confessor (d. 662), in
his *Commentary on the Our Father*, says that the disciple "advances toward
God free and uncontrolled by any attachment to beings at all, simple in his
desire [ἁπλοῦς τε τὴν ἔφεσιν] and uncomplicated in his intention, and makes
his dwelling with the one who is simple by nature [ἁπλοῦν τῇ φύσει] through
general virtues spiritually harnessed to each other as fiery horses."[113] For
Maximus monastic life is single-mindedness.[114]

Conclusion

Though monasticism is associated historically with celibacy and other forms
of asceticism (such as poverty, stability, and unwavering obedience), single-
mindedness is another consistent element of monasticism, and the one that
seems to be more essential in the earliest tradition: "For the Greeks *monachos*
described the way of life of a man devoting his life to a singleness of purpose: devotion to and contemplation of God. . . . The *monachos* might lead
a solitary life, but in any event would maintain a single focus, undeflected by
material considerations."[115] Though the word μοναχός is often seen as synonymous with "one who is single/celibate," that is not the oldest understanding
of the word, especially if one, like Cassian and Augustine, draws a straight
line between early monasticism and Acts 2 and 4. What these early believers
had in common was *not* celibacy but the sharing of material resources and a
common exercise of spiritual practices. Thus, to be a monk is to be one, not
divided; to be unified in one's goal of coming into union with God. Though
many believers live in a multitudinous manner, a μοναχός will set herself apart
by living simply and singly. A monk is single-minded.

112. Guillaumont, *Monachisme chrétien*, 58. See Philoxenos of Mabbug, "Letter to Patricius
of Edessa" 35, in Lavenant, "La lettre à Patricius d'Édesse," 782–83.
    113. Maximus the Confessor, *Selected Writings*, 109. Greek text in PG 90:871–910C.
    114. See also Maximus the Confessor, *Ambigua*, in PG 91:1368B.
    115. Hunt, "Monk as Mourner," 28.

Two

The Monk in History

To broaden the discussion begun in chapter 1, in this chapter I will examine historical texts in which the author is suggesting something akin to an "interiorized monasticism" (discussed in greater detail in the next chapter), or at least exploring the idea of how nonmonastic forms of life could be monastic. In the previous chapter the goal was to show that "monk" did not necessarily mean one who lives alone or in a community following a rule and some form of vows (such as the Benedictine vows of obedience, stability, and *conversatio morum*, i.e., a conversion of life). Here I hope to show that throughout Christian history, in different places at different times, there were differing visions of what monasticism was, *even if* these texts were produced in an environment that continued to promote more traditional expressions of monasticism. That is, if one understands monasticism to be recognizable by traits A, B, and C, then one will look for A, B, and C in ecclesiastical history and conclude, "Ah, there is monasticism." However, if monasticism is not reducible to a number of particular traits, then one must take seriously an author's expression of his understanding of monasticism. Examples include Symeon the New Theologian's (d. 1022) *Hymn 27*, Robert de Sorbon's (d. 1274) treatise on marriage as a monastic order, the medieval prose allegory *The Abbey of the Holy Ghost* (ca. 1350), and Walter Hilton's *Mixed Life* (ca. 1390). These examples are geographically diverse, from the Byzantine Empire to medieval France to late medieval England. They are also linguistically diverse: Symeon wrote in Greek, Robert de Sorbon in Latin, and *The Abbey of the Holy Ghost* and the *Mixed Life* are in English (though *The Abbey* is from a French original). Thus, across a wide geographical and linguistic span we have a good representation of thinking about the monastic life as an interior singleness of heart. And this diversity is important to demonstrate that monasticism has never been viewed monolithically but has expressed itself in a host of ways and in a host of places. This is obvious when one investigates Christian history, but it is not always acknowledged in modern overviews of monasticism, which often prefer orderliness to variation.

Symeon the New Theologian's *Hymn 27*

Symeon the New Theologian was born in Galatia, Asia Minor, in 949 but moved to Constantinople as a teenager, destined for a life in politics and imperial service. Thanks to a well-placed uncle, Symeon was given the office of *spatharokoubikoularios* and granted senatorial rank.[1] However, in 977 he became a monk at the well-known Stoudios monastery in Constantinople. This conversion to monasticism is, in part, the result of Symeon coming under the influence of a Constantinopolitan monk named Symeon Eulabes (or Symeon the Stoudite; d. 986/87) and experiencing, in 970, a powerful spiritual vision of the elder Symeon (discussed below).[2] Within three years Symeon was the *hegoumenos* (i.e., abbot) of the monastery of St. Mamas in Constantinople, rebuilding the monastery materially and spiritually. Because of conflict with the church's hierarchy and with the imperial court, Symeon was exiled in 1009, spending the last thirteen years of his life rebuilding the monastery of St. Marina across the Bosporus from Constantinople, dying on March 12, 1022, as a simple monk.[3]

Symeon's literary output is quite extensive, comprising theological, ethical, and catechetical treatises; chapters; thanksgivings; epistles; and his "Hymns of Divine Love."[4] According to Daniel Griggs, "Symeon wrote the *Hymns* throughout his monastic career, though most of them probably date from his maturity, especially during his exile."[5] Of greatest interest for the present purposes is

1. Though the duties of this office are unclear, it was traditionally given to eunuchs. For this reason (and others), H. J. M. Turner has argued that Symeon was a eunuch (*Symeon the New Theologian*, 18–19).
2. Described by Symeon in his *Catecheses* 22.70–116, in Krivochéine, *Syméon le Nouveau Théologien*, 370–74. For an English translation see Symeon the New Theologian, *Discourses*, 245–46. According to the life of Symeon by Nicetas Stethatos, Symeon had already attempted to enter the Stoudios monastery as early as 963 but was refused. See Hausherr, *Un grand mystique byzantine*, 6.
3. Symeon was dismissed as the *hegoumenos* of St. Marina in 1005.
4. In the life Stethatos refers to them as Τῶν θείων ὕμνων τοὺς ἔρωτας, literally "Loves of the Divine Hymns" (Nicetas Stethatos, *Vie* 111.8, in Hausherr, *Un grand mystique byzantine*, 154).
5. Griggs, introduction to Symeon the New Theologian, *Divine Eros*, 10. See also Koder, *Hymnes* 1–15, 76–77.

Hymn 27: "What sort of person a monk must be; what is his practice, progress, and ascent."[6] This hymn of 170 lines is divided into two parts, according to Johannes Koder: "The first describes Symeon's ideal (1–118): the solitary does not live alone, he lives with Christ. On the contrary, without Christ, every person remains alone, even if he lives in the midst of crowds (1–38). Living with his God, the solitary already lives in Paradise (38–118). The second part is a passionate exhortation to pursue this ideal (118–170). This magnificent life is possible for all (118–150), but it requires generosity: the life of the solitary is not a life of quiet death. Everything ends with prayer (150–170)."[7]

From the outset the hymn talks about the monastic life as an interior disposition. It is concerned not with the outward forms of the institution of monasticism (e.g., vows and rules) but with the proper understanding that the monk is primarily a monk because of his inner nature. For a monk (μοναχέ) to be a monk, he must be alone (μονάζων), though this aloneness is actually aloneness with God, for "you are not really alone, for you are with the King" (204.6), and it is an interior aloneness, in "the house of your soul" (204.1).[8] At the same time, however, the monk has separated himself from other monks, though this is perhaps more of a spiritual separation than a physical separation:

> you are alone with respect to us, since you are away [ὑπάρχων] from us, and separated [χωρισθείς] from the whole world, this is complete solitude. (204.7–8)

In Symeon's reckoning, one is only a monk if one is in communion with God the Trinity, because

> if one has not received the whole incarnate
> Logos God, then, alas, one has not become a monk at all.
> Hence this one who has been separated from God is alone [μόνος].
> (205.25–27)

6. Symeon the New Theologian, *Hymn 27* (*Divine Eros*, 204). The original Greek is found in Koder, *Hymnes 16–40*, 278–93. Another English translation is available in Symeon the New Theologian, *Hymns of Divine Love*. The titles of each hymn are the work of Alexis the Philosopher (see Koder, *Hymnes 16–40*, 22).

7. Koder, *Hymnes 16–40*, 278: "La première où Syméon décrit l'idéal (1–118): le solitaire ne vit pas seul, il vit avec le Christ. Au contraire, sans le Christ, tout homme reste seul, même s'il vit au milieu des foules (1–38). Vivant avec son Dieu, le solitaire vit déjà au Paradis (38–118). La seconde partie est une exhortation passionée à poursuivre cet idéal (118–170). Cette vie magnifique est possible à tous (118–150), mais elle suppose de la générosité: la vie de solitaire n'est pas une vie de morte quiétude. Tout s'achève par une prière (150–170)."

8. Parenthetical citations to *Hymn 27* are to the page number in Griggs's translation in *Divine Eros*, followed by the poem's line number.

A monk, therefore, is not someone who is truly alone (μόνος), in the physical sense, but someone who is in communion with the Father, Son, and Holy Spirit. With this logic it would appear that all Christians are monks, but given that the hymn was most likely written for a monk, perhaps even a *hegoumenos*, then there is certainly something more to Symeon's reasoning.[9] As is so often the case in Christian history, Symeon is creating a distinction between a "normal" Christian and a monk. The implication of the poem thus far would seem to suggest that not all Christians are in communion with the Trinity, but only those who are "monks," a kind of alone with the Alone.[10] Even if this is the case, however, I suggest that Symeon's view is instructive for understanding the nature of monasticism.

At its root, Symeon's theology of monasticism is about being alone with God, and—paradoxically—in this aloneness one is, in fact, not alone. But is this option not open to *all* Christians? Is not communion with God the very essence of Christian baptism? Symeon's own life is a testament to this reality. In 970 Symeon experienced a vision of his spiritual father (the elder Symeon) that he describes in *Discourse 22*, "On Faith":

> One day, as he stood and recited, "God, have mercy upon me, a sinner" *(Lk. 18:13)*, uttering it with his mind rather than his mouth, suddenly a flood of divine radiance appeared from above and filled all the room. As this happened the young man lost all awareness [of his surroundings] and forgot that he was in a house or that he was under a roof. He saw nothing but light all around him and did not know if he was standing on the ground. He was not afraid of falling; he was not concerned with the word, nor did anything pertaining to men and corporeal beings enter into his mind. Instead, he was wholly in the presence of immaterial light and seemed to himself to have turned into light. . . . His mind then ascended to heaven and beheld yet another light, which was clearer than that which was close at hand.[11]

Though Symeon was experiencing a vision of his spiritual elder, it is clear that he was having a divine experience, seeing the "immaterial light" of the Godhead and beholding "yet another light."[12] And this as a layman! Further, like most orthodox theologians before him, Symeon held that baptism marks

9. Koder, *Hymnes 16–40*, 279n1: "Cet Hymne est écrit pour un moine. C'est bien normal pour un higoumène." (This hymn was written by a monk. This is normal for a heguman.)

10. This is a paraphrase of Plotinus, *Enneads* 6.9.11.50, used by Symeon in *Hymn 27*, line 74.

11. Symeon the New Theologian, *Discourse* 22.4 (deCatanzaro, 245–46).

12. In a later vision, which occurred just before entrance into the monastic life, "we are meant to understand that he saw the radiance of Christ directly." McGuckin, "*Hymns of Divine Eros*," 184. See also McGuckin, "Luminous Vision."

a person's spiritual birth: "By Holy Baptism He [God] regenerates and re-fashions us, completely sets us free from condemnation, and places us in this world wholly free and not oppressed by the tyranny of the enemy. . . . We have been born again in Holy Baptism."[13] "At the same time Symeon emphasizes that 'perfect grace' is not automatically given to everybody in their Baptism: it must be acquired by good deeds," writes Hilarion Alfeyev.[14] In other words, there is room for good works throughout the baptized Christian's life, but they have been given the necessary preparation in baptism for those good works. This places all baptized Christians on equal footing before God, and if the layman Symeon can have a luminous vision of God, then it seems possible that this grace is open to all Christian believers. However, Symeon believes that many baptized Christians lose this original baptismal grace by their failure to keep God's commands. Consequently, they are in need of a second baptism, the baptism of the Holy Spirit, "which is the renewal of baptismal grace in those who have lost it. According to Symeon, it is not enough for salvation to be baptized 'in water': one should also be baptized 'in the Holy Spirit.'"[15] As a result of this thinking, "not all who are baptized received Christ through Baptism,"[16] but those who have the second baptism certainly have Christ. And nowhere does Symeon say that only monks have the second baptism. Nonmonastics, then, have Christ through second baptism and are, by Symeon's definition in *Hymn 27*, monks. In short, those who dwell with Christ and have the Holy Spirit are "monks" in the true sense of the word as used by Symeon since they are one with the One.[17]

Symeon continues by describing in general terms the way that all humanity will experience death, causing ultimate separation from others but eternal union with God, and he also emphasizes that in marriage the husband and the wife are united "once and for all" (206.50). Similar to marital union, each Christian is united to God, for "the soul is in God, and God in the soul" (206.55). This union with God, coupled with repentance, makes one a monk:

Thus are they united to God, those who purify
their souls through repentance in this world,
and they are appointed monks who are apart from others. (206.57–59)

13. Symeon the New Theologian, *Discourse 5*.10 (deCatanzaro, 100–101). See chap. 5 of this book for a further discussion on the place of baptism vis-à-vis monasticism.

14. Alfeyev, *Symeon the New Theologian*, 203.

15. Alfeyev, *Symeon the New Theologian*, 203–4.

16. Symeon the New Theologian, *Ethical Discourse* 10 (*On the Mystical Life*, 1:152). Greek text in Darrouzès, *Syméon le Nouveau Théologien*.

17. Further support for this is found in lines 18–19 of *Hymn 27* when Symeon writes, "But when one has Christ dwelling within, how, tell me, can it be said that one is alone?" To have Christ is to be a monk to the fullest degree.

It would seem that Symeon's second baptism is intimately linked to repentance, so much so that the second baptism *is* the life of repentance. In *Discourse 5*, "On Penitence," Symeon refers to the uselessness of monastic profession without repentance, emphasizing that even if he divested himself of all worldly wealth, forsook his family, and took the monastic habit, tears of repentance would still be necessary because of the residue of sin.[18] In the next section of the discourse he connects this explicitly to laypersons, saying that "it is possible for all men, brethren, not only for monks but for laymen as well, to be penitent at all times and constantly, and to weep and entreat God, and by such practices to acquire all other virtues as well. . . . This is possible for one who has wife and children. . . . He can receive the Holy Spirit [i.e., second baptism] and become a friend of God and enjoy the vision of Him."[19] Returning to *Hymn 27*, this would then make these laymen monks. Again emphasizing that to be a monk is not to be separated from others but to be united to God, Symeon poetically and elegantly writes,

> But I teach you how they [i.e., those united with Christ] live and in what manner
> they serve God, and sought Him alone
> before all else, and they found Him alone,
> and loved Him alone, and were united to Him alone,
> and became monks alone with the Alone,
> even if they were received among a multitudinous people. (206.70–75)

In the end, for Symeon a monk is anyone who is united to Christ; institutional connections and structures do not seem to factor into his definition of monasticism,[20] although he himself was a member of monastic communities.[21]

18. The connection between tears and baptism was made by John Climacus in the late sixth century when he wrote, "The fountain of tears after Baptism is greater than Baptism, even if it is somewhat bold to say so. For Baptism is just a washing away of evils which were in us before, whereas sins committed after Baptism are washed away by tears. As Baptism is received in infancy, we have all defiled it, but we cleanse it anew with tears." John Climacus, *Ladder of Divine Ascent* 7, quoted in Alfeyev, *Symeon the New Theologian*, 205.

19. Symeon the New Theologian, *Dicourses* 5.3 (deCatanzaro, 93).

20. I would suggest that this is due to the charismatic quality of Symeon's theology and vision of the Christian life against the "pessimists who preferred a formalist piety." Griggs, "Religious Experience," 85. Something similar can be seen in Macarius of Egypt (d. 391), who said, "In truth there is neither virgin nor married, neither monk nor secular, but God gives the Holy Spirit to all, according to the intention of each." Quoted in Ware, "Married Christian," 79–80.

21. Symeon's monastic "family" always included laypersons, something that he learned and inherited from Symeon Eulabes: "Sometime around 986–7 Symeon Eulabes died at the Stoudium monastery leaving Symeon as the new head and leader of his school of disciples, a circle that included both monastics and lay aristocrats" (McGuckin, *"Hymns of Divine Eros,"* 186).

Robert de Sorbon's Sermon on Marriage

Robert was born in Sorbon, a small town four kilometers north of Rethel and about two hundred kilometers northeast of Paris, to a poor family on October 9, 1201.[22] He received a basic education in language, grammar, and arithmetic at Rethel but then moved on to the monastic school of St. Denys in Reims at the age of twelve or fourteen to study rhetoric, grammar, and arithmetic, followed by study of the arts and theology at the University of Paris in 1235–36. He was subsequently appointed canon at Cambrai around 1250 and founded, in 1253 in Paris, a school for poor theological students.[23] These activities in Paris brought him to the attention of King Louis IX, who made Robert his priest-confessor in 1256. In 1258 Robert was made a canon at Notre-Dame de Paris and then chancellor of the University at Paris. He died on August 15, 1274, approximately five months after his more well-known theological colleague Thomas Aquinas.[24] Robert wrote a handful of works. For example: *On the conscience*;[25] *On the threefold way* (*De tribus dietis*; a treatise on confession that uses the image of the journey to Paradise); *On the holy and right way to confess*;[26] *On the manner of confession and how to hear a confession* (a guide for confessors);[27] *On the sense of taste* (*De saporibus*; a discussion of the multiple flavors of Eucharistic bread); and more than eighty sermons, especially *On marriage* (*De matrimonio*), which is of interest for our present purposes because it describes the "order of matrimony . . . in terms analogous to those used of the religious orders."[28]

22. This biographical sketch relies on Glorieux, *Aux origines de la Sorbonne I*, 11–29; Bériou, "Robert de Sorbon," 816–17; Verger, "R. de Sorbon"; and Chambon, *Robert de Sorbon*, v–vii.

23. Gabriel, *Paris Studium*, 73: Robert "wanted a house which could serve poor secular priests studying theology. His intention was to make them free from material worries while they were preparing for the highest degree at the University, the mastership in theology."

24. The thirteenth-century French monk-chronicler William of Nangis (d. 1300) made note in his *Chronicle of France* for the year 1264 that the most illustrious theologians at the University of Paris were Thomas Aquinas, Bonaventure, Gérard de Abbeville, and Robert of Sorbon: "Florebant hoc tempore Parisius insignes theologi, frater Thomas de Quina ordinis Praedicatorum, et frater Bonaventura ordinis Minorum, atque de saecularibus clericis magister Guerodus de Abbatis villa et magister Robertus de Sorbona, qui scholares Parisius primus constituit Sorbonenses." (Worthy theologians that flourished in Paris at this time were brother Thomas of Aquino of the Order of Preachers, and brother Bonaventure of the Orders of Friars Minor; and from the secular clerics master Guerodus of Abbatis Villa and master Robert de Sorbon, whose Parisian school first set up the Sorbon.) Bouquet, *Recueil des historiens*, 560.

25. Diekstra, "Robert de Sorbon's *De consciencia*."

26. Diekstra, "Robert de Sorbon's *Qui vult vere confiteri*."

27. Diekstra, "Robert de Sorbon's *Cum repetes*."

28. Diekstra, "Men, Women and Marriage," 69. For a full discussion of Robert's literary corpus, see Glorieux, *Aux origines de la Sorbonne I*, 54–59; and Bériou, "Robert de Sorbon," 821–22.

On Marriage is a work preserved in at least eight manuscripts, most at the Bibliothèque Nationale de France in Paris but one in Bruges, Belgium, and another in the Bibliotheca Apostolica Vaticana. In 1890 Jean Hauréau published the text, which was a transcription of some of the manuscripts. He claimed that the transcription was not of any particular manuscript but "a conflation made up selectively from manuscript versions that differ considerably in degree of elaboration and details of phrasing."[29] Nonetheless, "the eight surviving manuscript versions agree in their general outline and contents and we may be fairly confident that what we read represents Robert's views, though not necessarily his own authorized text or the verbal details of his oral presentation."[30] Though in some ways Robert's sermon is fairly normal, the sermon stands out in particular because of its positive assessment of women, or at least of women as wives.[31] In Robert's estimation a woman's significance is shown by the fact that she was created from man's rib, "not from the upper part or from the lower, but from the middle," whereas man is made from mud (189; *non de inferiori parte vel de superiori, sed de media . . . de limo terrae*).[32] Additionally, women come from a more exalted place than men, for women are from terrestrial paradise but men are from the earth (189; *virum fecit in terra, mulierem vero in paradiso terrestri*). Because of this, marriage should be esteemed even if virginity is still a more virtuous calling.[33] And this high regard for marriage leads Robert to offer an anecdote that places marriage on par with monasticism. Diekstra sums up the anecdote well using the Vatican version of the sermon:

> A married man is addressed by a university master with the salutation, "Good day, monk." At first the man is puzzled and looks about him expecting to see some nearby monk, but the other tells him: "It is you I am talking to, for you are a monk." The citizen can hardly believe his ears, assuming that it is a case of mistaken identity, and tells him: "I am not whom you think I am." But the master remains unperturbed, repeats his address and adds: "You are a monk. Do you wish to deny it?" upon which the citizen, understandably, gets annoyed and indulges in some rude language. The only effect is that the master now

29. Diekstra, "Men, Women and Marriage," 72. See also Hauréau, *Notices et extraits*, 188: "Nous en prévenons on ne trouvera dans le texte que nous allons donner au public la transcription fidèle d'aucun des manuscrits cites; il n'y a pourtant rien qui ne se lise dans les uns ou dans les autres." (We warn the reader that he will not find in the text that we are going to give to the public a faithful transcription of any of the cited manuscripts; there is nothing, however, that is not read in one or the other.)

30. Diekstra, "Men, Women and Marriage," 72.

31. Kooper, "Loving the Unequal Equal," 45.

32. Parenthetical references are to the page number in Hauréau, *Notices et extraits*.

33. Diekstra, "Men, Women and Marriage," 68.

evidently feels free to collar him for a disputation on the nature of his status in life. . . . The master tells him that since he is married, he is a member of an order, namely the sacramental order of matrimony, and proceeds to interrogate him on his knowledge of the rule of this order. The citizen has to confess that after twelve years of marriage he is still ignorant of the existence of any such rule, let alone its finer points. This leads the master to conclude that in addressing him as "monk" he had after all made too high an estimate of his status, assuming him to be of senior rank in his order; he should by now have been a novice-master engaged in instructing the young, but it appears that he does not even come up to the rank of a lay brother. He should have addressed him as "bad monk."[34]

Robert compares someone entering the order of matrimony to a novice entering the monastic life. Likewise, the Dominican Henry of Provins, preaching circa 1272, compares the "order" of marriage to the Franciscan and Dominican Orders,[35] and Guibert de Tournai (d. 1284), echoing Jacques de Vitry (d. 1240), says that marriage was created by God in Paradise as one of the original orders (*ordines*).[36] Thus, the crux of these comparisons hinges on the use of the word "order" (*ordo*).

Many scholars contend that the Western medieval world was divided into different *ordines*.[37] Sometime during the tenth century, in response to a feudal framework, the ideology of the three orders of life was firmly solidified, even if its rhetorical purposes and agenda were not always clear.[38] The schema was tripartite, often expressed as *oratores* (those who prayed), *bellatores* (those who fought), and *laboratores* (those who worked) or something similar, such as *dona* (those who make offering), *militia* (those in military service), and *orationes* (those who speak/pray).[39] One of the first extant Christian references

34. Diekstra, "Men, Women and Marriage," 68–69.

35. Bériou and d'Avray, "Comparison," 72: "*Vos videtis quod noster ordo et fratrum minorum non est diu quod incepit; et similiter alii ordines post incarnationem inceperunt; sed iste ordo incepit a principio mundi. Plus, quidam homo mortalis de Hyspania fecit nostrum ordinem; quidam homo de Lumbardia ordinem fratrum minorum; sed istum ordinem fecit ipse deus, et non de novo, sed a principio mundi*" (italics original). (You see that it is not long since our order and the order of the friars minor began; and similarly other orders began after the incarnation; but this order began from the beginning of the world. Further, a certain mortal man from Spain created our order; a certain man from Lombardy created the order of friars minor; but this order God himself created, and not recently, but from the beginning of the world.)

36. Bériou and d'Avray, "Comparison," 74.

37. The following is dependent on Peters, "Monastic Orders." On the origins of this division, see Oexle, "Tria genera hominum"; and Dubuisson, "L'Irlande."

38. See Duby, *Three Orders*.

39. On the latter three *ordines*, see Hallinger, *Corpus Consuetudinum Monasticarum*, 493.

to the tripartite *ordines* comes from the writings of King Alfred of England (d. 899) in his Anglo-Saxon translation of Boethius's *Consolation of Philosophy*: "Thus a king's raw material and instruments of rule are a well-peopled land, and he must have men of prayer (*gebedmen*), men of war (*fyrdmen*), and men of work (*weorcman*). As you know, without these tools no king may display his special talent. Further, for his materials he must have means of support for the three classes above spoken of."[40] This schema was adopted by other Anglo-Saxon authors, including Aelfric of Eynsham (d. ca. 1010) and Wulfstan II of York (d. 1023). In a letter to Wulfstan, Aelfric says that there are three orders in the church: *laboratores*, *bellatores*, and *oratores*. The first provide food, the second defend against enemies, and the third, those who pray, include priests, monks, and bishops.[41] Wulfstan used the same tripartite division as Aelfric in his own works. Outside England, the tripartite *ordines* are found in the mid-ninth-century commentary on Revelation attributed to Haimo of Auxerre (fl. 840–60)[42] and in a poem of Adalbero of Laon (d. 1090): "The house of God which is thought to be one is therefore triple. Now [some] pray, others fight, and others work."[43]

Another common grouping was that of clerics (those who ruled the church), monastics (monks and nuns who renounced the world), and laypersons (who lived and worked in the world). For example, Cistercian monk Aelred of Rievaulx (d. 1167) wrote that there are "three orders of human life. . . . The first is natural, the second necessary, and the third voluntary. The first is conceded, the second imposed, and the third is offered [to humankind]."[44] Elisabeth of Schönau (d. 1164) also details a tripartite division: "The three ways . . . express the nature of the three orders of the church, namely, the married, the chaste, and the leaders [i.e., *rectorum* = clerics]."[45] In like manner, Hildegard of Bingen (d. 1179), writing to a monk, says that the creatures of the Apocalypse (Rev. 4:7) represent the orders of society: the lion is monks, the calf is clerics, and the man is the laity. Theologian Peter Lombard (d. 1160) referred

40. Sedgefield, *King Alfred's Version*, 41. Translation slightly modified.
41. Whitelock, Brett, and Brooke, *Councils and Synods*, 1:252.
42. PL 117:953B: "A tribus scilicet ordinibus, qui forsitan erant in populo Judaeorum, sicut fuerunt apud Romanos, in senatoribus scilicet, militibus, et agricolis, ita et Ecclesia eisdem tribus modis partitur, in sacerdotibus, militibus, et agricultoribus, quae tribus amabilis dicitur." (From namely three orders which perhaps were among the people of the Jews, as they were among the Romans, namely, in the senators, soldiers, and farmers, so too the church, which is said to be lovable by the three, is divided by the same three modes in priests, soldiers, and farmers.)
43. Cited in Constable, *Three Studies*, 284.
44. Aelred of Rievaulx, *Mirror of Charity* 3.32.76 (Connor, 273). The first order is the laity, the second are clerics, and the third are monks.
45. Elisabeth of Schönau, *The Book of the Ways of God 5*, in *Complete Works*, 164.

to the "three orders of the faithful," as did Robert Pulleyn (d. 1146): "Three parts of the church, prelates, the continent and the married."[46] It would seem, then, that medieval society, at least in general, viewed the world as consisting of three orders. In the early Middle Ages this schema was that of workers, fighters, and prayers, but in the High Middle Ages it was laity, clerics, and monks. Such ordering and schematization is not a medieval innovation but a practice that predates the Middle Ages, going back to ancient Greece and Rome and to the early Christian church.

In the *Republic*, Plato (d. 347 BCE) uses the *ordines* of gold, silver, iron, and bronze, writing, "All of you in the city are brothers . . . but the god who made you mixed some gold into those who are adequately equipped to rule, because they are most valuable. He put silver in those who are auxiliaries and iron and bronze in the farmers and other craftsmen."[47] Subsequently, Pliny (d. 79) talked about the *tertius ordo* of senators, equestrians, and plebeians, later to be modified to senators, possessors, and plebeians. Theologians Clement of Rome (d. ca. 100) and Tertullian (d. after 220) were two of the earliest Christians to accept *ordines* in the church. Clement made a clear distinction between the laity and the clergy, and Tertullian spoke often about the "order of the church" (*ordo ecclesiasticus*) and the "order of priests" (*ordo sacerdotalis*).[48] Leo I (d. 461), bishop of Rome, acknowledges the *ordines* of monk, layman, and priest, while Sidonius Apollinaris (d. 489) spoke of monks, clerics, and the penitent. In Giles Constable's estimation, "By the fifth century, there was a well-established concept of a tripartite ordering of society in the Latin West."[49] By the High Middle Ages, the concept of *ordines* became particularly associated with the forms of monasticism that thrived across Western Europe.

Ordo had various meanings in the Middle Ages. It could mean the way things were or a mode of being; it was a legal term that described the way a government functioned; ecclesiastically, it referred to sacramental acts (such as marriage), to major and minor ecclesial ranks (e.g., deacon, priest, bishop, subdeacon, and lector), or to ecclesiastical canons and rules (e.g., the canons laid out in Gratian's *Decretum*). Most importantly, an *ordo* referred to a religious order (an *ordine religioso*) or to monks in particular as an *ordo* separate from priests. As we saw in chapter 1, Pseudo-Dionysius writes about the three clerical orders. For him bishops consecrate, priests enlighten through the sacraments, and deacons purify and discern among the laity. Dependent

---

46. For these and many more examples, see Constable, *Three Studies*, 251–341.
47. Plato, *Republic* 415a, in *Complete Works*, 1050.
48. E.g., Tertullian, *De idololatria* 7.3 and *De exhortatione castitatis* 7.2, respectively.
49. Constable, *Three Studies*, 269.

on these three *ordines* are the orders of those undergoing initiation: catechumens, so-called sacred people, and monks. Catechumens are those still being purified through instruction and formation, the sacred people contemplate sacred things because they are purified, and monks, who are purified of sin, possess a holiness allowing them to contemplate and commune with God.[50] Accordingly, medieval life was governed by *ordines*, and everyone fit into a particular *ordo*. "One entered into rather than received an order, which was marked by a way of life and an internal discipline as well as exterior distinctions and obligations," says Constable.[51] The *ordo* that saw thousands enter into its ranks was that of the religious (or monastic) order (*ordo monasticus*).

Christian authors such as Ambrose of Milan (d. 397), Augustine of Hippo (d. 430), and Gregory the Great (d. 604) employed a tripartite division when speaking about the church, asserting that there were the ranks of virginity, widowhood, and married life. As discussed above, by the Carolingian era this threefold distinction was articulated as laypersons, monastics, and clerics. Humbert of Silva Candida (d. 1061) said that the church has three kinds of people: doctors, continent, and the married; while Anselm of Laon (d. 1117) divided the church into the married, the continent in the active life, and the continent in the contemplative life. By the time of the High Middle Ages, the concept of monks as an *ordo* was an established reality, so much so that John of Salerno (d. ca. 950) could refer to "the order of monks,"[52] as could Peter Damian (d. 1072).[53] Because of differences in medieval monastic practices, it is proper to speak not only of a monastic order (singular) but also of monastic orders (plural).

One idea of monastic order in the medieval church refers to those monastics living together in a particular monastery that is part of a congregation, while another way of talking about a monastic *ordo* is to speak of those living under a rule, whether a particular *regula* (such as that of Benedict of Nursia) or a set of institutes and disciplines (such as the Canons of St. Victor in Paris).[54] A

50. Pseudo-Dionysius, *Ecclesiastical Hierarchy* 5–6.

51. Constable, *Three Studies*, 255.

52. John of Salerno, *Life of Odo of Cluny* 3.4, in Marrier and Duchesne, *Bibliotheca Cluniacensis*, 45D: "Sic enim apud nos ordo monachorum recidit." (For insofar as the monastic order among us has collapsed.)

53. Peter Damian, *Life of St. Romuald* 25 and 37, in Tabacco, *Petri Damiani*, 53: "Erat enim predictus imperator monastico ordini valde benivolus et nimia circa Dei famulos affectione devotus" (The aforementioned emperor was accustomed to show great benevolence to the monastic order and he was excessively devoted to the servants of God); and ibid., 78: "adeo ut putaretur totum mundum in heremum velle convertere et monachico ordini omnen populi multitudinem sotiare [sic]." (Truly one would think that Romuald wished to turn the whole world into a hermitage and make the multitude of people associates of the monastic order.)

54. For the various orders in the church, see in general Constable and Smith, *Libellus de diversis ordinibus et professionibus*.

third medieval use of the term *ordo* refers generally to a group of monastics living in a particular monastery whose life is legislated by a chapter—that is, monks meeting together to make decisions in common. Using these criteria, several definite *ordines* of monks are distinguishable in the Middle Ages. And this brings us back to Robert's sermon on marriage.

Diekstra believes that Robert is witty when presenting the *ordo* of matrimony as analogous to a religious order because it essentially allows Robert to show "that the rigours traditionally associated with the religious orders appear mild and humane in comparison with the hardships and restrictions that characterize the rule of the order of matrimony."[55] In Astrik Gabriel's estimation, "Robert appeals to the intelligence of married people and sets forth the reasons why matrimony is an honorable estate with proper rules to be observed in the conjugal order."[56] This rule begins by offering seven arguments for the honorableness of marriage, in the same way that a monastic rule may begin with a prologue before launching into specifics.[57] First, if a Benedictine or Cistercian monk is given respect because of their founders, then how much more should marriage be respected, whose founder is God the Trinity: "And the Lord God said: It is not good for man to be alone: let *us* make him a help like unto himself" (Gen. 2:18 Douay-Rheims; italics added).[58] Second, marriage is honorable because it was instituted in the prelapsarian garden of Eden, whereas the other sacraments have their origin in the fallen world. Third, the Son of God, at his incarnation, chose to be born to a married couple. Fourth, Jesus attended and performed his first miracle at a wedding, thus honoring the order of matrimony. In fact, for Robert, those who married are changing the waters of concupiscence into the wine of marital delight. Fifth, the honorableness of marriage is shown by Jesus's prohibition against its violation: "What therefore God has joined together, let not man separate" (Matt. 19:6). This inviolability is also shown by John the Baptist, though himself not married and thus not a partaker of the *ordo* of marriage, who died defending the sanctity of marriage. Sixth, the fruits of marriage (e.g., children and a woman giving her virginity rightly to her husband) argue for the honor of marriage. And seventh, marriage is honorable because it signifies the mystery of the union of Christ with his church (cf. Eph. 5).

55. Diekstra, "Men, Women and Marriage," 69–70. That Robert is equating the *ordo* of marriage with the *ordo* of monasticism is further evidenced when his contemporary and colleague Peter de Limoges (d. 1306) does the same. See Bériou and d'Avray, "Comparison," 73.

56. Gabriel, *Paris Studium*, 99.

57. E.g., the prologue of the *Rule of Benedict*.

58. Robert of Sorbon's Bible, the Latin Vulgate, reads: "dixit quoque Dominus Deus non est bonum esse hominem solum faciamus ei adiutorium similem sui."

The sermon then moves on to present the seven themes of the rule for the monastic order of marriage. Robert points out the foolishness of a Cistercian monk who does not know his order's rule and says that it would be just as foolish for a married person not to know the rule of his own order. Just as a Cistercian should know the rule before he enters the order, so too must a man and a woman know the rule of marriage before they enter it. First, those who enter the *ordo* of marriage must make their final vows on the day of their marriage, for they are not given the gift of a novitiate. Second, the bride and the groom each need to be in a state of grace because not even the pope can dispense them from their marriage vows once they are ratified and consummated, for what God has joined together cannot be separated. Third, if one (presumably the groom) has been involved in sexual relations prior to marriage and this creates grave problems of conscience, then the man and the woman must not cohabitate with one another lest they commit a mortal sin. One can partake fully in the marriage order only if one's conscience is clean. Fourth, no matter the situation, each spouse must pay the marriage debt if asked, for to do otherwise is to sin mortally.[59] Fifth, before entering the order of matrimony the man and the woman both need to have a clean conscience so as to enter into the *ordo* in a state of grace. Robert compares this proper preparation of the man and the woman to the priest's need to be fully prepared before ascending to the altar, or to a man's preparation for ordination. A man should desire an honest and chaste woman to marry (as opposed to a dancer or fornicator), and a woman should look in church for her husband and not at a dance or in a tavern. Sixth, the husband, in particular, must protect and provide for his wife. He must provide for her materially, and both are to encourage each other in their spiritual progress. The husband should remain faithful to his wife and allow her to attend Mass and the Daily Office. Furthermore, the husband should not let his wife converse with lascivious men or attend dances. Seventh, husbands and wives are to encourage each other to godly living and the pursuit of spiritual things, for the married life is simultaneously to live in Paradise and to pursue the good life. In other words, just as there is an essential and expected spiritual element to the monastic life, so there is in the *ordo* of matrimony.

Robert concludes the sermon by offering four reasons why someone would want to enter the monastic order of marriage. First, having children creates more people to serve God. Second, marriage helps both the bride and the groom avoid the sin of lust. Third, as with Mary and Joseph, the married

---

59. Robert goes so far as to say that even if one of the spouses has leprosy, the other spouse is still obligated to have sex if the spouse so desires.

couple is a help to each other. Fourth, marriage can be contracted to make peace between families, such as when nobles marry their daughters off to their enemies. Thus, there are both obligations and benefits in the *ordo* of marriage.

The Abbey of the Holy Ghost

The Abbey of the Holy Ghost is an English translation of a French original (perhaps a sermon,[60] but both may be translations of a Latin text) whose author is still unknown. The earliest French manuscripts of the text date to around 1300, whereas the earliest extant English manuscript dates to the mid or late fourteenth century.[61] *The Abbey* is a treatise on the spiritual life, akin to Walter Hilton's *The Mixed Life* (on which more will be said below), meant for those who have not and will not enter institutional religious/monastic life: "My dear brothers and sisters, I can well see that many wish to enter religion, but may not do so on account of poverty, or out of dread, or for fear of their relatives, or because of the tie of marriage. Therefore I here draw up a book of religion of the heart, that is, of the Abbey of the Holy Ghost, so that all those who may not physically enter religion may do so spiritually."[62] The treatise gives readers an opportunity to enter the religious life by following a spiritual journey into their interior monastery, finding their inner monk, if you will. As described by Julia Boffey, "The Abbey offers a programme of spiritual 'building,' figured allegorically as the construction of an abbey, and itemizes the constituent parts and personnel necessary for the project in ways that are designed to help readers towards some apprehension of true 'religion of the heart.'"[63]

The foundations for this abbey, constructed in the conscience, are dug by the maidens Humility and Poverty. Humility makes the foundation deep, and Poverty "makes it long and wide, by casting out from the heart everything connected with earthly things and worldly thoughts, so that although they have earthly possessions, they do not fasten their hearts on them with love."[64] Once the foundation is laid, Lady Obedience and Lady Mercy raise the walls, and Lady Patience and Lady Fortitude "raise up the pillars and underpin

60. Consacro, "Author," 16.

61. Consacro, "Critical Edition," cxxvi and cxxx–cxxxii.

62. Swanson, *Catholic England*, 96. Swanson's text is reprinted from Blake, *Middle English Religious Prose*, 88–102. Consacro, "Author," 16: "He addresses himself to all those who desire to pursue the contemplative life, but who, for one reason or another, cannot cut their ties with the active world."

63. Boffey, "Charter," 120.

64. Swanson, *Catholic England*, 96.

them so steadfastly and stalwartly that no wind of words or of anger or of spiritual temptations or of bodily lust, either inner or outer, may cast them down."[65] The treatise continues in this manner, assigning personified virtues to the different buildings and offices of the monastery (e.g., Prayer builds the chapel and Pity serves as the infirmarer). The point, of course, is that the monk constructing this abbey internally needs to cultivate these virtues in order to correctly build and adequately staff the monastery. To be virtuous is to be monastic. To cultivate virtue is to build a monastery.

The abbess of the monastery is Lady Charity, for "just as those who are in religion may do or say nothing, nor go into any place, nor take nor give without permission of the abbess, just so none of these things shall be done spiritually without permission of Charity."[66] The anonymous author of *The Abbey* is explicit here that the Christian life *is* the monastic life. Those who are in "religion" (i.e., vowed monastics) are under the obedience of an elected (or appointed) abbot or abbess, whereas those living in the Abbey of the Holy Ghost are under obedience to Lady Charity. This all harks back, of course, to the Great Commandment given by Jesus to his followers: "You shall love the Lord your God with all your heart and with all your soul and with all your mind. This is the great and first commandment" (Matt. 22:37–38). This commandment was issued to all Christians; therefore all believers are bound to abide by it, making Charity the perfect abbess and, by extension, making all Christians monks and nuns. Further, obedience to the abbess Lady Charity is important because though there are many "in religion," there are "too few religious."[67] It would seem, then, that part of the purpose of *The Abbey* was to increase the number of faithful monastics, those who were not just monks institutionally but monks internally, where it mattered most.

Ultimately, the purpose of this interior monastery is to ensure that she who possesses it engages in contemplation, that "burning to dwell with God in love, and with his delights to enhance the soul, and have a partial taste of the sweetness that God's chosen shall have in Heaven."[68] Such contemplation is aided by meditation, "good thoughts of God and of his works, of his words, and of his creation, of the pains he suffered, and of the heart-felt love that he had and has for us for whom he endured death."[69] In *The Abbey* the journey to perfec-

---

65. Swanson, *Catholic England*, 97.
66. Swanson, *Catholic England*, 97–98. The author of *The Abbey of the Holy Ghost* also connects it to an injunction attributed to the apostle Paul that "whatever you do or say or think in your heart, you should do it out of love."
67. Swanson, *Catholic England*, 98.
68. Swanson, *Catholic England*, 97.
69. Swanson, *Catholic England*, 101.

tion begins when the "monastic" thinks and meditates deeply on God and his works, which results in a devout longing love for God, accompanied by tears. In response God offers his comfort, which leads to contemplation. This inner abbey is similar to the ideal, pre-fall state of humankind because it is Satan's activities that bring decline to the abbey when he places into the monastery his four daughters of ill will (Envy, Pride, Complaint, and False-witness), whose purpose is to disturb and harm the abbey through wickedness. However, the prioress Lady Wisdom and subprioress Lady Humility take counsel with Lady Discretion so "that they should all fall into prayer to the Holy Ghost, who is visitor of this abbey, that he should hurry to come, as they had great need, to help them and visit them with his grace."[70] The Holy Spirit responds to this request by visiting the house and cleansing it. Thus, as with all monasteries, there is always the chance that the inner abbey of the Holy Ghost will find itself under attack, only to be rescued in the end by God. Just as monks and nuns give in to sin, so too do those who house an inner abbey. For there is not much of a difference, at least spiritually, between a monk living in a monastery proper and a "monastic" dwelling in the Abbey of the Holy Ghost.

Though there was a strong current in the High Middle Ages that the *vita activa* (active life) was in tension with, and perhaps even incompatible with, the *via contemplativa* (contemplative life), there was also a school of thought that insisted the two were not so much contradictory as complementary.[71] In many ways this was a uniquely monastic discussion: Was the *telos* of monastic life the contemplation of God or active service to one's neighbor? Should monks stay cloistered behind a monastery's walls, engaged in concerted study and prayer, or should monks leave the monastery regularly in order to minister to the needs of those in society? This debate even manifested itself institutionally. For example, the Carthusians, founded in 1084 by Bruno of Cologne (d. 1101), are perhaps the most austere monastic order, essentially never letting monks leave the enclosure and rarely allowing nonmonastics admittance to the charterhouse. They are the epitome of the contemplative life. Then there are the Franciscans, founded in 1209 by Francis of Assisi (d. 1226), whose very *raison d'être* is non-enclosed service to others, primarily through preaching, teaching, and hearing confessions. They are the epitome of the active life. As expected, there are other monastic/religious orders that do not fit neatly into this contemplative-active taxonomy, but this way of thinking about monastic orders has had a long and enduring history. Significantly for our present purposes, this taxonomy is one

70. Swanson, *Catholic England*, 103–4.
71. See Constable, "The Interpretation of Mary and Martha," in *Three Studies*, 1–141; and C. Butler, *Western Mysticism*, 157–223.

that also gained traction vis-à-vis nonmonastics (those engaged in the active life) and monastics (those engaged in the contemplative life). In other words, there was an active-contemplative distinction among monastic orders, while at the same time there was an active-contemplative distinction in the larger society between the laity and monastics. The end of this vision of the spiritual life is summarized well at the end of *The Abbey*: "Now I pray you all, through the charity of God, that all who read or hear of this religion be obedient with all their power and allow all the good ladies named before to do their duties spiritually each day within your hearts. And let everyone actively take care that you do no offence against the rule or obedience of this religion."[72]

Walter Hilton's *Mixed Life*

For a text like *The Abbey of the Holy Ghost*, conventional distinctions were being blurred. The anonymous author says that (1) nonmonastics can, in fact, be monastics if they construct an interior abbey; and (2) now that they are monastics, they can pursue a life of contemplation. At about the same time that *The Abbey* was making these claims, another author was saying something similar, also in English. Walter Hilton (d. 1396) was a Cambridge University–educated civil and canon lawyer who became an Augustinian Canon around 1386,[73] though he had lived prior to that as a solitary.[74] Despite his affinity for the deeply contemplative Carthusians, he chose the more active order of the Augustinian Canons.[75] In his *Mixed Life* (*Medeled Liyf*) Hilton addresses himself "to a wealthy layman who has all the responsibilities of a parent, master of a household and landowner, but who feels himself called to devotion. Hilton's treatise aims to dissuade its recipient from attempting to imitate the contemplative life of a vowed religious. He should instead follow the path to holiness that is practical to his position, not resenting the inevitable interruptions from his secular commitments, in which he may serve God by serving others, and accepting the boundaries to contemplative life in his circumstances."[76]

Though Hilton understands that the full contemplative life will likely demand a full contemplative existence (i.e., life in a contemplative community),[77]

72. Swanson, *Catholic England*, 104.
73. On Augustinian Canons, see Postles, "Augustinian Canons."
74. Clark and Taylor, *Walter Hilton's Latin Writings*, 1:103.
75. For Hilton's defense of vowed religious life, see his *On the Usefulness and Prerogatives of Religion*, a letter written to Adam Horsley, who became a Carthusian in 1386. See Clark and Taylor, *Walter Hilton's Latin Writings*, 1:119–72.
76. Windeatt, *English Mystics*, 109.
77. Hilton, *Mixed Life* 6.

he does not shy away, similar to *The Abbey*, from suggesting that the contemplative life is open to noncontemplative laypersons. He writes, "You should mix the works of the active life with spiritual works of the contemplative life, and then you do well. . . . You should understand that there are three ways of living: one is active, another contemplative, the third consists of both and is the mixed life."[78]

Importantly for Hilton, this mixed life is not unique to laypersons but also characterizes the life of ecclesiastical prelates and parish priests. Their ecclesial responsibility makes it impossible for them to engage fully in the contemplative life, but their vocation also demands some modicum of contemplative practices. In this way they are like most laypersons. Thus, they are ideal candidates for living the mixed life. In the end Hilton concludes,

> And assuredly, for such a man who has the spiritual authority of a prelacy, with care and government over others as prelates and holders of cures have, or in temporal authority like worldly lords and masters are, I consider this mixed life best and most appropriate for them, as long as they are obliged thereto. But for others, who are free and not bound to temporal or spiritual administration, I trust that the contemplative life alone, if they can truly achieve it, is the best and most rewarding, fairest and most expedient, and most fitting for them to undertake and engage in, and not to be left willfully or for any external acts of the active life, except for great necessity and great relieving and comforting of other men, whether in their bodies or in their souls.[79]

Thus, in *The Abbey* there is an intentional monasticization of the Christian life, making it possible for all believers to become monks and nuns, at least internally. And in the *Mixed Life* there is an intentional clericalization of all believers, leveling the spiritual life, if you will, in a similar manner to *The Abbey*. The significance of these treatises is that they are reimagining the boundaries of the spiritual life for nonmonastic, nonclerical women and men. Whereas nonmonastic laypersons were often thought of as a kind of second class of Christians, these texts chose to imagine things differently.

Conclusion

While Symeon the New Theologian was writing his hymns, while Robert de Sorbon was preaching sermons on marriage to learned university students

---

78. Walter Hilton, *Mixed Life* 2 and 3, in Swanson, *Catholic England*, 107.
79. Walter Hilton, *Mixed Life* 6, in Swanson, *Catholic England*, 110.

and graduates, and while the author of *The Abbey of the Holy Ghost* and Walter Hilton were writing vernacular spiritual treatises for laypersons, the "traditional" institution of monasticism continued to flourish. Though there may have been a sort of crisis of monasticism in the twelfth century, no real crisis in the Middle Ages ever threatened the extinction of monasticism as an institution.[80] It continued to thrive. For example, circa 1500 there were approximately 900 monastic houses in England with nearly 12,000 monks, nuns, canons, and friars, up from a total of approximately 6,500 monastics in 1400.[81] The authors discussed in this chapter were not attempting to do away with, nor had an inclination even to undermine, monasticism per se. They accepted the institution of monasticism as it had come down to them in history, and even shared many of the presuppositions about monasticism that were common in their time. These authors were not radicals, seeking to destroy monasticism; rather, they were offering alternative ways to view monasticism. They saw the good that was there and sought to add to it, not to detract from it.

What they do illustrate, however, is a vision of monasticism that was not shackled to any particular form. They were not advocating for some monolithic expression of monasticism but were pushing the boundaries out a bit further than they had been pushed for some time. Like most institutions, monasticism, at some point in its history, stabilized around a common core of practices and beliefs. No two monastic rules are exactly alike, but they parallel one another in unsurprising ways. In fact, a lot of people, when they speak about "monasticism," are mostly speaking about those women and men who have vowed poverty, chastity, and obedience and live together under a common rule of life.[82] Yet Benedictines do not vow poverty, chastity, and obedience. Rather, they vow stability, obedience, and conversion of life (*conversatio morum*). Because of these distinctions, then, it is always valid to ask, What is monasticism? Who are monks and nuns? Christian history demonstrates that the answers to these questions do not always lie in the common form of institutional monasticism but are more related to a Christian's inner being and disposition. One who seeks God single-mindedly can do this interiorly while living an active life punctuated by seasons of contemplation. And in the end that may be a more historically and etymologically accurate way of being a monk than taking prescribed vows and living in an abbey.

80. Cantor, "Crisis of Western Monasticism."
81. James Clark, *Religious Orders*, 7.
82. This is a main weakness of Vatican II's document on the religious-monastic life, *Perfectae caritatis*, which understands the religious life as helping "members follow Christ and be united to God through the profession of the evangelical counsels" (i.e., poverty, chastity, and obedience).

Three

Interiorized Monasticism

In Fyodor Dostoevsky's *The Brothers Karamazov*, Alyosha, the youngest of the Karamazov boys and a novice monk, undergoes a crisis of vocation. In the midst of this crisis, his dying spiritual elder, Zosima, says to him, somewhat prophetically, that Alyosha will leave the monastery: "You will go forth from these walls, but you will again sojourn in the world like a monk."[1] This, of course, is likely not what Alyosha (or Dostoevsky's readers) would have expected to hear from the (supposedly) saintly Russian monk-elder. For why would a monk encourage another monk to leave the monastery? Or why would a monk not understand that "the world" (*miru*) and the monk are ostensibly opposed to each other?[2] Zosima's words are later confirmed, however, when Madame Khokhlakov says to Alyosha (who has left the monastery), "I've regarded you as a monk, though you do look lovely in your new suit."[3] Monks, of course, do not wear suits; they wear habits.[4] So, somehow, Alyosha, though living in the "world" and wearing nonmonastic clothing, is still a monk.

This sentiment regarding a worldly monk is not unique to Dostoevsky but is common in the Russian Orthodox tradition. In 1763 well-known monk Tikhon of Zadonsk (d. 1783) was informed by his superior that a tradesman desired

---

1. Dostoevsky, *Brothers Karamazov*, 285.
2. The Russian word for "world" (*mir*) used here is the same word used in the Russian Synodal Bible (i.e., the translation in use in Dostoevsky's day) in 1 John 2:15 ("Do not love the world or the things in the world. If anyone loves the world, the love of the Father is not in him." [*Ne liubite mira, ni togo, chto v mire: kto liubit mir, v tom net liubvi Otchei.*]), suggesting that Zosima's use of it carries a negative connotation.
3. Dostoevsky, *Brothers Karamazov*, 572.
4. In the Russian Orthodox tradition, the habit is called a *schema*.

to enter the community. Tikhon replied, "Do not be in a hurry to multiply the monks. The black habit does not save. The one who wears a white habit and has the spirit of obedience, humility, and purity, he is a true monk of *interiorized monasticism* [*nepostrizhennyi monakh*]."[5] Zosima was certainly influenced, if you will, by Tikhon since Dostoevsky was well acquainted with Tikhon's life.[6] Yet what is this interiorized monasticism?

Throughout the history of the church there have been at least two ways to think about monastic life vis-à-vis sanctification: as superior to all other forms of Christian living or as one kind of Christian life among other, more or less equal, forms of Christian life. For example, the anonymous third-century sermon *The Hundredfold, Sixtyfold and Thirtyfold Reward*, interpreting Matthew 13:3–9, says that the hundredfold reward went to martyrs, the sixtyfold to virginal ascetics, and the thirtyfold to "married persons who had renounced sex upon receiving baptism."[7] Notice there is no reward for the sexually active married believer. Though Cyprian of Carthage (d. 248) taught the same regarding the hundredfold and sixtyfold, he quietly omitted the thirtyfold, though "he insisted that 'the greater sanctity and the reality (*veritas*) of the second birth' belonged to virgins 'who no longer have desires of the flesh and of the body.'"[8] By the time of Jerome (d. 420) there was a standard interpretation that asserted that the thirtyfold referred to marriage, the sixtyfold to widowhood, and the hundredfold to virginity/monasticism.[9] In short, you reaped the greatest spiritual and heavenly rewards when you became a monk and remained virginal. You reaped the least (and possibly nothing) when married.

On the other hand, some writers were insisting that the married life was good and was in no way a hindrance to salvation and sanctification. For example, Augustine of Hippo (d. 430), though often accused of being overly pessimistic about the goodness of sex and therefore marriage, saw it more positively in his earlier writings.[10] David Hunter recounts how the young, newly Christian Augustine still subscribed to a Platonic or Neoplatonic view in which the body was a prison.[11] However, the mind could ascend in such a way as to overcome this bodily imprisonment. This began to change as Augustine immersed himself more and more into the Pauline Epistles, finding in them

---

5. Quoted in Evdokimov, *Ages of the Spiritual Life*, 139 (italics original). See also Gorodetzky, *St. Tikhon of Zadonsk*, 48, where the phrase "interiorized monasticism" is translated more literally as "untonsured monasticism." The Russian text is in Gippius, *Sviatoi Tikhon Zadonskii*, 15.
6. Ziolkowski, *Hagiography*, 146–47.
7. Hunter, *Marriage, Celibacy, and Heresy*, 114.
8. Hunter, *Marriage, Celibacy, and Heresy*, 122.
9. Hunter, *Marriage, Celibacy, and Heresy*, 181.
10. See Hunter, "Augustinian Pessimism?," 153–54.
11. Augustine of Hippo, *Soliloquies* 1.14.24.

a new sense of the "pervasiveness of sin."[12] Though he continued to see sin as the choosing of a lower good (marriage) over a greater good (celibacy) or the greatest good (God), he came to understand that his sensuality was not just about embodiment but was the result of a divided will. Thus, the bishop of Hippo came to the "new idea of original sin as a division within the self," and this "had immediate consequences for his views of sex, marriage and celibacy."[13] In this view it is grace, and grace alone, as opposed to the work of the mind, that makes it possible to renounce sex, and this grace is not given to all Christians. So "for Augustine celibacy is not something that can be demanded, or even expected, of most Christians."[14]

In light of this change in his theology of sin, Augustine was now able to write a treatise titled *On the Good of Marriage* and another titled *On Holy Virginity*. Augustine said later that these two treatises were written primarily against Jovinian, who gained a following in the 390s, especially in Rome. Jovinian taught the good of both marriage and celibacy and claimed "that the superiority of celibacy over marriage could not be maintained except by condemning marriage."[15] In *On the Good of Marriage* Augustine does teach that marriage is a good while still maintaining that celibacy is also a good. In the end, however, the good of celibacy is better "because of the fact that to achieve the perfection of marriage is surpassed, rather than the sin of marriage avoided."[16] In other words, both marriage and celibacy are true goods, but celibacy is simply a better good. Nonetheless, marriage is a good, primarily in the context of "the bonding of society (*connexio societatis*) in the natural good of friendship."[17] In particular, there are three goods in marriage, according to Augustine: the procreation of children, marital fidelity, and that it is a sacrament.[18] Though it would be tempting to think that Augustine is merely pacifying his readers by claiming that marriage is a good, his works on marriage and virginity show that he is convinced of the ontological goodness of marriage, though it still is a lesser ideal than celibacy. Not a lesser good in the Augustinian sense but less than ideal. Hunter sums it up well: "Within Augustine's mature vision marriage serves as a fragile, though effective, social bond, a *societas*, that brings some stability and unity to the human race suffering from the instability and disorder wrought by sin."[19]

12. Hunter, "Augustinian Pessimism?," 155.
13. Hunter, "Augustinian Pessimism?," 157.
14. Hunter, "Augustinian Pessimism?," 157.
15. Hunter, "Augustinian Pessimism?," 158.
16. Augustine, *On Holy Virginity* 21.21, in *Marriage and Virginity*, 79.
17. Hunter, "Augustinian Pessimism?," 160.
18. Cf. the discussion of the sermon of Robert de Sorbon in chap. 2 of this book.
19. Hunter, "Augustinian Pessimism?," 170.

Historical Examples of Interiorized Monasticism

Moreover, early theologians believed that it was possible to be married while monastic at the same time, the sentiment that would later be labeled as "interiorized monasticism." Paul Evdokimov writes, "Since its advent, monasticism has been an integral part of the Church, because it expresses a spiritual norm that is *universal*, a normative value for *every* believer."[20] If it is universal and normative for *every* believer, then there needs to be some way to think about how one can be a married monk. Syncletica, a fourth-century desert mother, said, "It is possible to be a solitary [μονάζειν] in one's mind while living in a crowd."[21] This claim, albeit modest, opens the door to other perspectives that give credence to an interiorized monasticism. John Chrysostom (d. 407) writes explicitly that "the scriptures . . . want everyone to live the life of monks, even if they should happen to have wives,"[22] and elsewhere he says "monastics and the lay person must attain the same heights."[23] This sentiment is echoed in John's contemporary Basil of Caesarea (d. 379), who says that "obedience to the Gospel is required of us all, both married and celibate [μοναχοί]."[24] In the ninth century Theodore the Stoudite (d. 826) provided a robust understanding of the relationship between monasticism and the laity, including the married: "These and similar things are of the true Christian. Do not think, my Lord, that what I have said only concerns the monk. Although it affects the monk more intensely all these things equally affect the lay person."[25]

Similar strands of thought appear in writings from the Western church too. Bernard of Clairvaux (d. 1153) says that the Christian "must not suppose this paradise of inner pleasure in some material place: you enter this garden not on foot, but by deeply-felt expressions."[26] The abbot of Clairvaux is speaking here of contemplation, the particular task of the monk, saying that contemplative rest is not found in a material place, such as the monastery, but is in the affections and, thus, something open to all believers. Thomas à Kempis (d. 1471) bluntly writes, "The habit and tonsure by themselves are of small significance; it is the transformation of one's way of life and the complete mortification of the passions that make a true Religious."[27] Thomas's

---

20. Evdokimov, *Sacrament of Love*, 81 (italics original).

21. Ward, *Sayings of the Desert Fathers*, 234.

22. John Chrysostom, *Adversus oppugnatores vitae monasticae* 3.14, in Hunter, *Two Treatises*, 157.

23. Cited in Evdokimov, *Ages of the Spiritual Life*, 137.

24. Basil of Caesarea, *Sermo de renunciatione saeculi* 2 (FC 9:17).

25. Theodore the Stoudite, *Epistle* 464, quoted in Cholij, *Theodore the Stoudite*, 227.

26. Bernard of Clairvaux, *Ad clericos de conversione* 13.25, in *Sermons on Conversion*, 59.

27. Thomas à Kempis, *Imitation of Christ* 1.17 (Sherley-Price, 45).

thought seems similar to that of Catherine of Siena (d. 1380), who believed that the most important place for the Christian soul to dwell is in the "cell of self-knowledge." That is, all Christians, including the married, are monks in that they need to be enclosed "in order to know better God's goodness."[28] But it was the twentieth century, and the work of Paul Evdokimov in particular, that gave full breadth to the concept of interiorized monasticism.[29]

The Interiorized Monasticism of Paul Evdokimov

Evdokimov (d. 1970) was born in 1901 in St. Petersburg, Russia. Before the revolution of 1917 he began studying theology in Kiev but then fled Russia with his family, settling ultimately in Paris, home to many Russian émigrés. He graduated in the first class of the newly founded Institut de Théologie Orthodoxe Saint-Serge while also completing a degree in philosophy at the University of Paris-Sorbonne and, in 1942, completing a doctorate in philosophy at Aix-en-Provence. He taught at various institutions over the years, including, from 1953 until his death, Saint-Serge and, from 1967, the Ecumenical Institute at Bossey, Switzerland, and the Institut Supérior d'Études Œcuméniques in Paris. He was also an official observer at the second session of the Second Vatican Council in 1964.

Throughout his theological career, Evdokimov returned repeatedly to the interrelated topics of women, marriage, and interiorized monasticism. It is likely that he first encountered interiorized monasticism in the writings of Dostoevsky since his doctoral thesis and first book dealt with the problem of evil in the Russian novelist's works. In the 1960s, when Evdokimov was writing, it seemed that monasticism in the Orthodox world, especially on Mount Athos in Greece, was dying out. Evdokimov's response was to postulate, along with John Chrysostom, Tikhon of Zadonsk, and others, that what was needed was an interiorized monasticism, a monasticism common to both the traditional monk and the married man. Andrew Louth explains well the genesis of Evdokimov's interiorized monasticism when he writes that in *The Brothers Karamazov* the

> Grand Inquisitor has developed his parody of Christianity by turning the three temptations of Christ on their head. Whereas Christ refused to turn stones into bread by miracle, refused the mystery of leaping from the pinnacle of the Temple and landing safely in the Temple court, refused to acknowledge

28. Catherine of Siena, *Dialogue*, prologue 1 (Noffke, 25).
29. Michael Plekon says that Evdokimov's concept of interiorized monasticism is the "most inventive of his theological contributions." "Paul Evdokimov," 99.

Satan's authority in return for power over the nations of the earth, the religion of the Grand Inquisitor is precisely based on "miracle, mystery, and authority," in doing so depriving ordinary humans of freedom, a freedom he claims they are all too ready to relinquish. The three monastic vows of poverty, chastity and obedience are based on Christ's response to the three temptations, Evdokimov claims, and goes on to argue that they can be taken out of the cloister, as it were, and become the basis of an interior monasticism, lived in the world.[30]

Thus, contrary to Ivan in *The Brothers Karamazov*, who says that humankind is unable to handle freedom and would prefer to surrender their freedom (hence the overreach of the Grand Inquisitor in Ivan's narrative),[31] Evdokimov says that the three monastic vows bring great freedom and, in turn, this freedom creates all of the space necessary for one to mature spiritually. Poverty delivers the believer from materialism; virginity, or chastity, brings freedom from carnal desires; and obedience liberates one from the ego.[32] He writes in sum, "*While the empire found its secret temptation in the roots of Satan's three invitations, monasticism was openly built on Christ's three immortal answers. . . . The three monastic vows reproduce exactly the three answers of Jesus.*"[33] So much so, in fact, that Evdokimov refers to Jesus as "monk." It would seem, then, that to be a Christian is to be a monk.

Before going further, it will be helpful to note that Evdokimov was not alone in the Orthodox Church in thinking about monasticism in this way. He was not being idiosyncratic but expressing an emerging belief among Orthodox theologians. Evdokimov's mature reflection on interiorized monasticism was published in French in the mid-1960s. In 1968 another highly influential Orthodox theologian, Alexander Schmemann (d. 1983), also a product of the Russian émigré community and Saint-Serge in Paris, gave a lecture to a conference of Orthodox university students that was later adapted and published as a small pamphlet bearing the title *The Mission of Orthodoxy*.[34] In this work Schmemann was seeking to answer a rather straightforward question: What is the role of Orthodox Christians in America? He was

30. Louth, *Modern Orthodox Thinkers*, 172. See Evdokimov, *Ages of the Spiritual Life*, 139–53.

31. See Dostoevsky, *Brothers Karamazov*, 246–65.

32. Evdokimov also ties these three vows into the structure of the Lord's Prayer: "*obedience* to the will of the Father, the *poverty* of one who is hungry only for the substantial and eucharistic bread, and *chastity*, the purification from evil." *Ages of the Spiritual Life*, 139 (italics original).

33. Evdokimov, *Ages of the Spiritual Life*, 143 (italics original).

34. Available from Conciliar Press or in full at http://www.peterandpaul.net/schmemann -missionoforthodoxy. The following quotations from *The Mission of Orthodoxy* are from the online version, which lacks pagination.

concerned that the first generation of Orthodox émigrés to the United States was prone to a kind of ghettoism along national, cultural lines and that the later generations would become so Americanized (i.e., secularized) that they would cease to be functionally Orthodox Christians. Hence, he argued for a kind of middle ground, placing a lot of hope in the college-aged adults whom he was addressing.

The middle ground would be found in what Schmemann called the "twofold missionary perspective," in which Orthodox believers (1) "must maintain at all costs that which many people today contemptuously call the Christian institution," and (2) "must be a faithful remnant which relates to the world as it is today." This "remnant," he goes on to describe, is a "movement." He writes, "What the Church needs today, as it has needed it on several occasions in the past, is a dynamic movement of young men and young women, a kind of 'order' to fulfill the tasks that institution alone cannot and must not fulfill." Of course, once Schmemann uses the word *order*, he is now thinking about a kind of monasticism, which he expressly states in the next section: this movement "looks in some way like a new form of monasticism without celibacy and without the desert, but based on specific vows."[35] Interestingly, these vows are fairly Benedictine in nature.

First, prayer: the "first vow is to keep a certain well-defined spiritual discipline of life, and this means a rule of prayer." Schmemann tells his listeners that it is not enough to discuss spirituality and read books about it but that they must actually make an effort to pray, and to pray regularly. And by doing so they would be imitating early monasticism. Importantly, this rule of prayer is not something so difficult that only cloistered monastics can keep it but rather a rule "which could be practiced and followed by all and not only by some."

The second vow is obedience. Because we live in "a climate of radical individualism," obedience is not common among present-day Orthodox believers, says Schmemann, though "the whole spiritual literature emphasizes obedience as the condition of all spiritual progress." What Schmemann has in mind is obedience to the movement itself and not some appointed leader of the movement. It is obedience "in small things, humble chores, the unromantic routine of work." In short, this is a vow of doing, opposed to the individualistic "I feel" or "I don't feel."

The third vow is acceptance. Though Schmemann uses the word *acceptance*, his description of this vow makes it sound like the more traditional vow of stability, especially when he writes "that ascetical literature is full of

---

35. On the concept of the desert in Orthodox spirituality, see Damian, "Desert as a Place."

warnings against changing places, against leaving monasteries for other and 'better' ones. . . . Again, what we need today is to relate to the Church and to Christ our lives, our professions, the unique combination of factors which God gives us as our examination and which we alone can pass or fail."

Notice that these vows are not the traditional monastic vows; rather, they are, as Schmemann recognizes, vows for a noncelibate, nondesert monasticism. And the purpose of these vows and this lay monastic movement would be to "help people . . . to experience and live their Orthodox faith." The movement would also help Orthodox believers gain knowledge about the content of their faith and "its implications for their entire life." Finally, these lay monks could care about the needs of people in ways that a parish or diocese could not, such as reaching youth, "finding the total place and function of the Church in our world," and accepting the challenges of modern culture. This remnant of lay monastics would, in essence, keep the church from becoming a ghetto or becoming overly individualistic and secular.

Evdokimov is up to something similar in his own conception of interiorized monasticism, which he develops, in particular, in two important works: *The Sacrament of Love* and *Ages of the Spiritual Life*.[36] I will examine each of these texts in due order and then attempt to synthesize Evdokimov's thought. Evdokimov's first task in *The Sacrament of Love* is to demonstrate that marriage is not an inferior state to monasticism, which, we have seen, is a common misconception throughout Christian history. Because the gospel is addressed to all people, "trying to prove the superiority of one state over the other is therefore useless" since both concern themselves with "the intensity of the love of God"[37] and "the monk and the layperson must attain the same heights."[38] At issue, of course, is the lingering fallacy that sexual intercourse is inherently sinful and, therefore, celibacy is superior. Evdokimov counters this inheritance by insisting that the "married as well as the monastic state are two forms of chastity, each one appropriate to its own mode of being."[39] In ancient Russian monasticism the monastic novitiate was equated with marital engagement, and couples at their wedding took vows similar to those taken by monks at their profession.[40] In sum, "monastic holiness and married holiness are the two faces of Tabor; the Holy Spirit is the limit of the one and the other."[41]

36. A much shorter treatment is found in Evdokimov, "Le monachisme intériorisé."
37. Evdokimov, *Sacrament of Love*, 65.
38. Evdokimov, *Sacrament of Love*, 67.
39. Evdokimov, *Sacrament of Love*, 67.
40. Evdokimov, *Sacrament of Love*, 68.
41. Evdokimov, *Sacrament of Love*, 73.

The main element that monasticism and marriage have in common, according to Evdokimov, is a calling to asceticism.[42] Jesus's teaching that if the believer would be perfect, she must go and sell what she possesses, give to the poor, and then follow him forms the backbone of this universal Christian asceticism. For humankind "had fallen below himself, but asceticism elevates him above himself and gives him back his human dignity, an astonishing one, that of a new creature in Jesus Christ."[43] Asceticism, then, is about restoring our true humanity; it is about becoming authentic human beings. Thus, it is not an optional task but a task proper to the baptismal state because "asceticism is not a system of merely moral rules, but a system of exercises implying spiritual gifts that is offered to every Christian life."[44] Evdokimov concedes that this call to asceticism is lived to different degrees by those who are married and those who are monks: "The magnificent meaning of monasticism lies precisely in this dynamism, this violence, this maximalism that aspires only to the ultimate."[45] Thus, to be a monk is to be a maximalist—that is, to be dedicated wholeheartedly to the ascetic life that is common to all Christian believers. Just as martyrs were maximalists of a different sort, so are monastics.[46] All Christians are called to die for the faith just as all Christians are called to engage in ascetic struggle. Martyrs and monks are simply those who go to the utmost extremes, and they do so vocationally, not accidentally. Marriage is a vocation too; therefore it must be lived maximally by those called to such an estate. In other words, all married people must live fully into their marriage vows in the same way that all monks must live into their monastic vows. Both are maximalized callings and therefore eschatological callings.[47]

Evdokimov returned to the concept of interiorized monasticism just two years later in his *Ages of the Spiritual Life*.[48] The context here, though, is not the sacrament of marriage but a presentation of the spiritual life; hence Evdokimov takes a slightly different approach. Here he argues that the institution of monasticism is in a state of crisis, suggesting "that an historic cycle is coming to a close." Therefore, for the good of preserving the institution, or at least the good practices of the institution, "we must guard against simplification and

---

42. Asceticism will be dealt with in greater detail in chaps. 4–5. Evdokimov (*Sacrament of Love*, 80) defines asceticism as "the mastery of the spiritual over the material and psychic, without destroying anything in them."

43. Evdokimov, *Sacrament of Love*, 77.

44. Evdokimov, *Sacrament of Love*, 81.

45. Evdokimov, *Sacrament of Love*, 78.

46. Evdokimov, *Sacrament of Love*, 75.

47. See Phan, "Mariage, monachisme et eschatologie."

48. *The Sacrament of Love* was first published in French in 1962 and *Ages of the Spiritual Life* in 1964.

distinguish between changeable forms and the permanent principle, between the transmission of the essential message of the Gospel and the appearance of new witnesses."[49] So what, then, is the "permanent principle" of monasticism? It is the gospel testimony that is so eloquently represented in monasticism. That is, monasticism makes explicit the gospel's demand to be fully human and to be a witness to the transformative power of the gospel and baptism: "When humanity had sunk below itself, monastic asceticism raised it above its nature. . . . The dreadful Thebaid, cradle of so many spiritual giants, the arid and burning desert, was illuminated with their light. These astonishing masters taught the refined art of living the Gospel."[50] Paraphrasing Russian Orthodox theologian Georges Florovsky (d. 1979), Evdokimov makes the point that monasteries were provisionary in character, a necessary presence until the conversion of all people to the Christian faith. But since history has not vindicated this hope, monasticism is necessary, hence the problem with a monasticism that is in crisis. Nonetheless, says Evdokimov, "the baptized world is sufficiently Christian to hear the monastic message and to assimilate it in its own way. Here is the problem. As formerly, martyrdom was transmitted to the monastic institution, so today, it seems, monasticism evokes a certain receptivity in the universal priesthood of the laity. The testimony of the Christian faith in the framework of the modern world necessitates the universal vocation of *interiorized monasticism*."[51] In short, the crisis of monasticism is such that though it has been historically driven by its close association with early Christian martyrdom, it is now necessary to connect it not just with the vocation of martyrdom but with the universal priesthood of all believers. This universalizes monasticism to be particular to all baptized Christians; all the baptized are therefore monks and nuns, at least interiorly.[52]

For Evdokimov interiorized monasticism is a new way of looking for a solution to the old problem of living out the gospel commands fully. The first solution was that of monasticism proper. Institutionalized Christian monasticism preaches "a complete separation from a society which lives according to 'the elements of this world,' and from its economic, political and sociological problems."[53] This flight into the desert, if you will, results in autonomous communities that care for their own members (e.g., Mount Athos) and is not an option for all people. It radicalizes the gospel of Jesus Christ but in such a

49. Evdokimov, *Ages of the Spiritual Life*, 133.
50. Evdokimov, *Ages of the Spiritual Life*, 134–35.
51. Evdokimov, *Ages of the Spiritual Life*, 135 (italics original).
52. For a fuller discussion of the priesthood of all believers (i.e., the universal priesthood), see chap. 5 below.
53. Evdokimov, *Ages of the Spiritual Life*, 135–36.

way as to create a distinction and a division between those who are the whole-hearted followers of the gospel (i.e., monastics) and those who are not (i.e., everyone else). This is the very problem that Evdokimov has already argued against in *The Sacrament of Love*. Another solution has been "the attempt to Christianize the world without leaving it in order to build the Christian City of God." These "theocracies," however, end up "under the ambiguous forms of empires and Christian states. The resounding failure of this attempt proves that one can never impose the Gospel from above, nor prescribe grace as a law."[54] This kind of Christian empire/nation-state ghettoism is the very thing that Schmemann is concerned about in *The Mission of Orthodoxy*. Thus, Evdokimov concludes, there must be a better way, and that better way is interiorized monasticism. He ultimately concludes, "The monasticism that was entirely centered on the last things [i.e., the maximal monasticism of *The Sacrament of Love*] formerly changed the face of the world. Today it makes an appeal to all, to the laity as well as to the monastics, and it points out a universal vocation. For each, it is a question of adaptation, of a personal equivalent of the monastic vows."[55]

In these two works Evdokimov seems to be doing two things vis-à-vis interiorized monasticism. First, he is attempting to remove the false spiritual dichotomy between marriage and monasticism. One of these forms of life is not superior to the other since both are rooted in the gospel's command to be perfect. Second, he is attempting to find a way in which believers can live out the gospel commands without everyone becoming a monk or nun in the traditional sense or without the nation-state becoming legalistic and thereby legislating the precepts of the gospel as a *sine qua non* of citizenship. The result is interiorized monasticism, a new thing but not without precedent. And why something new? As Michael Plekon has suggested, "For [Evdokimov] it was wrong to try to repristinate the exact forms of any spirituality of the past, for different times require adaptations to those forms."[56] But make no mistake: this interiorized monasticism is still a vowed monasticism. To be exact, it is characterized by the standard monastic vows of poverty, celibacy (or, in this instance, chastity), and obedience.

Evdokimov sees monastic vows as "a great charter of human liberty."[57] As was stated above, monasticism is about being fully human, and these vows allow fallen humankind to live as true humans inasmuch as they are human persons

54. Evdokimov, *Ages of the Spiritual Life*, 136.

55. Evdokimov, *Ages of the Spiritual Life*, 139.

56. Plekon, "'Interiorized Monasticism,'" 244. See also Plekon, "Monasticism in the Market-place."

57. Evdokimov, *Ages of the Spiritual Life*, 139.

free from the ascendency of the material (vow of poverty) and the carnal (vow of chastity) and from idolatry of the ego (vow of obedience). The biblical basis of these vows is Jesus himself, "the prototype of the monk."[58] When Jesus overcame the temptations of Satan in the desert, he showed the way in which each human could live monastically. Importantly, this initial monastic impulse was an "event," meaning that it was not a movement toward an institutionalization of Jesus's example but, rather, a pneumatological response to God's offer of grace.[59] And Evdokimov seems to think that interiorized monasticism is a return, a recapturing of this pneumatological monasticism that is more authentic to the life of Jesus. The three responses of Jesus to the demonic temptations of Satan in the desert form the basis of the three monastic vows, which in turn form the basis of the three vows of interiorized monasticism.[60]

The first vow made by the interiorized monk is the vow of poverty. Evdokimov states that when Jesus rebuffed Satan by claiming that his followers "shall not live by bread alone," he was prioritizing the spiritual over the physical. In the old covenant folks labored by the sweat of their brow, but in the new covenant the spiritual person would choose to sit at the feet of Jesus à la Mary rather than to slave away at a meal à la Martha. The believers' primary sustenance now was the Eucharistic bread and wine, the so-called bread of angels (cf. Ps. 78:25). For the interiorized monk who, by design, lives in the world, it is imperative that she strive to make real a global economy that is based on need and not on profit. In this economy, "absence of *need to have* becomes a *need not to have*."[61] This makes it possible to appreciate all that we have as a gift from God. This "monastic ideal does not preach formal poverty but a wise frugality of needs."[62] Evdokimov continues by stressing that this poverty is not so much a poverty of deprivation as a poverty of use. Interestingly, he does not have to do much here to make "traditional" monastic poverty correspond meaningfully with interiorized monastic poverty, because historic monastic poverty was never a complete lack but rather a wise, godly, and prudent use of resources.[63]

58. Evdokimov, *Ages of the Spiritual Life*, 140.

59. Throughout his corpus Evdokimov seems to waver when thinking about the goodness of the institutionalization of monasticism. At times it is presented as a positive early Christian development, but more often he presents it negatively. For example, the early monastics were *staurophores* (cross-bearers) and *pneumatophores* (Holy Spirit–bearers), "the first charismatics before democratization was necessitated by the increasing numbers of monastics, and before the need for organization led to the imposition of harsh monastic law." *Ages of the Spiritual Life*, 144.

60. See also Plekon, "'Interiorized Monasticism,'" 246–48.

61. Evdokimov, *Ages of the Spiritual Life*, 146 (italics original).

62. Evdokimov, *Ages of the Spiritual Life*, 146.

63. There is not space here to address the reality that throughout much of monastic history poverty was the exception rather than the norm in many Christian monasteries. In both the East and the West there were houses whose material possessions were vast, including movable

The second vow made by the interiorized monk is the vow of chastity. How this vow is connected to Jesus's second response (Matt. 4:6) is a bit more indirect. Evdokimov interprets Satan's second temptation to be an inducement to covet more power than that granted by God to humankind. For example, Satan's words are a temptation to have dominion over space, for throwing oneself down from the temple and living would be to overcome earth's gravity and to rule the heavens and the spirits. Ultimately, says Evdokimov, this is a desire to want to be a "micro-god."[64] This leads to a desire to use magic powers to hypnotize, charm, and dominate, violating the mystery of nature, profaning "the sacredness of the cosmos, the creation of God."[65] Chastity, on the other hand, is not merely a physiological virtue "but expresses the entire and chaste structure of the human spirit. It constitutes the charism of the sacrament of marriage. In a wider sense, it inspires the meaning of the sacredness of every particle of God's creation, inviolable in its expectation of salvation that is to come from one who is chaste." Chastity, then, is the opposite of the power of magic "and signifies the return to the true 'supernaturally natural power' of paradise."[66]

This desire to be chaste and Edenic was manifested in the writings of the monastic fathers, says Evdokimov, as "the purification of the heart," a striving on the part of the monk to transcend one's physiological state. Outside the desert, in the sacrament of marriage,

> chaste love is attracted by the heart that remains virginal beyond every physical consideration. According to the Bible, there is a total "knowledge" of two beings, a conversation of spirit with spirit in which the body strikingly appears as the vehicle of the spiritual. This is why St. Paul says that man should learn "to take a wife for himself in holiness and honor." As pure material, suitable for liturgical use, the chaste man is entirely, body and soul, the matter of the *sacrament* of marriage, with the sanctification of his love. The charism of the sacrament effects the transcendence of the self. This is the transparent presence of one for the other, of one toward the other, so that both can offer themselves together as a single being to God.

---

property (e.g., vestments and gold vessels) and immovable property (e.g., land and tithes). There are, of course, also many examples of individual houses and individual monks who lived in extreme poverty, even to the detriment of the monk's health. Nonetheless, poverty is a historic and standard monastic vow no matter how it was interpreted at any given time and place in history.

64. Evdokimov, *Ages of the Spiritual Life*, 147.
65. Evdokimov, *Ages of the Spiritual Life*, 148.
66. Evdokimov, *Ages of the Spiritual Life*, 148.

Chastity—*sophrosyne*—integrates all the elements of the human being into a whole that is virginal and interior to the spirit.[67]

In these dense paragraphs Evdokimov is saying that chastity is an interior disposition that has more to do with the heart than it does with the sex organs. Chastity, biblically, is interiorized; it is an issue of purity of heart.[68] In this way, a married couple can still practice interiorized monasticism, because their chastity is inward in the same way that a nonmarried monastic is celibate.[69] In sum,

> "To throw himself from the pinnacle of the temple" means to alienate himself and to render himself useless. To this temptation and to the *concupiscence* that inclines a man to seize the power that Christ possesses, even over the angels, the response is chastity. "To cast himself down" designates the movement from the high to the low, from heaven to hell. This was Lucifer's exact itinerary and that of the fall of man which brought about concupiscence. Chastity is an ascension. It is the Savior's itinerary, from hell to the Father's Kingdom. It is also an inward ascension toward the burning presence of God. It is in the spirit that one casts oneself into the presence of God, and chastity is only one of the names of the nuptial mystery of the Lamb.[70]

In the end, chastity is the antidote to an improper zeal for authority, especially an authority over the created world, whose only Lord and Master is God himself.

The third and final vow of the interiorized monk is the vow of obedience. Humankind, as liturgical beings, says Evdokimov, are not passive since we engage in such acts of worship as singing the "Holy, Holy, Holy." That is, we are exercising our obedience to God by freely fulfilling the law of Christ in which we subject ourselves to the all-powerful, all-knowing God. Though God's law is, at times, expressed in "You shall not" statements, these are balanced by the "You shall" statements of the Beatitudes and the Great Commandment,

67. Evdokimov, *Ages of the Spiritual Life*, 149 (italics original). Evdokimov quotes from 1 Thess. 4:4.

68. Though Evdokimov does not quote Matt. 5:28, he is saying the same thing as Jesus, who pronounced that "everyone who looks at a woman with lustful intent has already committed adultery with her in his heart." Though adultery is a physical sin (i.e., a man and a woman who are not married have sex), Jesus extends it to include the immaterial "lustful intent" in one's heart.

69. Unfortunately Evdokimov does not consider the situation of nonmarried, nonmonastic men and women, though he surely thought of them as being able practitioners of interiorized monasticism.

70. Evdokimov, *Ages of the Spiritual Life*, 151 (italics original).

for example.[71] Evdokimov rightly notes that in the gospel obedience is tied to truth, which is what frees the otherwise sin-bound believer to live a holy life. Hence, writes Evdokimov, "This is why God does not issue orders, but he makes appeals and invitations: 'Hear, O Israel.' 'If anyone wills . . .' 'If you wish to be perfect . . .' It is an invitation to find freedom again: 'If anyone wishes to come to me and does not hate his . . .'"[72] Evdokimov continues by showing how this obedience in the gospel is enshrined in early Christian monasticism, particularly that in the deserts of Egypt, in the elder-disciple relationship as well as in the more modern conception of a staretz.[73] For interiorized monastics the equivalent of a staretz might be a spiritual director or a "soul friend."[74] But this obedience, of course, is not directed to the elder, staretz, or spiritual director but is an obedience to God through the elder, staretz, or spiritual director: "Every counsel of a *staretz* leads one to a state of freedom before the face of God." Moreover, "obedience crucifies our own will in order to arouse the final freedom—the spirit listening to the Holy Spirit."[75]

In his discussion of the traditional monastic vows, Evdokimov seems to have succeeded in accomplishing his two tasks in defending interiorized monasticism: to remove the false spiritual dichotomy between marriage and monasticism and to find a way in which believers can live out the gospel commands without everyone becoming a monk or nun in the traditional sense. He has shown that one does not need to choose marriage *or* monasticism but that there is a compatibility between the two; they are complementary, not contradictory. He has also shown that the demands of the gospel are not just met by the spiritual elite but are meaningfully met by all Christian believers who live fully into the vows of poverty, chastity/celibacy, and obedience. While Evdokimov was formulating and publishing his theology of interiorized monasticism, a similar sentiment was being formed and then articulated in the work of Roman Catholic priest-theologian and champion of interreligious dialogue Raimon Panikkar (d. 2010).

Raimon Panikkar's Monk as Universal Archetype

Panikkar, who was born in Spain to a Roman Catholic mother and a Hindu father and who studied and/or taught in Spain, Germany, Italy, and the United

---

71. Albeit the "You shall" aspect of the Beatitudes is not explicit.
72. Evdokimov, *Ages of the Spiritual Life*, 151.
73. *Staretz* is the Russian word for "elder." See Ware, "Spiritual Father."
74. Leech, *Soul Friend*.
75. Evdokimov, *Ages of the Spiritual Life*, 153.

States, was part of the symposium "The Monk as Universal Archetype" convened in November 1980 by the North American Board for East-West Dialogue (NABEWD). In the words of NABEWD chairman Armand Veilleux, a Trappist Cistercian monk, "The stimulating contribution of Raimundo Panikkar and the reflections of the participants led to a clearer awareness of the fact that there is a monastic archetype or a contemplative dimension innate in every human being. All those who are called monks . . . have chosen that dimension as the center around which their whole existence is" built.[76] Panikkar does not think of this monastic archetype in the sense that there is an ideal monk and then all other monks approximate this archetype to some degree. Instead, "to speak of *the archetype of the monk* . . . assumes that there is a *human* archetype which the monk works out with greater or lesser success. Traditional monks may have reenacted in their own way 'something' that we too may be called upon to realize, but in a different manner which expresses the growth and newness of the *humanum*."[77] For Panikkar there is a monk in each of us, and Panikkar understands his own being in this way: "Since my early youth I have seen myself as a monk, but one without a monastery, or at least without walls other than those of the entire planet . . . [and] without a habit, or at least without vestments other than those worn by the human family."[78] In the end, "monkhood" has two meanings: it is (1) "something special, difficult, even sometimes queer, with tinges of social nonconformity," but it is also (2) "something so very much human that it is ultimately claimed to be the vocation of every human being, what everybody should be or is called to be."[79] Panikkar, like Evdokimov, understands that he is saying something new, that he is enlarging the historical and traditional discourse about monks and nuns, and this is a good thing inasmuch as it is not just a "modernized imitation" of established monasticism but an "emerging mutation . . . a new *metanoia*, a new *conversion*."[80]

Panikkar defines a "monk" (*monachos*) as "that person who aspires to reach the ultimate goal of life with all his being by renouncing all that is not necessary to it, i.e., by concentrating on this one single and unique goal. Precisely this singlemindedness (*ekāgratā*) . . . distinguishes the monastic way from other spiritual endeavors toward perfection or salvation."[81] An essential element of

76. Veilleux, foreword to Panikkar, *Blessed Simplicity*, x.
77. Panikkar, *Blessed Simplicity*, 7 (italics original). Panikkar's contributions to *Blessed Simplicity*, with a new introduction, are printed in Panikkar, *Mysticism and Spirituality*.
78. Panikkar, *Blessed Simplicity*, 6.
79. Panikkar, *Blessed Simplicity*, 7.
80. Panikkar, *Blessed Simplicity*, 7 (italics original). Evdokimov had also referred to monasticism as a "metanoia" (i.e., changed way of life). See Evdokimov, *Sacrament of Love*, 76.
81. Panikkar, *Blessed Simplicity*, 10.

the monk as an expression of an archetype of human life, for Panikkar, is the reality that "monkhood" is one dimension of the *humanum*, which he understands as the "core of humanity or humanness that can be realized in as many fashions as there are human beings."[82] To be a monk is to *be*; it is not to *do* or to *acquire*. Because monkhood is one dimension of *humanum*, then everyone has the potential of realizing this dimension. Monkhood is not the only dimension but one dimension among many, for the "*humanum* is multidimensional, and no single dimension can encompass the complexity of human life."[83] It is in this way that the monk is the universal archetype, but it is not the only way. Monasticism is also universal because it "is not a specifically Christian, Jaina, Buddhist, or sectarian phenomenon; rather, it is a basically human and primordially religious one."[84] In Panikkar's thought, monkhood is prior to the "quality or qualification" of being Christian, Buddhist, and so on. I may live out my monastic dimension according to a particular religious form (e.g., Christian), but monkhood itself is prior to how I live it out.

Since monasticism is simply one dimension of the *humanum* and is due to the primordial character of monasticism, it is not inherently a form of life that can or should be institutionalized. Like Evdokimov, Panikkar is skeptical of the institutionalization of monasticism. Evdokimov thought that the institutionalization of monasticism radicalized the gospel of Jesus Christ in such a way as to create a distinction between the wholehearted followers of the gospel (i.e., monastics) and everyone else. Panikkar has a similar concern: "Once monkhood becomes institutionalized, it begins to become a specialization and it runs the risk of becoming exclusive. Not everybody can or should enter a monastery, but everybody has a monastic dimension that ought to be cultivated."[85] Once monasticism becomes a particular form of organized life, it loses its universality, which is what makes it one dimension of the *humanum*. Panikkar is fine with monasticism as an institution as long as it does not become institutionalized; he wants monastic communities to be organisms, not organizations.[86] Why? Well, if monkhood is a constitutive

---

82. Panikkar, *Blessed Simplicity*, 13.
83. Panikkar, *Blessed Simplicity*, 15.
84. Panikkar, *Blessed Simplicity*, 16.
85. Panikkar, *Blessed Simplicity*, 14.
86. Panikkar, *Blessed Simplicity*, 19. On the distinction between organism and organization, Panikkar says,

> The organization runs when there is money; the organism runs where there is life. . . . The organization needs a frame; the organism requires a body. The organization needs a boss, a leader, an impulse from the outside to let it function. The organism needs a soul, health, i.e., the harmonious interaction of all the parts of the whole. An organization is dientropic, an organism is diectropic. An organization equals the sum of its parts

human dimension, it will never find its full flowering in a closed institution. For Panikkar so much turns on the universality of monasticism, not only its existence as an institution but also its universal human dimensionality.

In the end, both Panikkar and Evdokimov are pushing for a nontraditional, noninstitutionalized form of monasticism, and though there are many differences in their theologies, there are common sentiments albeit with distinct terminology. Panikkar is greatly indebted to his study of non-Christian religions, whereas Evdokimov does not wander beyond his Eastern Orthodox heritage. Nonetheless, there is a shared center, and that center becomes important in any theology of monasticism.

Monasticism, the Priesthood of All Believers,[87] and Martin Luther

Though not exactly the same, Evdokimov's belief that the Christian doctrine of the priesthood of all believers is foundational to interiorized monasticism and Panikkar's conception of the universality of the monastic dimension of *humanum* as the foundation of monasticism's archetypicality share a mutual impetus: all human beings have something in common that manifests itself in a monastic lifestyle. One must make a kind of first-order theological commitment before one can say anything theologically meaningful about monasticism, and I believe that theological commitment is encompassed in the doctrine of the priesthood of all believers.[88]

As expressed by Evdokimov, the priesthood of all believers means that all Christian believers participate in the priesthood of Jesus Christ by virtue of

---

and each part is replaceable by an identical replica. An organism is more than the sum of its components and no component can be replaced by an exact duplicate, because each is unique. If at all, the organism has to regenerate itself from within when it has been wounded. An organism dies when the soul departs. . . . An organization has much more resistance because its structure is stronger and can function by inertia. (*Blessed Simplicity*, 19–20)

87. Here the doctrine of the priesthood of all believers will only be briefly discussed by way of Evdokimov and put into conversation with Martin Luther. A more detailed discussion of the priesthood of all believers will be given in chap. 5.

88. I do not think that Panikkar's universal monastic dimension is, in the end, a direct equivalent of Christian theology's priesthood of all believers. Yet I do think that they are getting at the same thing albeit with different terminology. Whereas Panikkar's terminology strives to be universal, the "priesthood of all believers" is strictly Christian and, therefore, exclusive. Elsewhere, and in a different context, Panikkar does put forward a theology of the priesthood of all believers when he writes that the "fundamental Christian attitude regarding the so-called non-Christian surroundings . . . *vis-à-vis* the world" is to stand "for the whole cosmos before God in action, contemplation and love. . . . This is the priestly vocation of every Christian (1 Pet. 2:9) sharing in the one only priesthood of Christ (Heb. 7:24, etc.)." "Christians and So-Called 'Non-Christians,'" 300–301. Accordingly, Panikkar does hold to a theology of the priesthood of all Christian believers.

our life of holiness.[89] This is not a functional priesthood but an ontological priesthood rooted in the fact that each baptized believer has been anointed by the Holy Spirit.[90] Evdokimov refers to it as one's priestly participation in the priesthood of Christ "by means of two priesthoods," the priesthood of each believer and the clerical priesthood.[91] All Christian believers are equal members of the people of God, and a *"functional difference* of ministries suppresses all ontological difference of nature and makes all separation between clerics and laymen impossible."[92] And "that is precisely why the laity develops the state of *interiorized monasticism."*[93]

Surprisingly, Evdokimov's theology of the priesthood of all believers, which underlies his vision of interiorized monasticism, is similar to the position that Martin Luther (d. 1546) took in the sixteenth century when offering his critique of monasticism, especially when considering that it is in baptism that a person is anointed priest. *The Judgment of Martin Luther on Monastic Vows* (written in 1521 but published in February 1522) was the German Reformer's most sustained criticism of monasticism to date. In 1521 a former Roman Catholic priest who now identified as on the side of Luther's Reformation married with the consent of his parish. His archbishop demanded that the local ruler turn over the priest to the ecclesiastical authorities, but the ruler refused. He instead referred the case to a commission of jurists. This led the Reformer Philip Melanchthon (d. 1560) to argue that the Scriptures and the Christian tradition allowed priests to be married. In response Luther wrote his *Theses on Vows* in 1521, arguing that clerical celibacy contradicts justification by faith, the Reformation's bedrock doctrine, and is therefore not binding on an individual. Furthermore, in the Reformation's wake many monks were leaving their monasteries, including the monks of Luther's own monastery, so much so that by spring 1522 the only person left in the monastery was the prior. Luther suspected that many monks were leaving to escape the discipline of the monastery because they could no longer keep their monastic vows. Thus, *The Judgment of Martin Luther on Monastic*

89. The phrase and concept of the priesthood of all believers is used to express the sovereignty of God over all created existence without distinction between priest/pastor and laity, or monastic and nonmonastic, for example. It holds that each person has direct access to God since it is Christ himself who is the "one mediator between God and men" (1 Tim. 2:5). As will be discussed in a later chapter, the priesthood of all believers is rooted in one's baptismal vows, making all baptized believers equal before God with regard to good works.

90. See Evdokimov, *Sacrament of Love*, 85.

91. Evdokimov, *Ages of the Spiritual Life*, 230.

92. Evdokimov, *Ages of the Spiritual Life*, 231 (italics original).

93. Evdokimov, *Ages of the Spiritual Life*, 233 (italics original).

Vows was intended to serve as a guide for those who had left the monastery or were thinking about doing so.[94]

Even before writing his treatise on monastic vows, Luther had expressed in more than one place his disdain for the monastic life *if* it were seen as a superior form of Christian life or as implying that monks and nuns were more sure of their salvation than the average nonmonastic believer. For example, he writes, "The pope or bishop anoints, shaves heads,[95] ordains, consecrates, and prescribes garb different from that of the laity, but he can never make a man into a Christian or into a spiritual man by so doing. . . . As far as that goes, we are all consecrated priests through baptism, as St. Peter says in 1 Peter 2[:9], 'You are a royal priesthood and a priestly realm.'"[96] In his *On Monastic Vows*, Luther never explicitly refers to the "priesthood of all believers," but he lays out his argument against monastic vows in five steps: (1) God's Word does not command monastic vows; (2) monastic vows are in conflict with faith; (3) monastic vows are compulsory and perpetually violate the freedom of a Christian; (4) monastic vows violate the Ten Commandments; and (5) monastic vows are contrary to common sense. In the first section, where Luther argues that monastic vows are against God's Word, he develops three points: (1) monastic vows are simply equivalent to baptismal vows; (2) scriptural commandments apply to all Christians since God makes no distinction between "counsels" and "precepts" like the Roman Catholic Church; and (3) virginity and celibacy are commandments given to all Christians inasmuch as individual believers are led to live virginal, celibate lives. It is this section that is apropos for the present topic.

Luther begins this section with a general principle: the Scriptures condemn whatever is a matter of rules, statutes, or orders, or whatever falls short of, is contrary to, or goes beyond Christ.[97] Because monastic vows, according to Luther, are a matter of rules and contrary to the gospel, they are to be condemned. Luther then presents Francis of Assisi (d. 1226) as someone who got it right but whose subsequent followers got it wrong. Luther thinks that Francis "wanted his brethren to live according to the gospel," and to do that they would "be as free from vows as from all human traditions. He wanted those little brothers to have the choice of living as celibates or as noncelibates on the strength of their vow and rule, and of remaining in monasteries and

94. For a full discussion of *The Judgment of Martin Luther on Monastic Vows*, see Peters, *Reforming the Monastery*, 19–37.

95. I.e., tonsures monks.

96. Martin Luther, "To the Christian Nobility of the German Nation Concerning the Reform of the Christian Estate" (*LW* 44:127).

97. Martin Luther, *The Judgment of Martin Luther on Monastic Vows* (*LW* 44:254).

under their own regulations as long as they wanted. Those who vowed the gospel vowed nothing other than this and could vow nothing else."[98] However, the *Regula bullata* (i.e., *Later Rule*), approved by the pope in November 1223, begins by saying that "the rule and life of the Friars Minor is this: to observe the holy Gospel of our Lord Jesus Christ by living in obedience, without anything of their own, and in chastity."[99] Luther thought this understanding wrong because it equated the gospel with the three traditional monastic vows: obedience, poverty, and chastity. Thus, Luther concludes, "This saintly man was deceived either by the great number of those in the world who despise the gospel, or by the misguided effort of procuring the support and approval of the pope. Consequently, he made the universal gospel intended for all the faithful into a special rule for the few."[100] And most important for Luther, "when a Franciscan takes his vow he vows nothing more than that which he already vowed at the start in his baptism, and that is the gospel."[101] That is, when a Franciscan takes his vows, he should be vowing nothing more than what he had already vowed and committed to at his baptism: "Francis must have been under an illusion when he taught his followers (if he ever did) to vow a second time that which both they and everybody else had vowed already at baptism, namely, that which we hold most in common, the gospel."[102]

Next Luther turns to the Latin church's tendency to divide the gospel into counsels and precepts. For Luther this means that the gospel is not meant for all, because if it was meant for all baptized Christians (i.e., all Christian priests), then it would not need to be divided into counsels and precepts. Historically in the West, monks followed the counsels, whereas nonmonastics were obligated to follow the precepts. By making this distinction, Luther concludes, "they do not know what the gospel really is."[103] For Luther the gospel "is simply the promises of God declaring the benefits offered to man";[104] therefore it is given to all people to follow the gospel commandments and exhortations. For Luther there is only one gospel, and it is binding on all Christians, regardless of one's state in life. For example, the commandments in the Sermon on the Mount

98. Luther, *On Monastic Vows* (LW 44:255).

99. *Regular bullata* 1.1, in Francis of Assisi and Clare of Assisi, *Francis and Clare*, 137. In all fairness, it was commonplace from the last part of the twelfth century for monastic rules to use the formula "to live in obedience, in chastity and without anything of their own" (or some combination thereof). In this way Francis and his followers were simply being traditional. See Hanron, "Commitment by Monastic Vow."

100. Luther, *On Monastic Vows* (LW 44:255).

101. Luther, *On Monastic Vows* (LW 44:255).

102. Luther, *On Monastic Vows* (LW 44:256).

103. Luther, *On Monastic Vows* (LW 44:256).

104. Luther, *On Monastic Vows* (LW 44:256).

are exactly that—"necessary commandments" that are "without a shadow of doubt, obligatory precepts taught by Christ."[105] Regarding virginity, which the Roman church termed a "counsel," Luther writes that "Christ did not counsel it, but rather discouraged it. . . . He neither invites anyone to take up celibacy, nor calls men to it. He simply refers to it."[106] Thus, Luther concludes,

> If celibacy is an evangelical counsel, what is the sense of your making a vow that goes beyond the gospel and makes a rigid commandment out of a counsel? For now you live not according to the gospel but beyond it. In holding this you even live contrary to the gospel and no longer have a counsel. If you obey the gospel, you ought to regard celibacy as a matter of free choice: if you do not hold it as a matter of free choice, you are not obeying the gospel. It is quite impossible to make an evangelical counsel into a precept, and it is equally impossible for your vow to be a counsel. A vow of chastity, therefore, is diametrically opposed to the gospel.[107]

When virginity is elevated to a higher state than that of the married life, as the Roman Catholic Church had done, the Christian life is divided into two states: perfection and imperfection. Monastics, of course, are the perfect, whereas all others are viewed as imperfect. Luther acknowledges that the Bible speaks against the sin of lust, but not the superiority of virginity over married life. Luther confesses that the unmarried are more effective servants of God, but the unmarried are praised by God not *because* they are unmarried but because they remain unmarried *for the sake of the kingdom of heaven*. Their end is not virginity as something to be praised but for the establishment of the kingdom of God. In a word, monastic vows are against God's Word because they deny the baptismal vows taken by all Christians, they wrongly divide the biblical commandments into counsels and precepts, and they elevate virginity to a place where it creates two classes of believers, the perfect and the imperfect.

Conclusion

We can see here that Luther's main contention against monastic vows is that they violate the gospel, which is for *all* believers, and that they create two classes of Christian disciples.[108] Luther concludes that the priesthood of all believ-

105. Luther, *On Monastic Vows* (LW 44:259).
106. Luther, *On Monastic Vows* (LW 44:261).
107. Luther, *On Monastic Vows* (LW 44:262).
108. This was not unique to Luther: "At the Reformation there was nothing which was rejected more resolutely than the belief that there were two grades of the Christian life with two standards

ers is central to understanding that God's commandments and exhortations are for everyone equally. And, again, in this way he is echoing the thoughts of Evdokimov and even Panikkar. What is ironic is that Luther is most often accused of hating the institution of monasticism to such an extent that he saw no use for it, but it turns out that his insight (i.e., that monastic vows are rooted in one's baptismal vows, in the gospel, and in the priesthood of all believers) is a stable foundation for interiorized monasticism. In his study of Evdokimov's thought on interiorized monasticism, Cho Phan concludes that the "interiorized monasticism of the laity is ultimately identical with the universal priesthood of the faithful."[109] In a sense Luther is saying the same thing; that is, to be a monastic is to live faithfully into one's baptismal vows, and to be a nonmonastic also means to live fully into one's baptismal vows. It is not an issue of a perfect versus imperfect life but one of location. Some men and women will be called into the monastery in order to live out their monastic calling in a particular way, according to a particular set of rules, whereas others will be called to be monks and nuns outside the cloister and the monastery walls. One is not better than the other; they are two sides of the same coin. In this light, it does not seem odd at all for Dostoevsky's Alyosha to be a monk wearing a nice new suit. For, according to Evdokimov, Panikkar, and Luther, many monks wear suits (or dresses).

---

of morality—one for priests and nuns, and another, less high, for ordinary folk working and living in the commonplace field of home and daily duty." Watt, *Priesthood of All Believers*, 3.

109. Phan, "Evdokimov and Monk Within," 58.

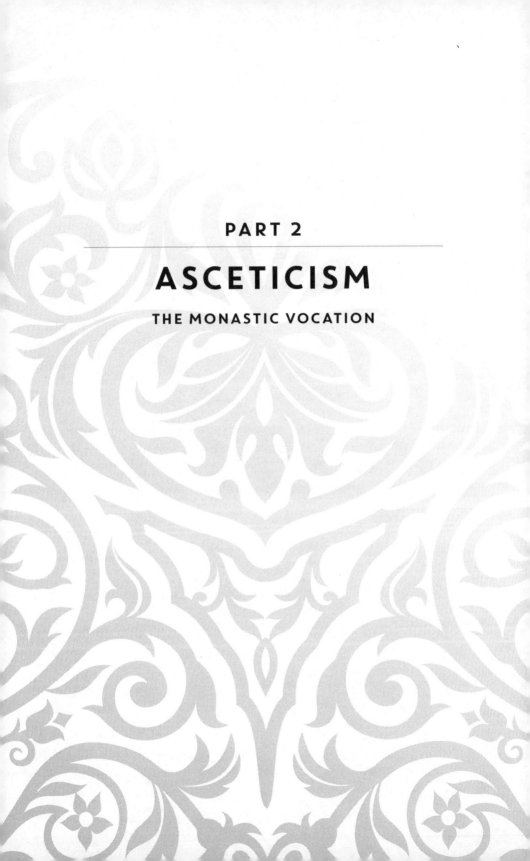

PART 2

ASCETICISM

THE MONASTIC VOCATION

Four

Defining Asceticism

In the earliest centuries of the Christian church there was a general conviction that any sins committed up to the point of baptism were forgiven by God at baptism. This being the case, it caused many Christians to delay baptism until the end of life, ideally on one's deathbed, when there would be essentially no additional time in which to sin against God.[1] In time, however, theologians concluded that an unbaptized baby would not go to heaven;[2] thus, it became impractical to delay baptism for fear of a person's damnation or eternal ambiguity in Limbo.[3] There was a need, then, to determine how a baptized person who continued to sin could live in communion with a holy God.[4] The answer, at least in part, was the development of a penitential system that took sin seriously but had procedures for how sinful Christians could restore proper communion with God. One of the earliest attempts at

1. One of the most well-known examples of this practice was Emperor Constantine (d. 337). See Eusebius of Caesarea, *Life of Constantine* 4.61–64.

2. This view emerged in the fourth century, becoming prominent in the fifth century. For example, Gregory of Nazianzus (d. 390) wrote, "And I think that . . . [unbaptized infants] will also have to suffer, but less, because it was not so much through wickedness as through folly that they wrought their failure." "Oration 40: On Holy Baptism" (*NPNF²* 7:367). Augustine of Hippo (d. 430) wrote, "It may therefore be correctly affirmed, that such infants as quit the body without being baptized will be involved in the mildest condemnation of all. That person, therefore, greatly deceives both himself and others, who teaches that they will not be involved in condemnation." "A Treatise on the Merits and Forgiveness of Sins and on the Baptism of Infants" (*NPNF¹* 5:22–23).

3. For example, Dante Alighieri (d. 1321) places unbaptized children in Limbo (alongside the virtuous pagans), which is just inside the gates of Hell, where there is "sorrow, without punishment." *Inferno* 4.28 (Esolen, 35).

4. This question was taken up as early as the second century in the Shepherd of Hermas 31.

developing a workable penitential system was through excommunication, in which sinning members of the church would be excluded from the most sacred portions of the liturgy. Basil of Caesarea (d. 379) even drew up a series of letters that list the offenses that merited excommunication and how long the excommunication would last. Yet the "practice of excommunication slowly gave way to a more active approach" in which a sinner confessed directly to a priest or elder, who would recommend an appropriate penance.[5] With this approach, though, came the need for guidelines. The appropriate penance for particular sins became a question of life and death, given that a person's eternal salvation was at stake. The answer, in part inspired by Celtic and Germanic legal practice, was found in the penitentials.

Collectively, the penitentials were manuals compiled between the fifth and eighth centuries that standardized penances performed (or paid) for one's sin, resulting in a penitent's restored relationship to the church and to God. These penitentials were rather wide-ranging in their coverage and in their imposed penances. For example, the sixth-century *Penitential of Finnian*, used in Ireland, begins by saying that "if anyone has sinned in the thoughts of his heart and immediately repents, he shall beat his breast and seek pardon from God and make satisfaction, that he may be whole."[6] By the end of the penitential, however, sexual sins merit a harsher set of penalties: "If any layman defiles his neighbor's wife or virgin daughter, he shall do penance for an entire year on an allowance of bread and water, and he shall not have intercourse with his own wife; after a year of penance he shall be received to communion, and shall give alms for his soul."[7] The *Penitential of Cummean* (ca. 650) says that a drunken priest or monk must live on bread and water for forty days, whereas a layman guilty of the same sin does so for only seven days. A fornicating bishop is to do penance for twelve years, whereas a monk-priest performs seven years of penance for the same sin. This penance includes asking pardon hourly; fasting every week except during Eastertide; when not fasting eating only bread and butter, vegetables, eggs, cheese, and milk; sleeping on a bed with only a small amount of hay; deploring one's guilt at all times; adopting an obedient attitude; and not partaking of the Eucharist until a year and a half into one's penance.[8] In the end, a study of these penitentials shows that a main form of penance for sin was bodily affliction, especially fasting and sexual abstinence but also including flagellation, for

5. Dysinger, "Asceticism and Mystical Theology." My thanks to Fr. Dysinger for providing me with a prepublication copy of his article.
6. McNeill and Gamer, *Medieval Handbooks of Penance*, 87.
7. McNeill and Gamer, *Medieval Handbooks of Penance*, 94.
8. McNeill and Gamer, *Medieval Handbooks of Penance*, 101–3.

example. Is it any wonder, then, that asceticism garnered a negative reputation? In the infamous words of Friedrich Nietzsche, "Read from a distant star, the majuscule script of our earthly existence would perhaps lead to the conclusion that the earth was the distinctively *ascetic planet*, a nook of disgruntled, arrogant, and offensive creatures filled with a profound disgust at themselves, at the earth, at all life, who inflict as much pain on themselves as they possibly can out of pleasure in inflicting pain—which is probably their only pleasure."[9] Nonetheless, asceticism is, historically, a *sine qua non* of monastic life; that is, to be monastic is to be ascetic.[10] But what does that mean, and can asceticism only be understood pejoratively with reference to penance or self-punishment?

The Proper Nature of Asceticism: Natural versus Unnatural

By the end of the first paragraph of the introduction to his *Asceticism in the Graeco-Roman World*, Richard Finn already connects the concept of asceticism to monasticism and acknowledges that different ascetic practices will be observed by those living different kinds of lives. For Finn, asceticism is "voluntary abstention for religious reasons from food and drink, sleep, wealth, or sexual activity. Such abstention may be periodic or permanent."[11] And this seems to get at the heart of most understandings of asceticism—that it is an abstention. Luke Dysinger adds to this concept of abstention the fact that, etymologically, ἄσκησις refers to the training necessary to acquire a skill, that is, "any exercise necessary for the development of a profession, artistic skill, or special lifestyle."[12] In the later Greek and Roman philosophical systems, this training or exercise was often, though not always, for the purpose of acquiring moral excellence (i.e., virtue). According to Finn, not all pagan asceticism "constituted an asceticism understood as a moral or physical training." In fact, "strictly limited forms of abstention from food and sex served largely to demarcate sacred places and times, to mediate a safe entry into, or communication with, the sacred realm of the gods, and to sanction the social order where sex and food had their normal places within household and city."[13] Nonetheless,

9. Nietzsche, *Genealogy of Morals*, 117 (italics original).
10. In the words of Henry Chadwick, "The ascetic ideal has found its institutional expression in monasticism." "Ascetic Ideal," 1.
11. Finn, *Asceticism*, 1. For a brief history of asceticism in general, see the editorial introduction to Wimbush and Valantasis, *Asceticism*, xix–xxxiii.
12. Dysinger, "Asceticism and Mystical Theology."
13. Finn, *Asceticism*, 18.

"some physical asceticism was a characteristic part of the holy life" even in pagan philosophy and religion.[14]

According to Michel Foucault, Christian asceticism is often viewed as an interior morality contrasted with the exteriority of pagan asceticism, though he thinks that this misses the essential elements of both. For him both kinds of asceticism are "a particular mode of relationship with oneself . . . albeit in a very different form,"[15] and both forms involve a particular kind of ἄσκησις, or training. Yet what might give asceticism a more specific Christian connotation is that it is an abstention for a particular end, such as union with God or cultivating charity.[16] Kallistos Ware says it well when he writes, "Asceticism . . . leads us to self-mastery and enables us to fulfill the purpose that we have set for ourselves, whatever that may be. A certain measure of ascetic self-denial is thus a necessary element in all that we undertake, whether in athletics or politics, in scholarly research or in prayer. Without this ascetic concentration of effort we are at the mercy of exterior forces, or of our own emotions and moods; we are reacting rather than acting. Only the ascetic is inwardly free."[17] This places Christian asceticism "in a wholly positive light. It is an essential component of spiritual growth analogous to the athlete's quest to achieve peak physical efficiency."[18] In the end, "all these different forms of [Christian asceticism, at least before Origen (d. 254),] owed little to the philosophical asceticism of Greek philosophy."[19] If this is the case, that Christian asceticism is for a particular end, and a positive one at that, and that it is not just a Christian copy of a pagan antecedent,[20] then it is important to understand what exactly Christian asceticism is.

14. Finn, *Asceticism*, 33.
15. Foucault, *Use of Pleasure*, 63.
16. See Guibert, "La notion d'ascèse, d'ascétisme," 937.
17. Ware, "Way of the Ascetics," 3.
18. Dysinger, "Asceticism and Mystical Theology."
19. Finn, *Asceticism*, 98.
20. Though there are interesting parallels between many aspects of pagan asceticism and Christian asceticism, I agree with Finn (and others) that the latter is not just a baptized version of the former. From a monastic-history point of view, however, there are two items raised by Finn to note. First, there is a pagan ascetical precedent to adopting a particular style of dress (i.e., the Christian monastic habit): "By the first century AD, Diogenes and his supposed teacher Antisthenes could each be attributed with first adopting the cloak . . . , the sack and the staff, as their characteristic garb." Finn, *Asceticism*, 19–20. Second, some pagan ascetics were thought of as cenobites and anchorites, particularly popular Christian monastic historical terms: "Pythagoreans at Kroton are described as not only students of the master's philosophy but 'coenobite' (*koinobioi*) sharing in a common life. After the sage's death some followers became solitaries in lonely places." Finn, *Asceticism*, 31. There is no doubt that pagan ascetic practices influenced Christian asceticism (and monasticism), but the influence is not as certain as it has been historically depicted.

Ware makes a distinction between natural asceticism and unnatural asceticism that goes back to the scholarship of Cuthbert Butler. Both of these kinds of asceticism are in relationship to the body. "Natural asceticism reduces material life to the utmost simplicity, restricting our physical needs to a minimum, but not maiming the body or otherwise deliberately causing it to suffer. Unnatural asceticism, on the other hand, seeks out special forms of mortification that torment the body and gratuitously inflict pain upon it," explains Ware. Thus, in Ware's examples, wearing cheap and simple clothing is natural asceticism, whereas wearing hair shirts and fetters with iron spikes piercing the body is unnatural. Similarly, it is natural asceticism to sleep on the floor but unnatural asceticism to sleep on a bed of nails; natural to live in a cave versus a nice house but unnatural to stand permanently on a pillar; natural to refrain from marriage and sexual activity but unnatural to castrate oneself; and natural to eat only vegetables and not meat, drink water and not wine, but unnatural to make our food and drink repulsive.[21] Moreover, "unnatural asceticism . . . evinces either explicitly or implicitly a distinct hatred for God's creation, and particularly for the body; natural asceticism may do this, but on the whole it does not. The official attitude of the church, especially from the fourth century onwards, has been entirely clear. Voluntary abstinence for ascetic reasons is entirely legitimate; but to abstain out of a loathing for the material creation is heretical."[22] Asceticism that reduces one's needs to a minimum in order to provide greater self-sufficiency for holy living (αὐτάρκεια) is to be favored over excessive and/or feigned self-control (ἐγκράτεια). Or, to say it in slightly different terms, better the ascetic be frugal and simple (εὐτελής) than to be luxurious and extravagant (πολυτέλεια). Thus, asceticism, as an essential component of spiritual growth, is the voluntary abstention from food and drink, sleep, wealth, sexual activity, and so on (for a period of time or permanently), for the purpose of maintaining inner attentiveness to God and achieving union with God.[23]

Christian Asceticism: A Case Study of Clement of Alexandria

Richard Finn writes that "Christian writers fiercely debated the degree and form of restraint they were to show with respect to food, drink, and sexual pleasure. Asceticism of some kind was integral to their faith in the first two centuries, but there was no agreement as to what form it should take."[24]

21. Ware, "Way of the Ascetics," 9–10. See also C. Butler, *Lausiac History of Palladius*, 1:188.
22. Ware, "Way of the Ascetics," 10.
23. See Dysinger, "Asceticism and Mystical Theology."
24. Finn, *Asceticism*, 97.

Because the earliest Christian theologians and philosophers had been influenced not only by pagan asceticism but also by Jewish asceticism[25] and biblical revelation, it was inevitable that these early formulators of Christian faith and practice would borrow from what had come before them. But instead of picking piecemeal at which exact practices they should adopt or adapt, some early Christian authors established helpful criteria to guide ascetic practice. It was obvious that certain practices would be observed, such as fasting and sexual continence, because they were prescribed by the Christian Scriptures. But the Scriptures often provided only a latitudinal understanding of ascetic practice and did not speak with great specificity.[26] Thus, some early Christian theologians did the same, such as Clement of Alexandria (d. ca. 215).

Clement was born circa 140–50 in either Alexandria or Athens to a pagan family. He received an excellent philosophical education from teachers in Greece, Assyria, Palestine, and Egypt, becoming in time a well-known teacher in Alexandria, his most famous pupil being Origen. He was the author of a number of important early Christian texts, particularly the *Protrepticus* (translated as *Exhortation to the Greeks*), *Paedagogus* (lit. "the teacher" but most often translated as *Christ the Educator*), and the *Stromata*. At the beginning of *Christ the Educator* Clement outlines a three-stage education: (1) the Logos of God establishes the fundamental beliefs that lead to conversion; (2) the Logos then teaches the believer how to act in a Christlike manner; and (3) the Logos explains how the believer moves from moral formation to *gnōsis*, or perfect knowledge of God. *Christ the Educator* is concerned with the second stage—how to act:[27] "In three books, [it] is addressed to a readership of baptized persons, who now need to be taught a way of life consistent with their Christian state, and this before moving on to a formation in 'knowledge.'"[28] The first book of *Christ the Educator* is devoted to establishing principles vis-à-vis divine pedagogy, while books 2–3 "contain a repertory of practical moral rules (*to biōpheles tēs paidagōgias*, 2.1.1)."[29]

25. Finn, *Asceticism*, 34–57; and Fraade, "Ascetical Aspects."

26. This perspective is evidenced well in Jesus's words that "when you fast, do not look gloomy like the hypocrites, for they disfigure their faces that their fasting may be seen by others" (Matt. 6:16). Fasting is assumed by Jesus, but no further details are given as to the frequency of fasting or which foods or drinks to avoid.

27. Clement is picking up on the Hellenistic understanding of a *pedagogus* as the slave who accompanies a young boy to school and oversees his behavior while the teacher provides instruction.

28. Moreschini and Norelli, *Greek and Latin Literature*, 1:254.

29. Moreschini and Norelli, *Greek and Latin Literature*, 1:256. It is generally acknowledged that Clement is greatly indebted to Stoic philosophy; nonetheless, as a Christian his presentation

At the beginning of book 2, Clement sets out a general principle that guides his theology of asceticism. Discussing bodily asceticism, Clement writes,

> Other men, indeed, live that they may eat, just like unreasoning beasts; for them life is only their belly. But as for us [i.e., Christians], our Educator has given the command that we eat only to live. Eating is not our main occupation, nor is pleasure our chief ambition. Food is permitted us simply because of our stay in this world, which the Word is shaping for immortality by His education. Our food should be plain [ἁπλῆ] and ungarnished [ἀπερίεργος], in keeping with the truth, suitable to children who are plain and unpretentious, adapted to maintaining life, not self-indulgence [οὐκ εἰς τρυφὴν ἐπιτήδειος]. Viewed in this sense, life depends upon two things only: health [ὑγείας] and strength [ἰσχύος]. To satisfy these needs, all that is required is a disposition easily satisfied with any sort of food; it aids digestion and restricts the weight of the body. Thus, growth and health will be fostered; not the unbalanced and unhealthy and miserable state of men such as athletes fed on an enforced diet. Surely, excessive variety [πολυειδεῖς ποιότητες] in food must be avoided.[30]

In the context of food Clement makes a distinction between what is plain and ungarnished and "excessive variety." This is so, says Clement, because excessive, lavish variety will simply make a person indisposed or give him an upset stomach or, worse, create a taste for the finer foods, which will lead the overindulgent person into investing boundless amounts of money and effort into procuring the finest foods. And to what purpose? For in the end "these men hug their delicacies to themselves, yet after a while they must yield them to the privy."[31] Thus, he says, "Let the meal be plain [λιτόν] and restrained [εὔζωνον], of such sort that it will quicken the spirit. Let it be free of a too rich variety [ποικίλαις ἀνεπίμικτον ποιότησιν] . . . for it supplies ample provisions for its journey, that is, self-sufficiency [αὐτάρκεια].

---

of Stoic ideals has now been baptized, if you will. Thus, his philosophy needs to read not just as a re-presentation of Stoic thought but as a Christianization of Stoic philosophy: "It must be remembered that an author is not explained, or even fairly represented, by showing how much he may have derived from others, for in the last analysis his finished thought is his own, however extensive the foreign material employed in its construction." R. Casey, "Clement of Alexandria," 39. Moreover, John Behr notes that "Clement's asceticism is held in check by Christ, its motivation certainly lies elsewhere, in the ideal he establishes for Christian life, an ideal he found in the popular cultivated morality of his time. Christ's incarnation is consequently understood by Clement as enabling the exercise of the morality taught by the Greeks, who, despite having received a spark of the divine Word, were unable to practice it due to their weakness." Behr, *Asceticism and Anthropology*, 166.

30. Clement of Alexandria, *Paedagogus* 2.1.1–2 (FC 23:94). Greek text in Stählin, *Clemens Alexandrinus, Erster Band*.

31. Clement of Alexandria, *Paedagogus* 2.1.4 (FC 23:96).

Self-sufficiency, in dictating that food be limited to the proper amount, ministers to the health of the body."[32] In short, Clement advocates for self-sufficiency
over self-indulgence and believes that food, in particular, leads to a lack of
moderation, which results in three sins: "Gourmandising [ὀψοφαγία] . . . is
nothing more than immoderate use of delicacies; gluttony [λαιμαργία] is a
mania for glutting the appetite, and belly-madness [γαστριμαργία] . . . is lack
of self-control with regard to food."[33]

In the end, for Clement, the Christian is bound by the apostle Paul's admonition that "whether you eat or drink, or whatever you do, do all to the
glory of God" (1 Cor. 10:31), for "the Christian way of life is not achieved
by self-indulgence."[34] Thus, "we should shy away from foods that arouse the
appetite and lead us to eat when we are not hungry."[35] Clement advocates
for mere self-sufficient practices when he says that "the natural and pure
drink demanded by ordinary thirst is water," not wine, for the "excessive
use of undiluted wine is intemperance; the disorderliness resulting from it
is drunkenness; and the discomfort and indisposition felt after indulgence is
called the after-effect."[36] Christians should also avoid using fancy drinking
cups, such as those made of gold, silver, or glass, because they have no purpose other than to put on a display for the eyes, and the same can be said for
luxurious furniture, dishware, utensils, bedding, and women's makeup, for
"all these things are manifestations of vulgar self-indulgence."[37] Regarding
sleep the Christian must "still [be] mindful of the precepts of temperance
[σωφροσύνης]."[38] The same temperance and self-control is to be expected
in one's married sex life: "It is unmistakably sinful to give in to sexual pleasure or to become inflamed by our lusts or to be excessively aroused by our
unreasonable desires. . . . Sowing seed is permissible only for the husband.
. . . Against every other sort of self-indulgence the best remedy is reason."[39]
Though many more examples could be offered, Clement's point is easily
seen: a proper asceticism tends toward the simple, the natural, and what
is sufficient and proper. It is a mean between two extremes. In his words,
"The medium is good in all things . . . since the extremes are dangerous,

---

32. Clement of Alexandria, *Paedagogus* 2.1.7 (FC 23:98). The context of these comments
is the Christian Agape meal. Clement's point is that even a meal of this significance should
still be simple in its fare.
33. Clement of Alexandria, *Paedagogus* 2.1.12 (FC 23:103–4).
34. Clement of Alexandria, *Paedagogus* 2.1.14 (FC 23:106).
35. Clement of Alexandria, *Paedagogus* 2.1.15 (FC 23:106).
36. Clement of Alexandria, *Paedagogus* 2.2.19 and 2.2.26 (FC 23:110 and 116–17).
37. Clement of Alexandria, *Paedagogus* 2.3.35 (FC 23:124–25).
38. Clement of Alexandria, *Paedagogus* 2.9.77 (FC 23:159).
39. Clement of Alexandria, *Paedagogus* 2.10.102 (FC 23:178).

the middle courses are good. For to be in no want of necessaries is the medium, and the desires which are in accordance with nature are bounded by sufficiency."[40] This frugality (εὐτέλεια), in fact, was made a precept from the time of Israel receiving God's law.[41] John Behr sums it up: "The most apt term to characterize this state, although Clement does not in fact use it in the *Paedagogus*, is moderation (μετριοπάθεια)."[42] And Clement is not alone in viewing asceticism in these terms.[43] Moreover, in the centuries following Clement asceticism became the particular practice of monks and nuns, which is not to say that nonmonastics were not expected to be ascetical, but men and women who joined monasteries were, in large part, signing up to practice asceticism robustly.

Monastic Asceticism: The Example of the *Rule of Benedict*

Benedict of Nursia (d. 547) says that the "life of a monk ought to be a continuous Lent."[44] As Terrence Kardong notes, "Benedict's chapter on Lent is one of his most successful efforts and also quite surprising in its tone. In a monastic Rule that often has to emphasize asceticism, one might expect that if there is to be a discussion of Lent, it will be super-ascetical or even grim. That is far from the case with RB 49."[45] However, Benedict's predecessor, known to us only as the "Master," was much more severe in his expectations of the monks at Lent. In the end, however, it was the RB that gained popularity and had a greater impact on Western Christian monasticism and, therefore, monastic asceticism. According to Conrad Leyser, "the *Rule* for beginners acquires monumental status, being hailed for over a thousand years as the definitive formulation of the monastic life." And it did this because it "solves the problem of asceticism and community that had specifically defeated John Cassian: how experts and beginners could live together in a community."[46] Sociologist Max Weber sums it up well when he writes, "In the Rule of St. Benedict . . . [Christian asceticism] has become a systematically developed method

---

40. Clement of Alexandria, *Paedagogus* 2.1.16, in Behr, *Asceticism and Anthropology*, 162. This is an important but difficult passage to translate: ἀγαθὴ μὲν ἡ μέση κατάστασις ἐν πᾶσι μέν . . . ἐπεὶ αἱ μὲν ἀκρότητες σφαλεραί, αἱ μεσότητες δὲ ἀγαθαί. μέσον δέ ἐστι πᾶν τὸ ἀνενδεὲς τῶν ἀναγκαίων. αἱ γὰρ κατὰ φύσιν ὀρέξεις αὐταρκεία. Stählin, *Clemens Alexandrinus, Erster Band*, 166.
41. Clement of Alexandria, *Paedagogus* 2.1.17.
42. Behr, *Asceticism and Anthropology*, 162.
43. See, e.g., Cassian, *Institutes* 6.23.
44. Benedict of Nursia, *Regula* 49.1, in Fry, *RB 1980*, 253. Benedict's *Regula* will hereafter be abbreviated as RB.
45. Kardong, *Benedict's Rule*, 408.
46. Leyser, *Authority and Asceticism*, 101.

of rational life conduct, with the goal to overcome the *status naturae*, to free man from the power of irrational impulses and his dependence on the world and nature, to bring him under the supremacy of purposive volition, to subject his action to constant self-control and the consideration of the ethical consequences [of his deeds]."[47] So what constitutes this influential Benedictine, monastic asceticism?

Having defined asceticism above in terms of abstention from food and drink, sleep, wealth, sexual activity, and other bodily mortifications, we can now observe the ways in which Benedict legislated for his monks in these areas. Regarding food, it is immediately apparent that Benedict is seeking to be neither too harsh nor too lenient, seeking a middle way similar to that expounded by Clement. First, no matter when the main meal of the monastery is taken, assuming it is not a fast day, there are to be "two kinds of cooked food because of individual weaknesses [*diversorum infirmitatibus*]" (39.1; 239).[48] This gives the monk an option: should he not be able to eat the one kind of food (perhaps due to his constitution or tastes), he can eat the other, and any monk may eat from both. A third dish of fruit and/or raw vegetables can be provided if such foods are available in the area. Further, each monk is provided daily with a "generous pound of bread" (39.4; 239). As Kardong notes, it is difficult to determine the exact size of this "pound" (most likely a kilo, which is about 2.2 pounds), but what is certain is that bread, as the staple of a medieval diet, was necessary for the performance of manual labor; therefore it was to be generously weighed (i.e., not skimped on). Depending on the manual labor to be done that day by the monks, the abbot could decide "to grant something additional, provided that it is appropriate, and that above all overindulgence [*crapula*] is avoided, lest a monk experience indigestion. For nothing is so inconsistent with the life of any Christian as overindulgence [*crapula*]" (39.6–7; 239).[49] Benedict is reasonable in understanding that if someone was going to engage in extra manual labor, then he would need the strength to do so, but he is also concerned that the monks not eat too much; that is, he is trying to walk a fairly narrow middle way. Evidence of overindulgence, however, would reveal itself gastronomically in indigestion. A monk with indigestion is an overfed, overindulged monk, and this is inconsistent with the Christian life. Last, younger boys living in the monastery (who may or may not become professed monks in adulthood) could eat the same kinds

47. Quoted in Kaelber, *Schools of Asceticism*, 100.
48. The first number refers to the chapter and verse of the RB cited, followed by the page number in Fry, *RB 1980*. The times of the main meal are set forth in RB 41.
49. The Latin word *crapula* in classical Latin meant "drunkenness," but it is used by Benedict here in a manner akin to gluttony.

of food but smaller amounts.[50] In the end, Benedict's perspective on food is summed up concisely when he writes, "In all matters frugality [*parcitate*] is the rule" (39.10; 239).[51]

Concerning drink, Benedict says that he is hesitant to legislate anything since everyone's needs are different. Nonetheless, Benedict recommends a *hemina* of wine a day will suffice or less for those "to whom God gives the strength to abstain" (40.4; 241).[52] A greater amount is allotted by the abbot if necessary because of local conditions, such as heat or the amount of daily manual labor, but as with overindulgence in food, he must "take great care lest excess or drunkenness [*satietas aut ebrietas*] creep in" (40.5; 241). A drunken monk is a sign of overindulgence in the same way as an indigested monk. Again, Benedict is striving for moderation: "Let us at least agree to drink moderately [*parcius*], and not to the point of excess [*ad satietatem*]" (40.6; 241). He concludes the chapter by asserting that those who are given less or none at all should not complain and grumble but bless God, ostensibly because their asceticism is exemplary. In both food and drink Benedict lays out the same ascetic principle, in line with Clement: neither eat nor drink too little or too much but only what is necessary to meet nature's need. For Benedict there is no glory in excessive fasting or overindulgence: "That asceticism of the cenobite is not based on striving for ever greater austerities, but on cheerful acceptance of the common issue, whether it be of food or drink or anything else. This does not preclude personal fasting norms that go beyond the ordinary, but it merely states the principle that the asceticism of the common life is the life itself."[53]

Concerning sleep, Benedict says that the monks are to sleep in separate beds made up of "a mat, a woolen blanket and a light covering as well as a pillow" (55.15; 263), with bedding appropriate to each monk's personal ascetical practice provided by the abbot (22.1).[54] Ideally, there should be a common dormitory, not individual rooms, in which a lamp burns through the night. The monks sleep clothed, seemingly to be ready at a moment's notice to go

50. They are allowed, though, to eat more frequently: "Since their lack of strength must always be taken into account, they should certainly not be required to follow the strictness of the rule with regard to food, but should be . . . allowed to eat before the regular hours" (37.2–3; 237).

51. That Benedict takes the monk's diet seriously is illustrated well when he legislates that monks on errand outside the community for the day "must not presume to eat outside" the monastery (RB 51.1; 255).

52. Fry, *RB 1980*, translates *hemina* as "half a bottle of wine" (approx. half a pint or eight ounces), which Kardong notes is "ridiculously small." Kardong, *Benedict's Rule*, 329. There is no consensus on the meaning of *hemina*, but Kardong leans toward it meaning about half a quart.

53. Kardong, *Benedict's Rule*, 330.

54. See Kardong, *Benedict's Rule*, 225; and Vogüé, *La règle de Saint Benoît*, 653–54.

pray, but given Benedict's concern that the "younger brothers [*adulescentiores*] should not have their beds next to each other, but interspersed among those of the seniors" (22.7; 219), full clothing seems to be a deterrent to sexual misconduct and/or so that the senior monks will be able to assist the drowsy (*somnulentorum*) younger brothers, who naturally need more sleep, should they fail to wake up quickly for prayers. Benedict legislates the amount of sleep each night on the basis of the time of year (i.e., the time of sunrise and sunset and the number of daylight hours for performing manual labor). Sleep is not kept to an unhealthy amount but is appropriate, as is food and drink, to the work of the monks and the time of the year.

When he discusses the question of wealth, Benedict does not have a lot to say about the amount of money a monastery is allowed to possess or accumulate, much less about how a monastery is to steward its financial resources. What seems clear, and what was often the case anyway, is that a monastery would possess those resources necessary to support the life of its monks and to rightly perform the community's liturgical duties. In time Europe's monasteries became some of the wealthiest landowners, coming close at times to having monopolies on certain forms of trade.[55] Nonetheless, Benedict initially sought to mitigate a monastery's wealth by ensuring that it had what it needed to support the community but little more. The RB states that the tools and goods of the monastery are under the watchful eye of the cellarer, a monk carefully chosen for the office because of his wisdom, maturity, and temperance. It is his job to "regard all utensils and goods of the monastery as sacred vessels of the altar, aware that nothing is to be neglected. He should not be prone to greed, nor be wasteful and extravagant with the goods of the monastery, but should do everything with moderation [*mensurate*] and according to the abbot's orders" (31.101–12; 229). All that the monastery owns is to be viewed as precious à la the Eucharistic vessels and should be of sufficient quality to meet the needs of the community.[56] The RB consistently portrays the property of the monastery as belonging to everyone (i.e., no personal property; see RB 33), and the property is to be useful.[57] Those using the monastery's things must care for them carefully and keep them clean (32.4). Importantly, the community's goods are allotted to each monk on the basis of need, and the monk who "needs less should thank God and not be distressed, but whoever needs more should feel humble because of his weakness" (34.3–4; 231). Again, the

55. For example, the Cistercians of northern England controlled much of the wool trade. See Donkin, "Cistercian Sheep-Farming."

56. See Kardong, *Benedict's Rule*, 271–72.

57. Benedict even disallows small gifts from parents, seeing in them potential for division and one-upmanship. See RB 54.

emphasis is on balance and creating a system in which the individual monk's asceticism is appropriate to that monk's state of life and not unnecessarily uniform across the entire community.

Concerning clothing, the monk's habit(s) also belong to the monastery. The quality of the habit depends on the local climate, and each monk in temperate climates is given a cowl (*cucullam*) and tunic (*tunicam*) and a "woolen cowl" (*cucullam . . . villosam*; 55.5) in the winter. In the summer a thinner habit is given to the monk along with a scapular (*scapulare*) for work and both sandals and shoes (*pedules et caligas*).[58] The color and quality of these items must not lead to complaint, and they should be made of what is available locally and "at a reasonable cost" (55.7; 263). It is enough (*sufficit*) for each monk to have two cowls and two tunics so that he will have something to wear while one set is being laundered, "but anything more must be taken away as superfluous [*superfluum*]" (55.11; 263). Further, Benedict emphasizes again that a monk is not to possess any of these things privately; rather, the items are all to be provided by the abbot so that there will be no sense of necessity among the monks.[59] Finally, the crafts of the artisans in the monastery are to be sold in such a way that there is no fraud (57.4). In short, the monastery is to take care of its needs and those of its members, but it is not to accumulate wealth unnecessarily nor be ostentatious before others. Wealth is a means to an end and not an end in itself.

The last area to investigate is sexual activity, something that the RB says little about since it presumes celibacy on the part of its monks. Nonetheless, there is one passing reference mentioned previously that seems to say something about sexual activity: "The younger brothers should not have their beds next to each other, but interspersed among those of the seniors" (22.7; 219). Kardong does not think that this mixing of younger and older is due to a worry over sinful sexual activity, for if "the worry was sexual, then it would seem that mixing youths with mature men would be a dubious solution to the problem."[60] Even so, Benedict may have been concerned nevertheless to ensure that the younger monks (who were, theoretically at least, more libidinous) were not unnecessarily tempted by sleeping too close together. Benedict's reasoning for this sleeping arrangement may have been multipronged.

This brief and incomplete survey allows us to see that within the monastery asceticism was to be practiced by all members of the community and (in the case of communities following the RB, at least) that asceticism was not

58. For full descriptions of these garments, see Fry, *RB 1980*, 261–62.
59. Kardong thinks that Benedict's stance against private property is motivated primarily by his concern to root out any spirit of autonomy (Kardong, *Benedict's Rule*, 274).
60. Kardong, *Benedict's Rule*, 227.

necessarily uniform but matched, where possible, individual monks' ascetical sensibilities and abilities.[61] Unfortunately, in later centuries the thoughtful balance of the RB often gave way in certain monasteries to extreme and even unhealthy manifestations of ascetic practices. For example, the late eleventh- and early twelfth-century monastic reformer Robert of Arbrissel (d. 1116) moved into the forest, wore a hair shirt made of pigskin, shaved his beard without water, used only one blanket while sleeping, avoided wine and rich and fine food, and rarely slept more than half the night. His asceticism was so extreme that his biographer asks, "Who could worthily recount how completely and with what savagery he raged against himself, how many and severe tortures he inflicted on himself, with what grim horrors he weakened himself?"[62] Laying such excesses aside, by the early Middle Ages asceticism became the particular (though not the exclusive) practice of monks and nuns.[63]

When summarizing lay devotion in the Middle Ages, R. N. Swanson writes, "The concept of 'medieval religious life' almost inevitably conjures up visions of monasteries, nunneries, and friaries, of those formally committed to such regular lives which marked them off from ordinary people. Such visions are too restrictive."[64] And, of course, he is right. Historically, most Christians have not been monks and nuns; therefore, individual religious lives have been lived outside the walls of the monastery, necessitating a range of practices and devotions conducive to the nonmonastic, lay life. The practices that arose to meet these needs can, in one way, be thought of as ascetic, but in another way they were not ascetic in the same way that asceticism developed within monasticism. Gerhoh of Reichersberg (d. 1169), a canon regular, wrote,

> Whoever has renounced at baptism the devil and all his trappings and suggestions, even if that person never becomes a cleric or monk, has nonetheless definitely renounced the world. . . . Whether rich or poor, noble or serf, merchant or peasant, all who are committed to the Christian faith reject everything inimical to this name and embrace everything conformable to it. Every order and absolutely every profession, in the catholic faith and according to apostolic teaching, has a rule adapted to its character; and under this rule it is possible by striving properly to achieve the crown of glory.[65]

61. This survey is incomplete, for example, because it fails to look at the asceticism of silence and frequent prayer, both of which are legislated heavily in the RB.

62. Baudri of Dol, *First Life of Robert of Arbrissel* 11, in Venarde, *Robert of Arbrissel*, 12.

63. It was not, of course, limited to monks and nuns. In fact, Ross Posnock demonstrates that it was common among literary and artistic types too. See Posnock, *Renunciation*.

64. Swanson, *Religion and Devotion*, 103.

65. Cited in Swanson, *Religion and Devotion*, 103.

This renunciation of the world, or rejection of "everything inimical," is a kind of asceticism but not to the degree practiced in monasteries.[66] Laypersons exercised their Christian devotion through, for example, attendance at Mass, observance of saints' days, going on pilgrimage, saying their prayers, and providing financial resources to the church. Many of these practices may have involved ascetical acts (e.g., abstaining from sex or fasting from food on prescribed holy days), but the day in and day out reality of lay devotion was not excessively ascetical in the way that it would have been for monks and nuns.[67] This "mild" asceticism, if I may, was no match for the consistent and robust monastic asceticism that came to a head, in particular, in monastic orders such as the Cistercian Order of the Strict Observance (aka Trappists),[68] a Cistercian reform begun at the Abbey of Our Lady of La Trappe under the leadership of Armand Jean le Bouthillier de Rancé in 1664. Having undergone a profound conversion to the monastic life, Rancé instituted a radical regimen of penitential asceticism, culminating, it appears, in the premature death of a number of early members of the community.[69] By this time the moderate and tempered asceticism of Benedict was replaced with a much more intense and, at times, dangerous ascetical regimen. Though nonmonastics were eager to see in monastic practices examples of holiness, they were not in a position to emulate the monk's extreme asceticism. Nonetheless, there is a move today toward recovering the truth that asceticism is for *all* Christian believers, not just monks and nuns.

Liturgical Asceticism

David Fagerberg is currently professor of liturgical studies at the University of Notre Dame and architect of what he calls "liturgical asceticism." Fagerberg has long noted that the Christian "tradition once connected liturgy, theology, and asceticism easily and naturally and necessarily," though this has not

66. For a differing perspective, see Kaelber, *Schools of Asceticism*, esp. chap. 2.

67. There were exceptions to this, such as the flagellents common from the eleventh century, though this too originally started in the monasteries. See Cohn, *Pursuit of the Millennium*, 127–47; and Ramsey, "Flagellation." Groups that blurred the line between monastic and lay, such as the Humiliati, were also strongly ascetical, to the point of even influencing the rise of the mendicant religious orders. See Kaelber, *Schools of Asceticism*, 91 and 97–98.

68. See Zakar, *Histoire de la stricte observance*; Krailsheimer, *Rancé and the Trappist Legacy*; and Bell, *Understanding Rancé*.

69. Recorded in *Relations de la mort de quelques Religieux de l'Abbaye de la Trappe* (1677). This text was reprinted frequently, with the definitive text (in five volumes) published in 1755 (see bibliography under "*Relations*").

been the case in much of modern liturgical theology.[70] For "*liturgy* without asceticism and theology is a species of ritual studies; *asceticism* without liturgy and theology is athletic or philosophical training; *theology* without liturgy and asceticism is an academic discipline in higher education."[71] Fagerberg's objective is not only to understand this tradition but also to return to it. What liturgy does, says Fagerberg, is create "a Christian grammar in the people of God"; that is, it gives the liturgist (i.e., the person engaged in the liturgy)[72] words with which to speak theologically.[73] And these words are not about the ritual of the liturgy but about the person of God, who is the proper object of all liturgies.[74] Thus, liturgy leads to theology, and theology, when absorbed, leads to godliness. This theology is "discovered in the structure of the liturgy, which shapes the lives of the liturgists." There are, then, two aspects to the liturgy: (1) the structure, which Fagerberg calls "liturgical theology," and (2) "the process of shaping lives," which he calls "liturgical asceticism."[75]

Fagerberg defines *liturgy* densely as "the Trinity's perichoresis kenotically extended to invite our synergistic ascent into deification."[76] It is perichoretic because it comes from the Father and returns to him through the power of Christ and in the operation of the Holy Spirit. The Trinity extends its co-inhering love outward in creation, a kenotic (i.e., self-emptying) act that invites the creation to return to the Creator by loving God and others. Succinctly, liturgy "is living in that eternal circulation of love within the Trinity."[77] This return to God is not accomplished by sinful humankind apart from the finished work of Jesus Christ on the cross. According to Fagerberg, Christ "descended in kenosis all the way to Sheol where he found Adam and Eve shackled by mortality, then he broke their chains, trampling down death by death, and raised human nature to ascend with him. . . . When Christ ascended as the first fruits of humanity, he blazed a trail for all to follow." Liturgists "follow" this trail through "co-operation with the operation of the Holy Spirit; we

70. Fagerberg, *Theologia Prima*, 2.

71. Fagerberg, *On Liturgical Asceticism*, 10 (italics original). See also the essays written in response to Fagerberg in Keating, *Liturgy and Priestly Formation*.

72. Fagerberg, *Theologia Prima*, 8: "The word *liturgist* can be used as virtually synonymous with *baptized* or with *laity* to name the members of the mystical body of Christ" (italics original).

73. Fagerberg, *Theologia Prima*, 3.

74. Elsewhere Fagerberg writes, "Liturgical theology materializes upon the encounter at the altar, not upon the secondary analysis at the desk. God shapes the community in liturgical encounter, and the community makes theological adjustment to this encounter, which settles into ritual form." "Liturgical Asceticism," 203.

75. Fagerberg, *Theologia Prima*, 4.

76. Fagerberg, *On Liturgical Asceticism*, 9.

77. Fagerberg, *Theologia Prima*, 31.

synergize with divine energy" through our free will, enabled by grace.[78] In short, we are deified, and deification is union with Christ: "The reason for creation was so that creatures might delight in the Creator insatiably, not from a distance but by participation in the divine nature."[79] So, again, liturgy leads to theology that leads to godliness, making asceticism an essential element of liturgy in the life of every liturgist. Liturgy "creates the Church: a theological corporation . . . and practitioners of liturgy."[80] At its most basic, "liturgical asceticism is the path to stunning normality."[81]

Yet what is this "normality"? According to Fagerberg, it is a state of apatheia, which literally means "passionlessness" (a = without; $pathos$ = passion).[82] Fagerberg notes that the human condition is affected by a malady whose cure is asceticism, resulting in apatheia.[83] The malady of humanity is that we no longer walk upright and fear God. Instead, we are sinners prone to passions, resulting in sin. Though created to be in filial communion with God, humankind is not in proper communion because of sin, and in and by the liturgy we are restored to our proper place as worshipers of God. This is made possible because Jesus Christ, as the God-man, did for humankind what we were created to do, recapitulating everything under his headship. In short, we were created to worship God endlessly, but sin has made that impossible. The Word of God , however, becomes incarnate to show us how to be in proper communion with God and establishes the means to make that possible—namely, liturgy, especially the Holy Eucharist. For "in the liturgy, every human being sees what he or she is to become if only something did not stand in the way of fulfilling that vocation."[84]

In this context a passion "refers to a disoriented and discordant and diseased heart. . . . [It] refers to a state contrary to the divine purpose for a human being."[85] It is the inclination that leads to sin, "a movement of the soul contrary to nature," to quote Maximus the Confessor (d. 662).[86] Fagerberg, following early Christian teaching, emphasizes that passions are not connected

---

78. Fagerberg, *Theologia Prima*, 31.
79. Fagerberg, *Theologia Prima*, 2.
80. Fagerberg, *Theologia Prima*, 10.
81. Fagerberg, *On Liturgical Asceticism*, 26.
82. See Bardy, "Apatheia."
83. Fagerberg, *On Liturgical Asceticism*, 28: "This chapter will deal more generally with the passions (*pathe*), taken as a problem, so that in the next chapter we can consider the discipline of overcoming them (*askesis*), and after that the state of dispassion (*apatheia*) which is the goal of asceticism."
84. Fagerberg, *On Liturgical Asceticism*, 28.
85. Fagerberg, *On Liturgical Asceticism*, 29.
86. Fagerberg, *On Liturgical Asceticism*, 30.

to materiality in such a way as to say that our problem is with material things. Matter is not the problem; the problem lies in the human heart. It is not material things per se that are evil but humankind's misuse of these things. The Christian's use of material things affects her immaterial nature, her spirit, to such an extent that she is no longer able to worship well. The solution to this problem, then, is to mitigate the way in which one interacts with the world—that is, asceticism.

Fagerberg is not interested in commending a list of ascetical practices. Rather, he wants to explore why Christians must be ascetical at all. He writes, "Our purpose is apologetic, an attempt to understand the purpose of asceticism itself, and to argue that such a purpose must be observed from within the framework of life in Christ's Church, that is, liturgical life."[87] In other words, Fagerberg wants to demonstrate that liturgy is the Christian's asceticism—that is, that the liturgy is the edifice in which asceticism lives. To *do* asceticism, if you will, is to worship, to be a liturgist, for "asceticism is a liturgical activity, whether for monk or laic, because its goal is deification."[88] In this Fagerberg is in agreement with James K. A. Smith's philosophy of liturgy, desire, and formation. Briefly, Smith argues that we are what we love.[89] We are liturgical beings (*homo liturgicus*) who do not only think but, first and foremost, love through habituated practices. Because we are liturgical beings, we are going to be formed through liturgy, but the question is which liturgy—a secular cultural liturgy or a sacred Christian liturgy? For the "liturgy is a 'hearts and minds' strategy, a pedagogy that trains us as disciples precisely by putting our bodies through a regimen of repeated practices that get hold of our heart and 'aim' our love toward the kingdom of God."[90] Thus, we involve ourselves in Christian community precisely because we are going to be formed liturgically, and we want that formation to be done in us by a Christian liturgy, not a cultural liturgy of materialism. At the end of the day, says Smith, "intentional Christian worship that . . . draws upon a holistic tradition of worship that activates the whole body, is packed with formative power."[91]

Consequently, all baptized Christians are meant to engage in ascetical struggle, and that asceticism is part of the remedy for humankind's sinfulness. This asceticism, however, is not meant to go beyond that which could be termed

87. Fagerberg, *On Liturgical Asceticism*, 66.
88. Fagerberg, *On Liturgical Asceticism*, 163. "Laic" is Fagerberg's term, borrowed from Eastern Orthodox theologian Nicholas Afanasiev (d. 1966), for nonmonastic, nonordained baptized Christians. It is roughly akin to "layperson," but it is meant to carry a more positive meaning. It comes from the Greek λαϊκός (common, profane, or lay).
89. See Smith, *You Are What You Love*.
90. Smith, *Desiring the Kingdom*, 33.
91. Smith, *Desiring the Kingdom*, 208.

"natural" asceticism. It is primarily in the doing of liturgy that followers of Jesus Christ see what they were meant to be, and it is in the doing of liturgy that they are at their most ascetical. The end purpose of this asceticism by way of the liturgy is deification, or conformity to Christ, or apatheia. Moreover, asceticism is both a preparation for liturgy and an element of liturgy itself: "*Askesis* increases the measure by which we can participate in the liturgical life to which baptism initiated us. Liturgy is where the Kingdom is symbolized in its fullest capacity, and *askesis* enlarges the eyes of the perceiver; it cleanses the surface of the liturgist to reflect glory."[92] Importantly, this asceticism is not simply morality, or the keeping of commandments. Rather, it is about the divinizing work of the Holy Spirit through the liturgical and sacramental life of the church, something that pertains to and touches the lives of all Christian believers.

Fagerberg recognizes that it is monks and nuns who have practiced flight from the world (*fuga mundi*) historically, thereby mitigating their interaction with material things. Nonetheless, asceticism is not unique to monasticism. Fagerberg quotes Russian theologian-philosopher Vladimir Solovyov (d. 1900) favorably: "The highest aim for Christianity is not ascetic detachment from the natural life but its hallowing and purification. . . . The purpose of Christianity is not to destroy life, but to raise it towards God who comes down to meet it."[93] This divine charge and expectation is laid on all Christians, says Fagerberg, at their baptism: "We do not think the monk is an ascetic while the lay person is not; rather, the monk practices the common Christian baptismal asceticism in an exceptional way. The very purpose of calling it *liturgical asceticism* is to remember that it is the discipline incumbent upon all people of God created by Christ."[94] Monks are simply doing what all believers are called to do but in a special, unique way. As Aidan Kavanagh writes, "The monk is simply a baptized Christian whose witness or *martyria* is identical with the witness of every other baptized Christian."[95] The monk and the nonmonastic Christian are called to do the same thing, to overcome the malady that affects all followers of Jesus Christ. Both are to engage in asceticism.

The vocation of all Christians, both monastic and nonmonastic, is holiness, and the liturgy aids in the fulfillment of this vocation. In fact, the liturgy is the primary arena for living out that vocation to the fullest. Nonetheless, it is important to bear in mind that some Christians do this as laypersons and

92. Fagerberg, *On Liturgical Asceticism*, 206.
93. Fagerberg, *On Liturgical Asceticism*, 34.
94. Fagerberg, *On Liturgical Asceticism*, 37 (italics original). See also Fagerberg, *Theologia Prima*, 31.
95. Kavanagh, "Eastern Influences," 59.

others do this as professed monks. In the end, "all Christians are called to be ascetics [and liturgists], though not all are called to be monks."[96] Or, to say it differently, laypersons, as interiorized monks, are to engage in ascetic practices just as professed monks and nuns are expected and sometimes legislated (e.g., the Benedictines) to do, and they do this primarily through the liturgy. The way interiorized monks and nuns practice their asceticism, which is absolutely necessary to their monastic calling, is by way of the liturgy. As stated above, it is in the liturgy that all liturgists glimpse the glory of God in such a way that they are reminded of who they are called to be: sinless men and women in communion with the Triune God. And it is in the liturgy that sinful liturgists have their lives shaped according to God's will; that is, they are deified. Thus, liturgy is paradisiacal in that it offers liturgists a glimpse of their future glory; it shows them who they truly are and how things will be eschatologically. And though professed monks have entered the monastery for the express purpose of pursuing God single-mindedly, they are not granted a vision of God that is superior to or fundamentally different from the one given to all liturgists. In the words of Fagerberg, "The monk doesn't do something the laic shouldn't do, but he does it in a different way, and the laic benefits from seeing this *askesis* concentrated to such potency."[97] In Fagerberg's understanding, the professed monk is an example to the interiorized monk. As both strive for heaven, the professed monk "gives the laic a sighting of his destiny by living the angelic life on earth."[98]

So, as monks and laics live out their unique though complementary vocations, they do so as liturgical beings (*homo liturgicus*), with the liturgy (especially the Daily Office and the Holy Eucharist) as their primary liturgical actions. Regarding the Daily Office especially, all professed monks throughout Christian history have prioritized prayer, especially praying the Psalms. Though the structure and frequency with which a monk or community of monks prays vary in monastic tradition, there is a venerable history of the sevenfold Daily Office: "Seven times a day I praise you" (Ps. 119:164). This led many monastic communities to pray most of the biblical psalms in a day or, as was the case at the medieval Benedictine monastery of Cluny in France, to pray more than 150 psalms each day.[99] However, while professed monks were busy praying the Psalter, there was often no such expectation

96. Fagerberg, *On Liturgical Asceticism*, 133. On monasticism as a vocation, see chap. 7 of this book.

97. Fagerberg, *On Liturgical Asceticism*, 136.

98. Fagerberg, *On Liturgical Asceticism*, 136.

99. By the end of the eleventh century the monks at Cluny prayed 215 psalms a day. See Constable, *Abbey of Cluny*, 78.

for nonmonastics. Nonmonastics were expected to pray but not with the frequency of monks and nuns. In fact, because of illiteracy and prejudice a nonmonastic was often only expected to pray the Our Father and/or other such short prayers (e.g., Ave Maria) each day. This changed over the course of the Middle Ages with the development of the rosary and prayer books, though the latter still required literacy, which made it an option primarily for the educated.[100] It was only at the Reformation, particularly with the Anglican *Book of Common Prayer*, that nonmonastic men and women were expected to pray monastically, if you will.

Over the years scholars have noted that Anglicanism has a monastic quality to it that is, in some measure, attributable to its unique history. As John-Bede Pauley writes, "Anglican identity is the expression of a monastically influenced theology of prayer and worship."[101] Similarly, Bede Thomas Mudge says, "Anglican piety depends heavily on the pre-Reformation monastic influence in England, and particularly that of the Benedictine communities."[102] Further, much has been made of the liturgical similarities between monasticism and Anglicanism. Though it was most usual in the Middle Ages for monastics to pray seven times a day in community, the central services of worship going all the way back to the patristic era were morning and evening prayer.[103] These times of prayer, along with the Eucharist, became the central acts of worship in the Anglican tradition: "The [*Book of Common Prayer*] continued the basic monastic pattern of the Eucharist and the divine office, in the form of 'matins' (which basically combined the offices of vigils and lauds) and 'evensong' (drawing from the offices of vespers and compline) as the principal public forms of worship."[104] The daily celebration of matins and evensong in nonparochial churches, such as cathedrals, is documented from the late seventeenth century onward. Additionally, Pauley writes, "The seventeenth century was also an era of order in religious practice. This meant not only the order of the liturgical hours but also the order of other aspects of daily life in connection with prayer. Prayers were composed for everyday occasions: on walking, dressing, grace before meals, on starting a journey. This practice of prayers for the daily activities of life finds a counterpart in the RB. As the RB strives to cultivate an habitual sense of the presence of God in alternating periods of prayer

100. Getting an education in the Middle Ages was often tied to one's socioeconomic status. So one's ability to pray was, to some extent, dependent on one's financial situation.
101. Pauley, "Monastic Qualities," 261.
102. Mudge, "Monastic Spirituality in Anglicanism," 507.
103. See Taft, *Liturgy of the Hours*.
104. Pauley, "Monastic Qualities," 265.

and work, so does the [*Book of Common Prayer*]."[105] To be an Anglican in the Reformation and early modern era was to pray monastically.

But this is true only if the professed monk-laic distinction holds and is understood in a certain way—that is, that monastics and nonmonastics pursue utterly distinct vocations in which one is a more certain way of divinization or union with God. What Fagerberg is saying is that though there is a distinction between the monk and the nonmonastic, their obligation to prayer, asceticism, and spiritual growth (i.e., theology) is the same: they are both liturgists, and of the same kind. It is incumbent on both monks and nonmonastics to engage in the liturgy, and not just for the sake of the liturgy qua liturgy (i.e., a series of ritual actions), but in order to work out their respective ascetical vocations. To be monastic is to be ascetical, and to be ascetical is to be liturgical, and liturgy is for the whole people of God, monk and laic alike.

Conclusion

Throughout Christian history asceticism and, in many ways, liturgy were the special preserves of professed monks. Monks wrote the books that discussed the nature and practice of asceticism, and monks created the books necessary to pray seven times a day, in supposed imitation of the biblical saints. These monks engaged day in and day out in ascetic endeavors, and even their form of life (e.g., the RB) was arranged around an ascetic posture toward daily living. These monks also prayed day in and day out in ways that were not expected of nonmonastic men and women. Nonetheless, both monk and laic share the same problem of sin and its attendant disposition toward the passions, and both monk and laic share the same overall Christian goal: deification and union with God. As well, all monks and laics share the same solution to the problem of sin: the life of faith in Jesus Christ. And all monks and laics are called to be liturgists and practice liturgical asceticism. In this way professed monks and nonmonastics have much in common or, more properly, have nearly everything in common since they are liturgists, ascetics, and theologians. Yet these are not just shared commonalities in some external, abstract way; rather, they get at the heart of what it means to be a Christian. Monks and laics do what they do because of their baptism, and there is only one baptism common to all believers, whether monk or laic. Consequently, the liturgically ascetic life of both monastics and nonmonastics is rooted in the priesthood of all believers.

105. Pauley, "Monastic Qualities," 268.

Five

The Priesthood of All Believers

O ver the centuries, but especially during the twentieth century, there have been discussions and debates over when exactly during the Eucharist the bread and the wine become the body and blood of Jesus Christ.[1] Is it at the recitation of the institution narrative ("On the night he was handed over to suffering and death . . .")? Or is it at the epiclesis—that is, when the president/celebrant asks the Holy Spirit to bless and sanctify the gifts of bread and wine for the benefit of those who partake of them in a worthy manner? John McKenna concludes, after examining the theological development of this question in Christian history, that "an attempt . . . to fix theologically an exact moment of consecration . . . hardly seems acceptable. To attempt such precision seems to be, in effect, to attempt to pinpoint God's sovereign action."[2] I find myself, as an Anglican, in agreement with McKenna. Moreover, I would suggest that the entire Canon of the Mass is necessary for the proper consecration of the bread and the wine.[3] Why? Because it is not the priest's role alone to make the Eucharist, but it is the work of all the people of God—priest and congregation. Without the congregation's "Amen" (that is, "So be it") the consecration is incomplete; there is no Eucharist. Again, in the words of McKenna, "the whole eucharistic prayer is consecratory."[4] In

1. See McKenna, *Eucharistic Epiclesis*.
2. McKenna, *Eucharistic Epiclesis*, 203.
3. The Canon of the Mass is the central part of the Holy Eucharist (also known as the Eucharistic Prayer, anaphora, or Great Thanksgiving) that begins with the preface (i.e., "The Lord be with you. . . . Lift up your hearts. . . . Let us give thanks to the Lord our God") and concludes with a final doxology ("By him, and with him, and in him . . .") and Amen.
4. McKenna, *Eucharistic Epiclesis*, 205.

other words, the president/celebrant is a priest, and so are the members of the congregation. In fact, all Christian believers are priests; there is a priesthood of all believers. Thus, an examination of the doctrine of the priesthood of all believers is essential in light of David Fagerberg's liturgical asceticism discussed in the previous chapter, and this doctrine is at the core of a theology of baptismal vows and at the root of a proper understanding of (interiorized) monasticism.

The Priesthood of All Believers

The doctrine of the priesthood of all believers (also known as the "universal priesthood") is rooted in the scriptural witness. The passages most frequently cited to support the doctrine include 1 Peter 2:4–9; Revelation 1:6; and Revelation 5:10.[5] Apart from these particular verses, Uche Anizor and Hank Voss argue that "Scripture offers a bounty of material that goes toward funding a robust doctrine of the priesthood of all believers."[6] For example, "Adam is portrayed [in Gen. 2–3], against the later picture of the Israelite priesthood and temple, as the 'archetypal priest' who served in God's primal temple."[7] Israel, as God's chosen people, are said to be a kingdom of priests, assuming that they obey God (Exod. 19:5–6). David is to be "a priest forever after the order of Melchizedek" (Ps. 110:4), and the prophet Isaiah describes the royal priestly "servant" who will restore God's people to their rightful place and relationship with God (Isa. 52–66). Jesus Christ, as descendant of the priest-king David, is the ultimate fulfillment of Isaiah's servant; therefore the "royal priesthood of Christ is the basis and pattern for the priesthood of all believers."[8]

This connection between the priesthood of Jesus Christ and all believers is elaborated on by the apostle Peter: "As you come to him, a living stone rejected by men but in the sight of God chosen and precious, you yourselves like living stones are being built up as a spiritual house, to be a holy priesthood [ἱεράτευμα ἅγιον], to offer spiritual sacrifices acceptable to God through Jesus Christ. . . . But you are a chosen race, a royal priesthood [βασίλειον ἱεράτευμα], a holy nation, a people for his own possession, that you may proclaim the excellencies of him who called you out of darkness into his marvelous light" (1 Pet. 2:4–5, 9).

5. Some scholars, however, reject the relevance of 1 Pet. 2:4–9 to the discussion. See, e.g., Elliott, *The Elect and the Holy*.
6. Anizor and Voss, *Representing Christ*, 26.
7. Anizor and Voss, *Representing Christ*, 28.
8. Anizor and Voss, *Representing Christ*, 41.

Peter, writing to a gentile audience, is eager for his readers to embrace the Messiah; thus he quotes three passages from the Jewish Scriptures (Isa. 28:16; Ps. 118:22; and Isa. 8:14) that speak of the whole people of God in priestly terms. On the one hand, Peter's appropriation of these texts may be because he wants to emphasize that the congregations he is addressing are elect in the same way that Israel was elected by God; or he may want to emphasize that believers, like Old Testament priests, are to live holy lives, set apart for God's service. On the other hand, apart from using these passages to establish the status of Christian believers, Peter is interested in showing that, as priests, believers have a particular function in the church.[9] Historically, Christian theologians have elaborated on both of these: status and function. But it was only in the Reformation era that a theology of the priesthood of all believers became a bedrock principle of ecclesiology, especially for Protestant churches.[10]

Martin Luther on the Priesthood of All Believers

In the early sixteenth century as Martin Luther (d. 1546) was coming of age theologically, he began to question the Latin-speaking church's conception of how sinners came to saving faith in Jesus Christ. Convinced from the Scriptures (esp. Rom. 1:17) that works could not and do not save, Luther posited that a sinner is saved by grace alone, through faith alone.[11] This insight or, perhaps, recovery of Pauline teaching led Luther to conclude that if works were not essential to justification but were, in fact, the fruit of justification, then everyone, no matter how poor in spirit or how "secular," could be justified. And so began Luther's dismantling of the medieval sacred/secular dichotomy.[12] It was inevitable that in doing this Luther would come to question the nature of the late medieval priesthood as he had inherited it.

9. Muthiah, *Priesthood of All Believers*, 8–9.

10. This is not to say that there was no discussion of the concept during the early church or medieval eras, as we will see. In fact, there is a rich tradition of commentary and theologizing about the universal priesthood in these time periods. See, e.g., Dabin, *Le sacerdoce royal des fidèles*, 69–328 and 507–96; and Yarnell, *Royal Priesthood*, 17–83.

11. It is beyond the scope of this work to investigate the legitimacy of Luther's critique of the late medieval Latin church. What is clear is that he came to believe that the Latin church, with its pope in Rome, taught salvation by works and *not* by faith. For example, he wrote in 1520, "Many people pray, fast, and create pious endowments, do this and that, and lead respectable lives in the opinion of others; but if you ask them whether or not they are certain that God is pleased with what they do, they do not know or at least have their doubts. Moreover, they cite learned scholars who do nothing but teach good works and claim it is necessary to have such certainty. See here! All those good works are performed apart from faith; they amount to nothing and are completely dead." Luther, *Treatise on Good Works*, 19; German text in *WA* 6:196–276.

12. On this dichotomy, see Besserman, *Sacred and Secular*, 1–17.

There were a range of views in the decades leading up to the Reformation about what it meant to be a priest.[13] For some a priest was a mere confector of the Eucharist—that is, the one who said the right words and made the right actions over the bread and the wine so as to transubstantiate it into the body and blood of Jesus Christ. The priest's holiness was inconsequential to the action performed, and he was standing at the altar *in persona Christi* in ways that no layperson could ever hope to do. Yet as early as the thirteenth century there was the more pastoral image of the priest as the *medicus animarum*, a doctor of souls: "The priest will be discerning and prudent, so that like a skilled doctor he may pour wine and oil over the wounds of the injured one."[14] By Luther's time there were a variety of views about priests, but (risking over-generalization) common to most of those views was an understanding that a priest was a mediator, sacramentally and spiritually. He stood between those who were not ordained priests to offer the sacrifice of the Mass, and he stood between these same people and God by his right to "bind and loose" their sins in the sacrament of confession and to interpret the Word of God.[15] The priest was the sacred one and laypeople were the secular ones in this sacred/secular distinction. Luther's theology sought to reform that understanding.

Luther was not striving to get rid of duly ordained priests (i.e., a liturgical, cultic priesthood) and replace them with a priesthood of all believers, but he was attempting to protect the once-and-for-all self-sacrificed Jesus Christ from being resacrificed again and again on the altars of Western Europe.[16] As Norman Nagel sees it, "To suggest something other or more is to rob Christ of his having done it all."[17] Thus, beginning with his *Babylonian Captivity of the Church* (published in 1520), Luther began to offer a theology of universal priesthood. He writes, "For thus it is written in 1 Peter 2[:9]: 'You are a chosen race, a royal priesthood, and a priestly royalty.' Therefore we are all priests, as many of us are Christians."[18] Moreover, "Let everyone, therefore, who knows himself to be a Christian, be assured of this, that we are all equally priests, that is to say, we have the same power in respect to the Word and sacraments. However, no one may make use of this power except by the consent of the community or by the call of a superior."[19] Though Luther is committed to

13. See Swanson, "Apostolic Successors."
14. *Concilii quarti Lateranensis Constitutiones* 21, in Tanner, *Decrees*, 1:245.
15. See Council of Trent, Session 23, 15 July 1563, "Canons on the Sacrament of Order," chap. 1.
16. Council of Trent, Session 22, 17 September 1562, "Canons on the Most Holy Sacrifice of the Mass," are illustrative of this emphasis in sixteenth-century Roman Catholic theology.
17. Nagel, "Luther," 281.
18. Luther, *Babylonian Captivity of the Church* (LW 36:112–13). Latin text in WA 6:497–573.
19. Luther, *Babylonian Captivity of the Church* (LW 36:116).

the priesthood of all believers, he does not think that means that any or all Christians should preach or administer the sacraments. That is still reserved for those who are called by the Christian community and its leadership and subsequently ordained to such ministry. For Luther there is only "one single priest" in the New Testament: though there "is a spiritual priesthood, held in common by all Christians, through which we are all priests with Christ," there is only one high priest and one mediator, Jesus Christ.[20] Thus, because of Jesus Christ's priesthood there is no need for another nonspiritual priesthood, though all Christians are priests spiritually.

Luther's most well-developed theology of universal priesthood may be in a treatise cumbersomely titled *Answer to the Hyperchristian, Hyperspiritual, and Hyperlearned Book by Goat Emser in Leipzig—Including Some Thoughts Regarding His Companion, the Fool Murner*, published in 1521.[21] Jerome Emser (d. 1527) had served in various roles throughout his career: secretary to a Roman cardinal; secretary and chaplain to the duke of Saxony; university lecturer in Erfurt (where he had Luther as a student) and Leipzig; and editor of humanistic texts (such as Pico della Mirandola). On July 25, 1518, Luther preached in Dresden and attended a dinner at Emser's home wherein Luther made certain statements at the dinner that were later used against him. The following year Emser wrote an open letter to John Zack (administrator of the archbishopric of Prague) in defense of Luther, assuring Zack that Luther would not seek the support of the "heretical" Hussites in his fight with Johann Eck (d. 1543). However,

> when Luther read Emser's open letter to the Bohemian Catholics, he became convinced that it was a clever device to continue the intrigue Emser had launched at the Dresden banquet. On that occasion Emser had lulled Luther into making statements conservative Roman theologians could later use against him to substantiate their suspicion of heresy. Now Emser used his eyewitness account of the Leipzig Debate [held in June and July 1519] to create the impression that Luther had never agreed with the heretic [Jan] Huss, even though he had made some statements in Leipzig to that effect. Accordingly, to Luther Emser's falsification of the record of his debate with Eck [at Leipzig] was but another trap for him. If he accepted Emser's "defense," he would appear to have silently

20. Luther, *Misuse of the Mass* (*LW* 36:138). This text was written in 1521. German text in WA 8:482–563.

21. In German: *Auff das ubirchristlich, ubirgeystlich und ubirkunstlich buch Bocks Emszers zu Leypczick Antwortt D. M. L. Darynn auch Murnarrs seynsz geselln gedacht wirt.* English translation in *LW* 39:143–224; German text in WA 7:621–88. Luther referred to Emser as the "goat" because Emser's coat of arms included a shield and helmet adorned with a goat. This shield was on the title page of Emser's published writings.

recanted his statements on Huss; if he rejected Emser's interpretation, Emser would be justified in accusing Luther of heresy, since the Leipzig statements could then no longer be regarded as the emotional outbursts of a debater in trouble.[22]

Thus, Luther decided to publish a response to Emser titled *An Addition to Goat Emser* in late September 1519. This was met with a response by Eck titled *An Answer for Jerome Emser against Luther's Mad Hunt* (published in October 1519) and Emser's own *Assertion of the Goat against Luther's Hunt* (1519).[23] The next year, in December, Emser published his *Against the Un-Christian Book of the Augustinian Martin Luther, Addressed to the German Nobility*.[24] This was a response to Luther's *To the Christian Nobility of the German Nation* (published August 18, 1520). This elicited a quick response from Luther (*To the Goat in Leipzig*),[25] followed by Emser's *To the Bull in Wittenberg*,[26] which Luther countered with *Concerning the Answer of the Goat in Leipzig* (January/February 1521).[27] Emser felt the need, yet again, to respond, so he published a brief satirical piece titled *Reply to the Answer of the Raging Bull in Wittenburg*.[28] Moreover, the "fool" Thomas Murner (d. 1537) wrote three treatises against Luther in November and December 1520.[29] Instead of responding to him directly, Luther simply included him in his extensive response to Emser.

Despite its polemical genesis and highly charged, combative tone, Luther's *Answer to the Hyperchristian, Hyperspiritual, and Hyperlearned Book by Goat Emser in Leipzig* spends a great deal of space addressing the priesthood of all believers. Emser, himself an ordained priest, had defended the ordained priesthood by saying that there were two priesthoods: one spiritual and one churchly/ecclesiastical.[30] Using 2 Corinthians 3:6 to establish that biblical verses can be interpreted according to the letter and according to the Spirit, Emser applies this distinction to 1 Peter 2:9, writing, "He who interprets the words of St. Peter to mean that all Christians should be priests to the extent that

22. Eric W. Gritsch and Ruth C. Gritsch, introduction to Luther, *To the Goat in Leipzig* (*LW* 39:108).

23. Emser's extant treatises are printed in Enders, *Luther und Emser*.

24. Enders, *Luther und Emser*, 1:1–145.

25. Luther, *To the Goat in Leipzig* (*LW* 39:111–15). German text in *WA* 7:262–65.

26. Enders, *Luther und Emser*, 2:3–8.

27. Luther, *Concerning the Answer of the Goat in Leipzig* (*LW* 39:121–35). German text in *WA* 7:271–83.

28. Enders, *Luther und Emser*, 2:27–44.

29. Luther called him the "fool" because of his last name, Murner. *Murnarr* is German for fool.

30. To label Emser's position, Luther coined a new word, *Kirchisch* (churchly). Emser himself had used *ecclesiasticum*. See Enders, *Luther und Emser*, 1:21–33.

they are consecrated by bishops strikes with the sheath, takes the letter, and follows a deadly reasoning. For St. Peter speaks of the inward spiritual priesthood which all Christians possess, and not of the consecrated priesthood."[31] Thus, Emser agrees with Luther that Peter is talking about a spiritual (i.e., universal) priesthood but postulates that this does not mean that there is not also an ordained (or ecclesiastical) priesthood. Luther says that "this is sheer error and blindness" because this "invented priesthood" is not biblical, for "the New Testament . . . writes of no more than one spiritual priesthood."[32] In other words, the New Testament only ever refers to a spiritual priesthood because it does not teach that there is a churchly/ecclesiastical priesthood.

Next Luther turns to etymology to further prove his point. First, we are all equal priests, and what Emser calls "churchly priesthood" in the Christian Scriptures is called "ministry," "servitude," "dispensation," "episcopate," and "presbytery," but it is never called "priesthood" (*sacerdocium*) or "spiritual" (*spiritualis*). In fact, "the little word 'priest' [*priester*] stems from the Greek language in which *presbyteros* means *senior* in Latin and 'the elder' [*eldest*] in German. . . . Thus priest indicates age, not status; nor does it make one a cleric or a spiritual man."[33] Furthermore, says Luther, the word *bishop* "too stems from the Greek language. For he whom they call *episcopus* is called *speculator* in Latin and 'a guardian or watchman on the tower' [*warttman odder wechter auff der Wart*] in German. This is exactly what one calls someone who lives in a tower to watch and to look out over the town so that fire or foe do not harm it. Therefore, every minister or spiritual regent should be a bishop, that is, an overseer or watchman."[34] For Luther the word *priest* and *bishop* were only ever used to mean "elder" and "overseer"; therefore, they are not statuses in the New Testament. It is wrong, then, to call someone a priest if one means "churchly" priest in an Emserian sense, for the New Testament only uses "priest" to refer to all Christians, albeit some of those priests will be elders who give oversight to the younger priests.

Continuing his argument, Luther next turns to Emser's habit of using later Christian history to prove the existence and rightness of earlier practices, thus, thinks Luther, begging the question. In a surprising moment of antihistoricism and biblicism, Luther, perhaps going too far polemically, says that "when you

---

31. Luther, *Answer to the Hyperchristian, Hyperspiritual, and Hyperlearned Book by Goat Emser in Leipzig* (LW 39:152).
32. Luther, *Answer to the Hyperchristian, Hyperspiritual, and Hyperlearned Book by Goat Emser in Leipzig* (LW 39:153).
33. Luther, *Answer to the Hyperchristian, Hyperspiritual, and Hyperlearned Book by Goat Emser in Leipzig* (LW 39:154).
34. Luther, *Answer to the Hyperchristian, Hyperspiritual, and Hyperlearned Book by Goat Emser in Leipzig* (LW 39:154).

drag in by the hair some passages of the [early church] fathers to apply to your dreams, it does not move me at all."[35] For Luther this is a fight about the proper understanding of Holy Scripture, not a discussion about early Christian practices or beliefs.[36] Emser's mistake, says Luther, is a logical, philosophical one: "You should not prove the antecedent (*prius*) through the consequent (*posterius*) and beg the question (*principium petere*)."[37] Luther concedes that there is a historical churchly priesthood that has its own practices and works against "other common Christians," but, he asks, should that usage be enough to create "two kinds of priesthood in Christendom?" No, because "no usage can change or reinterpret anything in Scripture or in articles of faith." Usages apply to those things that are changeable—that is, offices and services within the church: "Consecration does not make a cleric, but it does make servants out of clerics: tonsure, chasuble, mass, and sermon are not the signs of a priest but rather of a servant and official of the common priesthood." Episcopal consecration does not create a new priesthood, but those consecrated become "stewards, servants, and administrators of the other priests."[38] In summary, Luther writes, "I really think it has been proven clearly enough that we are all priests. And these priests are not a different kind of priest; they are servants and officials . . . of the common priesthood. So there are not two kinds of priesthood in Christendom, as you have dreamed."[39]

As soon as Luther's text rolled off the printing press, Emser authored a reply called *Quadruplica to Luther's Recent Answer, Concerning His Reformation.*[40]

---

35. Luther, *Answer to the Hyperchristian, Hyperspiritual, and Hyperlearned Book by Goat Emser in Leipzig* (LW 39:156). Luther subsequently acknowledges that the churchly priestly estate was called "priesthood" by early Christian authors, including biblical authors (e.g., Heb. 5:1) but says that they had little option since it was already common to make a distinction between laymen and those chosen to rule or oversee others. He thinks that if the authors were to do it all over again, they would not have referred to it as priesthood.

36. Luther spends the bulk of the last two-thirds of the work talking about the superiority of the Scriptures over the early church fathers, going so far as to say that if Emser really wants to argue with him, he "should first prove that usage—even if it is good usage—and human teaching are valid." *Concerning the Answer of the Goat in Leipzig* (LW 39:162).

37. Luther, *Answer to the Hyperchristian, Hyperspiritual, and Hyperlearned Book by Goat Emser in Leipzig* (LW 39:157; parenthetical inclusions are original to the text).

38. Luther, *Answer to the Hyperchristian, Hyperspiritual, and Hyperlearned Book by Goat Emser in Leipzig* (LW 39:157).

39. Luther, *Answer to the Hyperchristian, Hyperspiritual, and Hyperlearned Book by Goat Emser in Leipzig* (LW 39:159). Also: "Thus you yourself must confess with me that this priesthood did not come out of Scripture. For whatever exists on the basis of usage is already known without Scripture and is without God's order. Likewise, if it is confirmed by the teachings of the fathers and men, it is known to be not from Scripture because usage and human teaching are something different from Scripture." Luther, *Answer to the Hyperchristian, Hyperspiritual, and Hyperlearned Book by Goat Emser in Leipzig* (LW 39:161).

40. See Enders, *Luther und Emser*, 2:130–83.

In this text Emser rearticulates his conviction that because the Christian tradition teaches a priestly estate, 1 Peter 2:9 must be interpreted as teaching a twofold priesthood: a spiritual priesthood (that includes all believers) and a physical one (that consists of the priestly estate).[41] In October 1521 Luther responded with his *Dr. Luther's Retraction of the Error Forced upon Him by the Most Highly Learned Priest of God, Sir Jerome Emser, Vicar in Meissen*.[42] Luther limited his ironic response to Emser's interpretation of 1 Peter 2:9. Not realizing Luther's irony, Emser responded again with a pamphlet titled *Reservation to Luther's Retraction*.[43] Luther chose not to respond, ending a two-year dispute. Despite Luther's polemics and, at times, biting sarcasm, his main argument is that all Christian believers are priests because this is what the Bible says in 1 Peter 2:9, a sentiment that is echoed elsewhere in Luther's corpus.

For example, already in 1520, a year before he wrote his *Answer* to Emser, Luther had made the priesthood of all believers an important part of his argument in *To the Christian Nobility of the German Nation Concerning the Reform of the Christian Estate*. This work, written to provide a theological rationale for calling on the nobility to help advance the Reformation, argues that the "Romanists" (*Romanisten*) have built three walls that need to be destroyed: (1) the view that the temporal power has no power over the church because the spiritual power is above the temporal power;[44] (2) the claim that only the pope can interpret the Scriptures correctly; and (3) the claim that only the pope can summon a council ("if threatened with a council, their story is that no one may summon a council but a pope").[45] Luther's main theological belief that undermines all three of these walls is the universal priesthood. Regarding the first wall, Luther contends that the distinction between the spiritual estate (e.g., the pope, bishops, priests, and monks) and the temporal estate (e.g., princes, lords, artisans, and farmers) is a "pure invention." The truth instead is that "all Christians are truly of the spiritual estate, and there is no difference among them except that of office . . . because we all have one baptism, one gospel, one faith, and are all Christians alike; for

41. Eric W. Gritsch and Ruth C. Gritsch, introduction to Luther, *Dr. Luther's Retraction of the Error Forced upon Him by the Most Highly Learned Priest of God, Sir Jerome Emser, Vicar of Meissen* (LW 39:227).

42. See Luther, *Concerning the Answer of the Goat in Leipzig* (LW 39:229–38). German text in WA 8:247–54.

43. See Enders, *Luther und Emser*, 2:199–221.

44. On the medieval development of this political theory, see Robinson, "Church and Papacy."

45. Martin Luther, *To the Christian Nobility of the German Nation Concerning the Reform of the Christian Estate* (LW 44:126). German text in WA 6:404–69. On conciliarism in general see Oakley, *Conciliarist Tradition*.

baptism, gospel, and faith alone make us spiritual and a Christian people."[46]
Further, though popes and bishops anoint, tonsure, ordain, and consecrate
individuals for particular offices, those actions do not make the recipient into
a Christian or into a spiritual person. Why? Because all Christian believers
are "consecrated priests through baptism, as St. Peter says in 1 Peter 2[:9]."[47]
For Luther, some Christians have a special calling or work (*Amt oder Werk*)
but *not* a special status (*Stand*).[48] In essence, all believers are equal in their
standing before God (they are all spiritual persons), though some have been
called to a particular work within the church, while others perform particular
works outside the church but they do so as spiritual persons. Hence, "those
who exercise secular authority have been baptized with the same baptism,
and have the same faith and the same gospel as the rest of us, we must admit
that they are priests and bishops and we must regard their office as one which
has a proper and useful place in the Christian community. For whoever comes
out of the water of baptism can boast that he is already a consecrated priest,
bishop, and pope."[49] This does not mean that everyone should exercise such
offices, Luther argues, but only those with the consent and the election to do
so. In like manner Luther goes on to dismantle the other two walls using the
same logic: if we are all priests, then we can all interpret Scripture, and any
priest (i.e., any Christian believer) can reprove and constrain the pope when
he violates the Scriptures.

What is of particular importance here is that Luther situates the priesthood
of all believers in the context of baptism. Christian believers come out of the
waters of baptism and are, then, all priests. For Luther, membership in the
universal priesthood of all believers is a consequence of baptism. He repeats
this in *Concerning the Ministry*, written in 1523 to Bohemian Christians:
"For a priest . . . was not made but was born. He was created, not ordained.
He was born not indeed of the flesh, but through a birth of the Spirit, by
water and Spirit in the washing of regeneration. . . . Indeed, all Christians
are priests, and all priests are Christians."[50] Thus, there is an essential link
between baptism and the priesthood of all believers. Again, Luther is not
the first Christian theologian to formulate a well-developed theology of the
universal priesthood,[51] but his is an important milestone in the history of

---

46. Luther, *To the Christian Nobility* (LW 44:127).
47. Luther, *To the Christian Nobility* (LW 44:127).
48. On Luther's concept of *Stand*, see chap. 7 below.
49. Luther, *To the Christian Nobility* (LW 44:129).
50. Luther, *Concerning the Ministry* (LW 40:19). Latin text in WA 12:169–95.
51. See Dabin, *Le sacerdoce royal des fidèles*; Eastwood, *Royal Priesthood of the Faithful*;
and Eastwood, *Priesthood of All Believers*.

Western theology, one that came to full fruition, in many ways, in the twentieth century, largely as a result of the Second Vatican Council.

The Priesthood of All Believers in Roman Catholic Theology

Having evaluated the documents of the Council of Trent concerning the priesthood of all believers, Nelson Minnich concludes that "Trent did not deny the existence of a universal priesthood of all believers. . . . The theologians and bishops of Trent held that the faithful are in a certain sense truly priests."[52] While Minnich acknowledges that Vatican II added important Eucharistic and missiological dimensions to Trent's understanding, he demonstrates clearly that Trent was addressing this central Lutheran tenet at more than one of its sessions, even though the council's understanding came in the form of anathemas.[53] Minnich ultimately concludes that the Council of Trent teaches that "priests were both those who were consecrated to God and those who administered the sacraments and treated the sacred things. The first group were interior or spiritual priests, namely, all the faithful. The others were external, visible priests, chosen from among the faithful for the sacred ministry. While all the faithful became spiritual priests by baptism, it was only those who were in the state of grace who properly possessed this priesthood."[54]

This Tridentine understanding appears to derive from the teaching of Thomas Aquinas (d. 1274). Because Jesus offered *himself* on the cross, as opposed to an animal, he established a ritual (*ritum*), derived from his own priesthood: "the whole rite of the Christian religion is derived from Christ's priesthood."[55] That is, "the worship and sacrifice begun by Christ are 'organized.' Christ has not simply put an end to positive religions in favour of a purely personal, human, inwardness; he has ushered in a worship and a sacrifice as a *positive, social, institutional religion*."[56] In short, by offering himself as a sacrifice, Jesus created the need for an external, ritualistic Christian liturgy that requires ministers (i.e., an order of priests): this "new worship . . . is not something purely personal, private and altogether inward: it is truly a religion, a worshipping and sacrificial order, with its high priest or head, Christ, the sole *verus sacerdos* [true priest]; it also has its ministers, its *sacramenta*, and its

52. Minnich, "Priesthood of All Believers," 341–42.
53. See, e.g., Council of Trent, Session 23, 15 July 1563, "Canons on the Sacrament of Order," chap. 1, in Tanner, *Decrees*, 2:743.
54. Minnich, "Priesthood of All Believers," 361–62.
55. Thomas Aquinas, *Summa Theologiae* III, Q. 63, Art. 3: *Totus autem ritus Christianae religionis derivatur a sacerdotio Christi*, in *Summa Theologica*, 4:2357.
56. Congar, *Lay People*, 143 (italics original).

faithful people are by implication ordered, consecrated, appointed and united to it."[57] All believers participate in Christ's priesthood in that they worship Christ as priest (i.e., Trent's notion of interior or spiritual priests), but institutional, sacramental worship of Christ requires ministers *in persona Christi*: "In the measure that Christ communicates to men the power to celebrate his priestly worship with him . . . he dedicates and deputes them by making them share in his priesthood [i.e., Trent's external, visible priests]. . . . Therefore, while all members are active in the sacramental worship it celebrates as the body of the high priest Christ, there are some who are specially described as ministers and . . . functionaries or 'liturgists.'"[58] Simply put, these "liturgists" offer prayers to God on behalf of the whole church.[59]

Importantly, both kinds of priesthood, for Aquinas, are rooted first and foremost in baptism. Aquinas believes that the principal effect of the sacraments is grace, but another effect of the sacraments is that they impart a "certain spiritual character."[60] This "character is properly a kind of seal, whereby something is marked, as being ordained to some particular end. . . . Now the faithful are deputed to a twofold end. First and principally to the enjoyment of glory. . . . Secondly, each of the faithful is deputed to receive, or to bestow on others, things pertaining to the worship of God."[61] Moreover, this character is indelible, as is Christ's priesthood (cf. Ps. 110:4); therefore, each believer has "a share in [Christ's] priesthood" by way of this sacramental character.[62] But it is only certain sacraments that imprint this character, "namely, Baptism, Confirmation, and [ordination to a Holy] Order."[63] Thus, both kinds of priesthood are rooted in the indelible character conferred on a person in baptism, which comes before confirmation and ordination. In this way Thomas is in complete agreement with early Christian theologians such as Augustine of Hippo (d. 430), who wrote that "just as we call all Christians 'Christs' in virtue of their mystical anointing (*chrisma*), so do we call them all 'priests' because they are all members of one Priest."[64] Yves Congar (d. 1995) concludes that, like Thomas, "Augustine expressly associates the priestly quality of the faithful with the sacrament of baptism."[65]

57. Congar, *Lay People*, 143 (italics original).
58. Congar, *Lay People*, 144.
59. See Thomas Aquinas, *Summa Theologiae* III, Q. 64, Art. 1, ad. 2; and III, Q. 64, Art. 8, ad. 2.
60. Thomas Aquinas, *Summa Theologiae*, III, Q. 63, Art. 1: *aliquot spirituali character*.
61. Thomas Aquinas, *Summa Theologiae*, III, Q. 63, Art. 3, in *Summa Theologica*, 4:2357.
62. Thomas Aquinas, *Summa Theologiae*, III, Q. 63, Art. 5, in *Summa Theologica*, 4:2359.
63. Thomas Aquinas, *Summa Theologiae*, III, Q. 63, Art. 6, in *Summa Theologica*, 4:2360.
64. Augustine, *City of God* 20.10 (Dyson, 992–93).
65. Congar, *Lay People*, 140.

In fact, Congar, one of the leading Roman Catholic theologians before and after Vatican II, also agrees with Thomas and, perhaps surprisingly, with Luther too. Like Luther, who was also a student of Thomas, Congar believes that "priest" and "high priest" are primarily used of Jesus Christ in the New Testament; therefore, Luther and other Reformers were not wrong to interpret πρεσβύτερος as "elder" and ἱερεύς as "sacrificer" and to back away from the late medieval notion that "priesthood" was always exercised in the context of the Eucharist. Nonetheless, because believers belong to Christ, they have a "spiritual and real . . . sacerdotal quality which, belonging properly to Christ, is communicated to all members of his body . . . by baptism."[66] This "sacerdotal quality," however, is not merely Eucharistic; that is, it is "not to be *defined* by a relationship with the eucharist."[67] Rather, the priesthood of all believers consists in being well ordered in relationship to God, living a holy life and an apostolic life of religion, prayer, dedication, charity, and compassion. Congar concludes that the

> fact of the matter is that the priesthood of the faithful is a reality so rich in context that no single aspect or statement exhausts it. . . . There is a moral priesthood, which consists in living and doing with a priestly soul, in a spirit of religion; there is a real but wholly inward and spiritual priesthood, that of prayer and ascetical life; there is a priesthood with a sacramental reference and import, associated not only with righteous life but with baptismal consecration, whose supreme activity is participation in the eucharistic offering. All these are authentic aspects of the tradition's deposit.[68]

Like Augustine, Thomas, and Luther, Congar roots this universal priesthood in baptism.[69] In the end Congar concludes with Thomas that there "are then two degrees [of priesthood], one linked with consecration by baptism (and confirmation), the other with consecration of holy orders, in the priestly quality through which the fellowship-body . . . of Christ celebrates on earth . . . the worship of the New Covenant."[70] In this way Congar is thinking not only with Thomas Aquinas but also with the council fathers of Vatican II.

On January 25, 1959, Pope John XXIII, only three months into his papacy, announced his intention to convene a new ecumenical council. Several months later a pontifical commission was set up to begin consultations with the

66. Congar, *Lay People*, 133.
67. Congar, *Lay People*, 137n2 (italics original).
68. Congar, *Lay People*, 138.
69. Congar, *Lay People*, 138, 140.
70. Congar, *Lay People*, 144–45.

church's leadership about issues that would be addressed at the forthcoming council. In June 1960 formal commissions were set up to begin preliminary work for the council, and on December 25, 1961, the pope officially summoned the council to begin meeting in 1962. The decree *Consilium*, published on February 2, 1962, set the start date of the council for October 11, 1962. Approximately 2,300 church fathers attended the council, which was divided into four periods, each lasting about ten weeks, ending in December 1965.[71]

Lumen gentium, the Dogmatic Constitution on the Church, was promulgated by Pope Paul VI on November 21, 1964.[72] In its introductory paragraph the document states that it "intends to declare with greater clarity to the faithful and the entire human race the nature of the church and its universal mission."[73] In the second chapter, "The People of God," the council fathers state that Christ the Lord, as the high priest chosen from among human beings, "has made the new people 'a kingdom, priests to his God and Father.'"[74] These "new people" are made priests "by regeneration and anointing of the holy Spirit" at baptism, becoming a holy priesthood.[75] Their main activity as priests is to offer spiritual sacrifices "and declare the powers of him who called them out of darkness into his marvelous light."[76] This priesthood of all baptized believers, however, does not displace an ordained priesthood. In agreement with Thomas Aquinas and Congar, the council fathers concluded that there is a "common priesthood of the faithful and the ministerial or hierarchical priesthood."[77] The two priesthoods are interrelated, stated the council fathers, "though they differ in essence and not simply in degree." They are interrelated because "each in its own particular way shares in the one priesthood of Christ."[78] *Lumen gentium* describes it this way: "The ministerial priest, through the sacred power that he enjoys, forms and governs the priestly people; in the person of Christ he brings about the eucharistic sacrifice and offers this to God in the name of the whole people. The faithful, on the other hand, by virtue of their royal priesthood, join in the offering of the eucharist, and they exercise their priesthood in receiving the sacraments, in prayer and thanksgiving, through the witness of a holy life, by self-denial and by active

---

71. Tanner, *Decrees*, 2:817–18.

72. Pope John XXIII, who convened the council, died on June 6, 1963. Paul VI was elected just two weeks later, on June 21.

73. *Lumen gentium* 1.1, in Tanner, *Decrees*, 2:849.

74. *Lumen gentium* 2.10, in Tanner, *Decrees*, 2:856. The quotation is from Rev. 1:6, one of the proof texts for the priesthood of all believers.

75. *Lumen gentium* 2.10, in Tanner, *Decrees*, 2:856.

76. *Lumen gentium* 2.10, in Tanner, *Decrees*, 2:856, citing 1 Pet. 2:4–10.

77. *Lumen gentium* 2.10, in Tanner, *Decrees*, 2:857.

78. *Lumen gentium* 2.10, in Tanner, *Decrees*, 2:857.

charity."[79] It is important to note that according to the council, like Augustine, Thomas, and Congar, the priesthood of all believers is conveyed through the sacrament of baptism and strengthened by confirmation and the Eucharist.[80]

In the end, this brief survey of significant theologians and a church council reveals that though Martin Luther may have moved the concept of the universal priesthood of all believers front and center, it was not wholly absent from medieval and later Roman Catholic teaching. What is important to note in each of these authors is that (1) the priesthood of all believers does not negate the fact that some believers will subsequently be called out of the community to exercise a ministry or be members of the hierarchical priesthood, and (2) that the priesthood of all believers is rooted in baptism. For Luther some believers will become ministers within the church in a unique way because of the consent of the faithful and their election by the church's membership. In Roman Catholic theology these individuals are made ministerial priests through the laying on of hands by a bishop in ordination. Though Luther rejects the distinction between the two kinds of priesthood, he still acknowledges that all believers are priests by virtue of their baptism, as do Roman Catholic councils. It appears then that the main disagreement between Luther and Trent (and perhaps Vatican II also) is not about the priesthood of all believers but about the hierarchical nature of the church.[81] In this way Luther and Roman Catholic conciliar teaching are not as dissimilar as might be expected.

Orthodox Theology and the Priesthood of All Believers

Orthodox theologian Andrew Louth, in his recently published *Introducing Eastern Orthodox Theology*,[82] never mentions the universal priesthood. In the bestselling *The Orthodox Church* by Bishop Kallistos (Timothy) Ware, it receives only one short statement: "Through Chrismation every member of the Church becomes a prophet, and receives a share in the royal priesthood

79. *Lumen gentium* 2.10, in Tanner, *Decrees*, 2:857. The council's decree on the ministry and life of priests, *Presbyterorum ordinis*, states something similar: in the mystical body of the church "all the faithful together become a holy and royal priesthood, offer spiritual sacrifices to God through Jesus Christ, and declare the wonderful deed of him who called them out of darkness into his marvelous light. . . . However, that the body might fit together into a unity . . . the same Lord appointed some as ministers who would have the sacred power of Order within the company of the faithful, to offer sacrifice and to forgive sins." *Presbyterorum ordinis* 1.2, in Tanner, *Decrees*, 2:1043.
80. *Lumen gentium* 2.11.
81. See Minnich, "Priesthood of All Believers," 357–59.
82. Louth, *Introducing Eastern Orthodox Theology*.

of Christ."[83] Paul Evdokimov, however, dedicates an entire chapter of *Ages of the Spiritual Life* to the topic. After establishing that the Bible makes no distinction between the laity and clergy, Evdokimov says that because of Jesus Christ's ministry the people of God, now united in Christ, share his priesthood; that is, "Christ has made all Christians 'a kingdom of priests.'"[84] This universal priesthood does not mean that there is not also, à la Roman Catholic theology, a "functional priesthood of the clergy."[85] In fact, "we can clearly see here the essence of the Eastern Church tradition. There is neither an anti-clerical egalitarianism nor a division of the clergy of the one Body into two parts, but the sacerdotal participation of all in the one divine Priest, Christ, by means of two priesthoods."[86] This will remain the case until the parousia, when there will be no further need of priestly mediation.

As it is in Luther, Thomas Aquinas, and Roman Catholic theology, this universal priesthood is rooted in and bestowed in the sacrament of baptism (and, for Eastern Orthodoxy, chrismation):

> By baptism . . . all are already priests, and it is in the heart of this priestly equality that the functional differentiation of charisma is produced. It is not a new "consecration" of a bishop or a priest, but an ordination for a new ministry of one who was already consecrated, already changed in his nature once for all, having already received his priestly character. The sacrament of the *anointing with chrism* (confirmation in the West) establishes all the baptized in the same hieratic, priestly order. From this equality, some are chosen, set apart and established by a divine act, as bishops and presbyters. A *functional difference* of ministries suppresses all ontological difference of nature and makes all separation between clerics and laymen impossible.[87]

All baptized Christians participate in the priesthood by offering up as a sacrifice their whole life and existence. Moreover, the "laity forms an ecclesial dimension that is, at one and the same time, of the world and of the Church." Though not all baptized Christians (i.e., the laity) have the power to administer the sacraments, they do bear "the power of the sacred in the world,

---

83. Ware, *Orthodox Church*, 279.
84. Evdokimov, *Ages of the Spiritual Life*, 228.
85. Evdokimov, *Ages of the Spiritual Life*, 229.
86. Evdokimov, *Ages of the Spiritual Life*, 230.
87. Evdokimov, *Ages of the Spiritual Life*, 231 (italics original). Similarly to Thomas Aquinas, Evdokimov notes that "initiation (the three great sacraments of the faithful [i.e., baptism, chrismation/confirmation, and Eucharist]) introduces every Christian into the order of sacred hierarchy of the People of God, differentiated solely by functional ministries." *Ages of the Spiritual Life*, 233.

celebrating the liturgy of the entire cosmos therein."[88] Thus, in Orthodox theology there is a similar understanding of the priesthood of all believers to what is seen in Luther, Thomas, and Roman Catholic theology: (1) there are two priesthoods—one proper to all believers and one by election/ordination; and (2) the priesthood of all believers is rooted in baptism.[89] In the end, there is a surprising consistency of thought regarding the universal priesthood across the three major expressions of the Christian faith.

Baptism, the Priesthood of All Believers, and Monasticism

The above survey demonstrates that not only is the priesthood of all believers present in the Christian tradition, but it is present in all three expressions of the Christian faith: Protestantism, Roman Catholicism, and Eastern Orthodoxy. In the words of John Elliott, "The association of this Petrine text [i.e., 1 Pet. 2:5, 9] with baptism, a general priesthood, the priesthood of Christ, and Christian holiness and service by no means originated with Luther but reflects a developing body of theological thought from the early Fathers onward."[90] For the present purposes this is significant given that monasticism, and the taking of monastic vows in particular, is rooted in baptism. Paul Evdokimov and David Fagerberg both draw out the implications of this doctrine.

Evdokimov adopts a historiography that says (wrongly) that monasticism replaced early Christian martyrdom.[91] Before the legalization of Christianity in the fourth century, the story goes, martyrdom was the clearest evidence of someone's full and total commitment to the Christian faith. They would die for it. After Christianity's legalization, however, the "Holy Spirit immediately 'invented' the 'equivalent of martyrdom.' In fact, the witness of the martyrs to 'the one thing needful' is passed on to monasticism."[92] Moreover, says Evdokimov, "monasticism's *metanoia*, or transformation, deepened Baptism's second birth which brought to life already the 'little resurrection.'"[93] In other words, it is presumed that a monk is a baptized Christian, for an "encounter

---

88. Evdokimov, *Ages of the Spiritual Life*, 238.

89. Though Luther rejects the notion of two priesthoods, he does so because he believes that the New Testament does not teach such a distinction. He does, however, acknowledge that Christian history, in fact, recognizes two priesthoods. Moreover, Luther's "minister" seems nearly identical to a Roman Catholic or Eastern Orthodox "priest" even if a Lutheran minister is simply one who is elected with the consent of the faithful versus being ordained by a bishop. The difference appears to be ecclesiological, not ontological.

90. Elliott, *1 Peter*, 450.

91. See also the introduction of this book.

92. Evdokimov, *Ages of the Spiritual Life*, 134.

93. Evdokimov, *Ages of the Spiritual Life*, 134 (italics original).

with God could not be made in the state of fallen nature. It presupposes a previous restoration of this nature in the sacrament of Baptism."[94] Likewise, Fagerberg, in asserting that monastics and nonmonastics (i.e., the monk and the laic in his terminology) are "coworkers in the vineyard," affirms that "their spiritual vocation comes from the same baptism."[95] He continues to say that the "same price will be exacted of both the monk and the laic: death. We must die to enter the Kingdom; that's why we're baptized."[96] Like Evdokimov, Fagerberg roots this theology in the transformation effected at baptism: "All vocations to holiness [i.e., the monk and the laic] begin in baptism."[97]

Both Evdokimov and Fagerberg continue this line of reasoning outward, until they arrive at the intersection of the priesthood of all believers, which is also rooted in baptism, and interiorized monasticism. Evdokimov believes that "monasticism evokes a certain receptivity in the universal priesthood of the laity. The testimony of the Christian faith in the framework of the modern world necessitates the universal vocation of *interiorized monasticism*."[98] Furthermore, there is a "perfect equality of nature in all the members of the church" that "corresponds to the fundamentally homogeneous character of Orthodox spirituality. . . . Prayer, fasting, the reading of the Scriptures and ascetic discipline are imposed on all for the same reason. That is precisely why the laity develops the state of *interiorized monasticism*."[99] Evdokimov also sees this theology evidenced in the Eastern Orthodox rite of tonsure that happens at baptism, which is "identical with that performed for one entering monastic life. . . . In undergoing the rite of tonsure, every lay person is a monk of *interiorized monasticism*, subject to all the requirements of the Gospel."[100] Fagerberg says the same thing when he quotes Evdokimov approvingly[101] and also when he quotes Pope John Paul II approvingly: "In the East, monasticism was not seen merely as a separate condition, proper to a precise category of Christians, but rather as a reference point for all the baptized, according to the gifts offered to each by the Lord; it was presented as a symbolic synthesis of Christianity."[102] Finally, Fagerberg sums up his thinking on the matter when he writes, "There are ascetics who make a vow, a profession—they are professionals. Professional ascetics live a visible life of renunciation in

94. Evdokimov, *Ages of the Spiritual Life*, 72.
95. Fagerberg, *On Liturgical Asceticism*, 158–59.
96. Fagerberg, *On Liturgical Asceticism*, 159.
97. Fagerberg, *On Liturgical Asceticism*, 221.
98. Evdokimov, *Ages of the Spiritual Life*, 135 (italics original).
99. Evdokimov, *Ages of the Spiritual Life*, 233 (italics original).
100. Evdokimov, *Ages of the Spiritual Life*, 234–35 (italics original).
101. Fagerberg, *On Liturgical Asceticism*, 38, 149.
102. Fagerberg, *On Liturgical Asceticism*, 220, quoting John Paul II's *Orientale lumen*, 9.

personification of the theological virtue of hope. The non-professionals, the layman and laywoman, exercise this virtue no less, only in different form."[103]

Yet oddly enough, though perhaps not unsurprisingly, it is Martin Luther who makes the most out of baptism and the priesthood of all believers vis-à-vis monasticism—in his criticism of monastic vows. As stated above, *The Judgment of Martin Luther on Monastic Vows* was written in 1521 but not published until February 1522. The preface to the work is a letter that Luther wrote to his father on November 21, 1521, in which Luther explains why he needed to enter into the monastic life and how now, in hindsight, he sees the folly of his decision. In 1505 Luther's father had wished to remove the young Martin from the monastery because he had been destined for a career in law; thus, Luther asks his father whether he seeks to remove him now from the monastery just as he had wished to do before. The younger Luther asks, "What difference does it make whether I retain or lay aside the cowl and tonsure? Do [they] make the monk?"[104] The younger Luther believes that the most important development in his thinking during his years as a monk was that he now realizes that the cowl and tonsure do not make the monk; rather, since God makes the monk, Luther's conscience is free: "I am still a monk and yet not a monk."[105] It appears that Luther, at this point, views himself as a monk not because he is under particular monastic vows but because he is choosing, in the freedom of Christ, to be a monk—it is an extension of his baptismal vows. Yet he also acknowledges that he is no longer a monk; God "has taken [him] out of the monastery" and placed him in his true service in the same way and to the same extent that all baptized Christian believers are in service to God.[106]

In *On Monastic Vows*, Luther makes the broad argument that since there are scriptural commandments that insist on vow keeping, the main issue at stake in the question of monastic vows is whether they are, in fact, vows at all. As noted in chapter 3, in describing the ways in which one can distinguish between true and false vows, Luther argues, among other things, that monastic vows are against God's Word.[107] In the first section Luther argues that monastic vows are against God's Word in three ways: (1) monastic vows are simply equivalent to baptismal vows; (2) scriptural commandments apply

103. Fagerberg, *On Liturgical Asceticism*, 220.
104. Martin Luther, *The Judgment of Martin Luther on Monastic Vows* (LW 44:334–35). Latin text in WA 8:573–669.
105. Luther, *On Monastic Vows* (LW 44:335).
106. Luther, *On Monastic Vows* (LW 44:335).
107. The work concludes with a discussion of the true nature of poverty, chastity, and obedience as well as an exposition of 1 Tim. 5.

to all Christians since God makes no distinction between "counsels" and "precepts," unlike the Roman Church; and (3) virginity and celibacy are commandments only for individual believers who are led to live virginal, celibate lives. It is his first contention that concerns us the most: monastic vows are simply equivalent to baptismal vows.

Luther is particularly concerned in *On Monastic Vows* not only that these vows are against the Scriptures but also that they are understood to be lifelong: "Neither the early church nor the New Testament knows anything at all of the taking of this kind of vow, much less do they approve of a lifelong vow of very rare and remarkable chastity."[108] Though Luther is aware that the Acts of the Apostles records that the apostle Paul and four other men took a vow (Acts 21:23–26), he insists that "it was a vow left over from the old law" and "it was only a temporal vow."[109] Moreover, Luther says that Anthony of Egypt (d. 356), "the very father of monks and the founder of the monastic life," also taught that nothing should be observed that is contrary to the Scriptures. Luther insists that Anthony "knew absolutely nothing about monastic vows and ceremonial of this kind, but willingly chose to live as a hermit, and of his own will chose to live unmarried, after the pattern of the gospel."[110] So neither the apostle Paul nor Anthony (i.e., two of the most important persons in biblical and early monastic history) advocated or practiced the taking of vows, much less lifelong vows. Returning to the apostle Paul, Luther writes that Paul never advocated that believers should follow him or his practices but rather that believers should follow him only because he is a follower of Jesus Christ. That is, by following Paul the faithful are following Christ. In the end Luther concludes, "These and similar pronouncements of Scripture are clearer than the light of day and utterly reliable. The Scriptures clearly compel us to condemn whatever is only a matter of rules, statutes, orders, schools of thought, and, in addition, whatever falls short of, is contrary to, or goes beyond Christ."[111] Thus, no one is at liberty to take monastic vows.

Luther's main point here is that all Christians are under obligation to follow Christ, and Christ alone. They are to live up to only those standards declared in the Scriptures and to go no further in their devotion. For how could one go further in devotion than following Jesus Christ, for any "other way is wrong, slippery, and dark."[112] Luther continues by commending Francis of Assisi (d. 1226), who "wisely said that his rule was the gospel of Jesus

108. Luther, *On Monastic Vows* (LW 44:252).
109. Luther, *On Monastic Vows* (LW 44:253).
110. Luther, *On Monastic Vows* (LW 44:253). See Athanasius, *Life of Antony*.
111. Luther, *On Monastic Vows* (LW 44:254).
112. Luther, *On Monastic Vows* (LW 44:254).

Christ."[113] Only later did his followers become "unbelievable hypocrites" and demand chastity of all who wanted to follow the way of Francis. Luther believes that Francis wanted to give his original followers the choice of living as either celibates or noncelibates because this would be consistent with the gospel. However, this was undone by Francis himself and certainly by later generations of friars. In Luther's estimation Francis "made the universal gospel intended for all the faithful into a special rule for the few. What Christ wanted to be universal and catholic, Francis made schismatic."[114] How so? Because he advocated the taking of particular vows that went beyond baptismal vows: "When a Franciscan takes his vow he vows nothing more than that which he already vowed at the start in his baptism, and that is the gospel."[115] In other words, the only proper rule of life, the only true monastic rule, is the gospel, and all believers vow to obey the gospel at their baptism.

Monastic vows, in Luther's estimation, are against the Christian faith. For Luther, following Romans 14:23, everything that is not of faith is sin. So if monastic vows are against faith, then they are sinful. Luther argues that they are not of faith because they are permanent vows, that is, lifelong and compulsory. Vows based on faith, on the other hand, allow someone "to keep them at one time or to renounce them at another."[116] Furthermore, returning to a theme he addresses elsewhere,[117] Luther says that good works are the fruit of faith; thus they "do not really pertain to the remission of sins and a serene conscience, but are the fruits of a forgiveness already granted and still present."[118] Works done before faith with the intention that they aid salvation are sins, whereas works done as a result of faith "are the fruits of a man who is already justified" and are motivated by faith and love.[119] As Luther sees it, a believer cannot expect works to assist in the remission of sins. Therefore, monastic vows taken with the assumption that they will aid justification are sins. Luther returns to the believer's baptismal vows, stating that they are the only true vows born of faith. Monastic vows, which undermine the baptismal vows of all Christians, were thought of erroneously, thinks Luther, by the late medieval church to be a kind of second grace over and above baptismal vows. Speaking to this, Luther concludes that "they think the grace of baptism has become worthless, and that now the shipwreck must be avoided by the 'second

---

113. Luther, *On Monastic Vows* (*LW* 44:255).
114. Luther, *On Monastic Vows* (*LW* 44:255).
115. Luther, *On Monastic Vows* (*LW* 44:255).
116. Luther, *On Monastic Vows* (*LW* 44:273).
117. E.g., in *The Freedom of a Christian*.
118. Luther, *On Monastic Vows* (*LW* 44:279).
119. Luther, *On Monastic Vows* (*LW* 44:279).

plank of penance' [i.e., the taking of monastic vows]."[120] In short, the only vows that matter to Luther are a believer's baptismal vows.

Conclusion

The history of Christian theology shows that the church's theologians have affirmed the place of the laity in the life of the church. Though there is debate about the nature and genesis of an ordained priesthood or duly elected ministers, there is agreement that all Christians are priests inasmuch as they participate in the priesthood of Christ by way of their baptism (and chrismation). Thus, baptism makes the priest. Yet it is also baptism that makes the monk, whether an interior one or an exterior, historic one. Though Roman Catholic and Eastern Orthodox theologians would disagree with Luther that monastic vows are unbiblical and thereby unnecessary, they would agree with him that the fundamental vows of all believers are those made at baptism. Thus, in the end, the primary vows of the monastic life are baptismal vows, and these are taken by all believers, making them priests in the church of God. By extension, would not these same vows make all believers monks in a similar manner? Evdokimov and Fagerberg think so, at least in a qualified sense. Luther would likely answer in the affirmative too, though he would prefer to say that all monks are believers rather than that all believers are monks. Nevertheless, there is an intimate connection between baptism, the priesthood of all believers, and monasticism, whether interiorized or historic. That connection, though, needs to be explored in greater detail.

---

120. Luther, *On Monastic Vows* (*LW* 44:280–81).

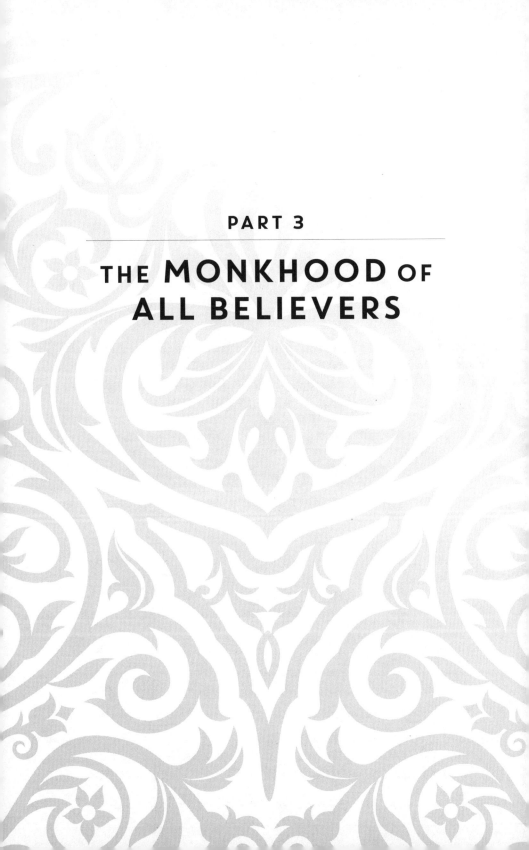

PART 3

THE **MONKHOOD** OF **ALL BELIEVERS**

Six

All Monks Are Christians and All Christians Are Monks

The Ladder of Divine Ascent by John Climacus (d. 649) is one of the most well known and popular spiritual texts in the Eastern Orthodox Christian tradition. In fact, "there is no work in Eastern Christendom that has been studied, copied and translated more often than *The Ladder of Divine Ascent*."[1] Orthodox monks read it or hear it read in the refectory every Lent, and it is popular among nonmonastic Orthodox Christians too. Not only is the text popular, but icons depicting the divine ladder are commonplace as well.[2] Perhaps the best known of the icons is that of the Saint Catherine's Monastery in Sinai from the late twelfth century. Against a brilliant gold, the ladder, ascending from the bottom left to the top right, dissects the icon into two regions, separating the heavenly realm from the worldly. The ladder has thirty rungs, one for each chapter of Climacus's *Ladder of Divine Ascent*, and is populated by monks making their way to heaven. At the top of the ladder is none other than John Climacus himself, being welcomed to heaven by Jesus. Surrounding the ladder, however, are a host of demons, some with bows and arrows and some with ropes, who are pulling climbers off the ladder into hell. In other words, not everyone successfully ascends the ladder and is saved. In the top left is a host of heavenly angels praying, we assume, for the successful ascent of the climbers. In the bottom right is a group of men, likely monks,

1. John Climacus, *Ladder of Ascent*, 1.
2. See Martin, *Illustration*.

who are both praying for those climbing the ladder and preparing for their own ascent. They look to those on the ladder for inspiration and guidance.

Some later versions of the icon, especially those of Russian provenance, depict a monastery in the lower right with John Climacus standing in the doorway, holding a copy of *The Ladder of Divine Ascent* on which is written, "Ascend, ascend, brothers." In the bottom left of the Russian version is an image of hell that contains not only monks but also kings and queens—that is, not only monastics but laypersons too. The message is clear: monastics and nonmonastics are all on the spiritual journey, and some will be saved, while others will fail and be damned. What is significant here is that the image of the ladder is an image of the spiritual life not just for monks but for *all* believers. Everyone is on an ascent to heaven (i.e., salvation), but only some monks and some nonmonastics will ultimately be saved. Though *The Ladder of Divine Ascent* was initially written for monks, its message is now one for all Christians. Climacus perhaps anticipated this when he wrote that "angels are a light for monks and the monastic life is a light for all men. Hence monks should spare no effort to become a shining example in all things."[3] As an example, monks demonstrate the way to union with God, a way that all Christians who seek to be saved must travel.

There is a similar message communicated by the thirteenth- to fifteenth-century frescoes in the Benedictine monastery at Subiaco in Italy. Around 500 CE Benedict of Nursia (d. 547) moved there to live alone in a cave, ostensibly escaping the worldliness of the city of Rome. According to his biographer/hagiographer Gregory the Great (d. 604), Benedict "was sent to Rome for a liberal education. But when he saw that some of his classmates were plunging into vice, he withdrew his foot that he had just placed on the threshold of the world. . . . So, abandoning his literary studies, and leaving his family home and inheritance, he sought to please God alone."[4] Accordingly, he settled into a cave, receiving his food from another local ascetic, who lowered it down to him in a basket tied to a rope. Though Benedict eventually left Subiaco for Monte Cassino, the current monastery traces its origins to the twelfth century. Because the monastery is built on the side of a cliff, its different elements are at various elevations. The larger, upper church is where most visitors enter today. Using a set of stairs, one can then descend into the smaller, lower church, which also grants one access to Benedict's original cave—the Sacro Speco. From there one can take the so-called Holy Stairs down to the lowest levels. The next lower level contains the Madonna Chapel, and just beyond

---

3. John Climacus, *Ladder of Divine Ascent* 26 (Luibheid and Russell, 234).
4. Gregory the Great, *Dialogues* 2.prologue, in Kardong, *Life of St. Benedict*, 1.

that, a few feet lower, there is a chapel that is used for the funerals of monks and the original crypt.

Climbing down the Holy Stairs is quite an experience, considering that on either side the walls are frescoed with vivid images.[5] On the right as you descend there is an image of Death on a horse, who is either riding over a group of individuals who have already died or killing them by riding over them. Your focus is drawn to Death's sword, which is striking down two noblemen mid-conversation. The message is clear: death will find you, perhaps even when you least expect it. The image on the left as you descend the steps is also a reminder that regardless of your station in life, you will die and, in time, decompose. Here a man (likely a monk) is speaking to three persons dressed as nobles. Two of the nobles are more interested in talking to one another, while only one is listening to the monk. Before the monk is an image of a deceased nobleman in three different stages of death: newly dead, early stages of decomposition, and, finally, skeletal. That two of the three noblemen are not listening to the monastic preacher indicates that they likely think that they are above death, or at least that death will not visit them soon. The message here is similar to the one across the stairs: everyone dies. No matter whether you are a monk or nobleman, death will find you, and it is important that you are spiritually ready when the time comes. In this sense, monastics and nonmonastics are the same—they are inhabiting the same world with the same temptations, and both need to make wise decisions so that in the end—and it will come!—they will be saved. Death is the great equalizer.[6]

What these images suggest is that there is a remarkable similarity between the monastic life and the nonmonastic Christian life. Both monastics and nonmonastics seek to ascend the proverbial divine ladder in order to be in union with God, because in the end everyone dies. The goal of the Christian life, however, is to die in communion with God, to be saved and not to be dragged through the gates of hell and damned forever. There is, of course, more to the Christian life, but these are its ultimate, eternal concerns. But is

5. For pictures of the monastery see "Italy, Subiaco," Flickr Hive Mind, https://hiveminer .com/Tags/italy,subiaco/Interesting (accessed August 30, 2017).

6. What the icons of the divine ladder and the frescoes of Subiaco teach is a common theme in Christian art. Another example would be the tympana of the great French Gothic cathedrals, such as Vézelay, Autun, and Notre-Dame de Paris. Each depicts scenes of the last judgment in which the fate of men and women from all stations of life (e.g., monks, nuns, kings, and queens) is being decided. As they are weighed in the balance, demons attempt to cheat the scales while angels fight back. In the end people from all stations of life are depicted as going either to heaven or to hell. Some monastics are going to heaven and others to hell, and the same is true for the nonmonastic individuals. Again, death and judgment shorten the (perceived) distance between monastic and nonmonastic life.

there really no distinction then between the kind of spiritual life that a monk should live and the kind that a mechanic should live? Is a nun actually like a nurse from the perspective of Christian spirituality and formation? Perhaps so.

Christian Spirituality Is Monastic Spirituality

As I wrote in chapter 1 of this book, John Cassian (d. mid-340s) described the origins of Christian monasticism in a way that is "historically worthless."[7] To review: In the preface to his *Institutes* Cassian says that monasteries were "founded by holy and spiritual fathers *at the time* when the apostles started preaching."[8] When this is compared to book 2 of the *Institutes*, it is clear that Cassian is connecting the Christian form of life described in Acts 4:32 ("Now the full number of those who believed were of one heart and soul, and no one said that any of the things that belonged to him was his own, but they had everything in common") with the origins of Christian monasticism. He makes this explicit in his *Conferences* when he writes, "The discipline of the cenobites took its rise at the time of the apostolic preaching."[9] Four hundred years later, by Cassian's time, however, this fervor of devout Christian living had cooled, so much so that "now it is difficult to find even a few like that in the cenobia."[10] Cassian's reason for this decline in devotion is illustrative:

> At the death of the apostles, the multitude of believers began to grow lukewarm, especially those who came over to the faith of Christ from different foreign nations. Out of regard for their rudimentary faith and their inveterate paganism, the apostles asked nothing more of them than that they abstain "from things sacrificed to idols, from fornication, from things strangled, and from blood." But this liberty, which was conceded to the pagans because of the weakness of their new faith, gradually began to spoil the perfection of the Church which was in Jerusalem, and, as the number of natives and of foreigners daily increased, the warmth of that new faith grew cold, and not only those who had come over to the faith of Christ but even those who were the leaders of the Church relaxed their strictness.[11]

Cassian goes on to say that it was the few who did continue to adhere to the ideals of Acts 4 who became the first monastics. And it is this monastic

---

7. Stewart, *Cassian the Monk*, 7.
8. Cassian, *Institutes*, preface 8 (ACW 58:14) (italics added).
9. Cassian, *Conferences* 18.5.1 (ACW 57:637).
10. Cassian, *Conferences* 18.5.2 (ACW 57:637).
11. Cassian, *Conferences* 18.5.2 (ACW 57:637–38). Cassian is quoting Acts 15:20.

historiography that is of little worth. Yet what is historically worthless can be theologically and spiritually valuable and illuminating.

What Cassian is saying is that the Christian life lived by the first generation of believers in Jerusalem is *the* perfect form of Christian living. It is Christian spirituality itself. If all followers of Christ had continued to live in this way, then there would have been no need for monasticism because all Christians would have been living the proper, ideal Christian life. But that form of Christian living had to become the *monastic* form of Christian living because of the lukewarm faith of early Christian believers and the church's leaders. In short, at the time of Acts 4, says Cassian, there was no distinction between *nonmonastic* spirituality and *monastic* spirituality because everyone was living a proper Christian life. Thus, Christian spirituality and what we might now call "monastic spirituality" were one and the same. There was one form of the spiritual life, and it was obligatory for all baptized followers of Jesus Christ. To say it differently: all Christians were monks and all monks were Christians. Though Cassian's depiction might not be an accurate historical representation of the origins of Christian monasticism, it is a Cassinese theology of Christian spirituality and one that echoes throughout the halls of Christian history.

Throughout the history of Christian spirituality there has often been a tension between the commands and demands of the gospel and the distractions and obligations of living in the *saeculum*. In fact, this friction is made explicit in the Scriptures themselves. Jesus prays to his Father, asking that though his followers will be *in* the world, they would not be *of* the world (cf. John 17:14–15). Jesus recognizes that there is a difficulty in being someone who is not of this world but obligated to live in it. The apostle Paul seems to be saying something similar when he admonishes the Christians in Rome to "not be conformed to this world [αἰῶνι]" (Rom. 12:2). These biblical texts are *not* suggesting that there is an incompatibility between that which is spiritual and that which is material (i.e., "this world"), for that is a not a Christian belief but a remnant of ancient Greek and Roman philosophy's influence on early Christian thought and practice. Because God the Father created everything material and saw that "it was good" (e.g., Gen. 1:10), then it *is* good. Material things are good in themselves and meant to be used (albeit in moderation) by all people, including Christian believers. In Christian theology the tension is not between materiality and spirituality but between being spiritual and being "of the flesh [σάρκινος]" (e.g., Rom. 7:14). Carnality is bad, but materiality is not. Nonetheless, there lingers in the Christian tradition a sentiment that says materiality is bad in that it forms the basis of those things that lead to temptation and sin. For example, Augustine of Hippo (d. 430) could only imagine sex, being the way to satiate one's lust, as a sin.

Midcareer, Augustine concluded that lust (Lat. *libido* or *concupiscentia*) is seated in both the body and the soul; thus, the seat of concupiscence is the entire person.[12] Yet the body is the fundamental outlet for concupiscence, and that outlet is primarily sexual: "There are, then, lusts for many things; yet, when the word 'lust' [*libido*] is used without any addition signifying the object of lust, the only thing that usually occurs to the mind is the lust that arouses the impure parts of the body."[13] So much so that lawful sex between married persons was still tainted with concupiscence; that is, a person was literally conceived in the sin of lust. A man and a woman lusted, became sexually aroused, and then were able to have sex—hence Augustine's theology that Adamic original sin is transmitted through the sex act.[14] As he writes in *The City of God*, "If sin had not come into being, therefore, marriage . . . would have produced children to be loved, but without the shame of lust."[15] Had Adam and Eve not sinned, then, they would have procreated through the will alone and not lustfully: "The seed of offspring, therefore, would have been sown by the man and received by the woman at the time and in the quantity needed, their genital organs being moved by the will and not excited by lust."[16] Simply put, Augustine sees an intimate connection between sin and the body. It was not supposed to be this way, concludes Augustine, but in our postlapsarian state that is the reality.

This kind of thinking runs counter, I think, to a healthy view of materiality and embodiment, like that depicted in the Christian Scriptures. Again, there was an expectation already in the New Testament that Christian living and the "world" would exist in tension with each other. But when a theologian the stature of Augustine of Hippo adopts an antimaterial perspective, even a mediated one, it is inevitable, perhaps, that others will follow his lead. And this is certainly the case given Augustine's vast influence on subsequent Christian theology, history, and spirituality. By the fourth century it was common to view the Christian church in spiritually hierarchical terms, and not just in terms of laity versus clergy, for example, but also in hierarchical terms vis-à-vis Christian spirituality.[17] Those most attached to embodiment and materiality were, frankly, the least spiritual, whereas those most distanced

---

12. Augustine of Hippo, *On the Literal Interpretation of Genesis* 10.12.30. See also Burnell, "Concupiscence," 226.

13. Augustine of Hippo, *City of God* 14.16 (Dyson, 614). On Augustine's conceptions of *libido* and *concupiscentia*, see Bonner, "Libido and Concupiscentia."

14. See Augustine of Hippo, *On Marriage and Concupiscence* 1.24.27.

15. Augustine of Hippo, *City of God* 14.23 (Dyson, 623).

16. Augustine of Hippo, *City of God* 14.24 (Dyson, 625–26).

17. See chap. 3 of this book for a discussion of this in terms of Matt. 13:3–9's hundredfold, sixtyfold, and thirtyfold reward, for example.

from materiality were the most spiritual.[18] Yet this is where an unnecessary division emerged in Christian faith and practice that continues to exist today, and it is a distinction that does more harm than good.[19]

As discussed above, by the time of the sixteenth-century Reformation it was common practice to think of monastics and clergy as more spiritual than all other Christians.[20] Though most baptized believers would be saved,[21] monks, nuns, priests, bishops, and popes were, it seemed, on a fast track to union with God.[22] The reasons for this are many, but one of them is certainly related to Augustinian notions of sex: those who are celibate (or at least supposedly celibate) are inevitably going to be more spiritual than those who are not. Thus, monastics and clergy are, because of their disengagement from sex, more spiritual. These same women and men were also holier because they dedicated their lives to handling holy things (e.g., the Holy Eucharist).[23] Nonmonastics and nonclerics were destined to be tainted by lust through sex and would handle unholy things (e.g., money).[24] The chasm, as noted in chapter 5 above, grew wider and deeper until theologians such as Martin Luther spoke up. And in their speaking up they were not just being polemical

18. In monastic history an egregious example of this thinking manifests itself in the conception that monks and nuns are living the "angelic life." See Frank, *Angelikos Bios*; and Leclercq, "Monasticism and Angelism."

19. Even when affirming marriage, Christian theologians often still thought of it as less spiritual than living as a monk. For example, John Chrysostom (d. 407) wrote, "Let your prayers be common. Let each go to Church; and let the husband ask his wife at home, and she again ask her husband, the account of the things which were said and read there. If any poverty should overtake you, cite the case of those holy men, Paul and Peter, who were more honored than any kings or rich men; and yet how they spent their lives, in hunger and in thirst. Teach her that there is nothing in life that is to be feared, save only offending against God. If any marry thus, with these views, he will be but little inferior to monks; the married but little below the unmarried." *Homily 20 on Ephesians* (NPNF[1] 13:151). Thomas Aquinas (d. 1274) is more blunt: "Entrance into religion [i.e., vowed religious life] is a greater good." Thomas Aquinas, *Summa Theologiae* II-II, Q. 189, Art. 10, in *Summa Theologica*, 4:2009.

20. In the words of John Colet (d. 1519), dean of St. Paul's Cathedral in London, the "priesthood is . . . greater than other [*sic*] the kings or emperors: it is equal with the dignity of angels." Lupton, *Life of John Colet*, 297, with modernized spelling.

21. I say "most" because certain medieval theologians, such as Dante Alighieri (d. 1321), think that some believers, including popes, will go to hell on the basis of their bad behavior. See, e.g., Dante Alighieri, *Inferno*, canto 19.

22. For example, the late medieval law collection known as the *Authenticum* says that monasticism cleanses one from all sin: *omnem quidem humanam eius maculam detergat. Novelle* 5, in Heimbach, *Authenticum*, 39. See also Thomas, *Secular Clergy in England*, 20–24, a section titled "The Exalted Status of Priests and Clerics."

23. O'Day, *Professions*, 50–54.

24. The debate over what constitutes "poverty" in second-generation Franciscanism is illustrative of this tension between holiness and the corruptive nature of something material such as money. See Burr, *Spiritual Franciscans*.

but attempting to set aright a listing ship. They were trying to recover the biblical vision of what it means to be a spiritually well-formed Christian.

In this book I have tried, up to now, to show two things in particular: (1) a "monk" is someone, anyone, who has a single-minded, interior focus on God rooted in her baptismal vows; and (2) asceticism, that most monastic of practices, is expected of all Christian believers by virtue of our baptism and is characterized primarily by balance and moderation. Like John Cassian commenting on Acts 4, I am trying to say that all Christians are monks and all monks are Christians. The latter half of that statement is intuitive, but the former half is not—or, at least, is not any longer. But Christian history shows us that there has remained, often just under the surface, a conviction that because death is no respecter of persons, it matters that all believers mature spiritually; that even if monks, nuns, and clergy are somehow better prepared for eternal salvation and sanctification, it is incumbent on nonmonastics to be just as prepared. And not because they are somehow lesser Christians who have to taint themselves with worldly, material things, but because they *are* Christians of the same sort as the men and women who enter monasteries and abbeys. It is a difference of vocation, not a difference of evangelical expectations.[25]

Christian formation and spiritual maturation begin at baptism: "Holy Baptism is the basis of the whole Christian life, the gateway to life in the Spirit . . . and the door which gives access to the other sacraments."[26] Furthermore, it is here that the believer commits herself to Jesus Christ and to walking in his holy ways.[27] In this sense baptism is the gate, the starting point for all further spiritual development.[28] So when Martin Luther insists that

25. See chap. 7 below.

26. *Catechism of the Catholic Church* 1213, accessed March 9, 2018, http://www.vatican.va/archive/ENG0015/__P3G.HTM.

27. In cases of infant baptism, it is the parents, sponsors, the parish, and/or the church who make these commitments on behalf of the baptizand. See, for example, the first question of "A Catechism" in the 1662 *Book of Common Prayer*, where the person being catechized, when asked what her godparents did for her at baptism, responds, "They did promise and vow three things in my Name. First, that I should renounce the devil and all his works, the pomps and vanity of this wicked world, and all the sinful lusts of the flesh: Secondly, that I should believe all the articles of the Christian faith: And thirdly, that I should keep God's holy Will and Commandments, and walk in the same all the days of my life."

28. Dante Alighieri acknowledges this in a rather interesting manner in the *Divine Comedy*. In Limbo, the first rim of hell, Dante meets a number of virtuous ancient poets and philosophers, including Homer and Aristotle. Virgil, Dante's guide and an inhabitant of Limbo, tells Dante that Limbo is a place without punishment, though it is sorrowful because those who are there long to ascend to Paradise. They are there, he says, because "baptism they did not have, the one gate to the faith which *you* believe." *Inferno* 4.35–36 (Esolen, 35, italics original). Because they lack baptism, they are unable to ever enter into God's presence.

all Christians are under the same evangelical obligations, he is insisting that it is one's baptismal vows that make this true, not a later set of evangelical counsels, such as poverty, celibacy, and obedience. Luther was not seeking to do away with monasticism completely, but he was attempting to reform it, to put it back onto the firm foundation of baptismal vows.[29] In fact, he saw value in the sanctifying nature of monasticism: "It would be a good thing if monasteries and religious foundations were kept for the purpose of teaching young people God's Word, the Scriptures, and Christian morals, so that we might train and prepare fine, capable men to become bishops, pastors, and for civil government, and fine, respectable, learned women capable of keeping house and rearing children in a Christian way."[30] But this monasticism *must* be based on baptismal vows, rooted in the priesthood of all believers. For monasticism to become anything other than a training ground for godliness makes it demonic to Luther: "As a way of seeking salvation, these institutions are all the devil's doctrine and creed."[31] Luther is talking about the institution of monasticism, that conglomeration of monastic houses of men and women that came, collectively, to be known as monasticism. He is talking not about particular forms of monasticism (e.g., Cistercian, Benedictine, or Carthusian) but about the institution as a whole. And there is a place for the institution of monasticism,[32] but the institution of monasticism is different from the reality that each baptized Christian believer is a monk inasmuch as she or he is a single-minded follower of God. In the language of Tikhon of Zadonsk or Paul Evdokimov, she or he is an interiorized monastic.

And this is what all baptized believers have in common, that they are interiorized monks; or, they are supposed to be. I noted above that Christian spirituality is *not* about being antimaterial; instead, it is about one's inner life, one's spirit (hence Christian *spirit*uality). At its most general, the word *spirituality* "refers to the deepest values and meanings by which people seek to live." Therefore, "'spirituality' implies some kind of vision of the human spirit and of what will assist it to achieve full potential."[33] But, more specifically, "spirituality refers to the way our fundamental values, lifestyles, and spiritual practices reflect particular understandings of God, human identity, and the material world as the context for human transformation. While all Christian spiritual traditions are rooted in the Hebrew and Christian scriptures . . . they are also attempts to reinterpret these scriptural values for specific

---

29. Peters, *Reforming the Monastery*, 19–37.
30. Luther, *Confession Concerning Christ's Supper* (LW 37:364).
31. Luther, *Confession Concerning Christ's Supper* (LW 37:364).
32. See chap. 7 below.
33. Sheldrake, *Brief History of Spirituality*, 1–2.

historical and cultural circumstances."[34] At the same time, though, Christian spirituality is just as much about what the person of the Holy Spirit is doing in the life of the individual believer. Spirituality is not just the study of how Christians have lived at times in various cultures or how they appropriated the Christian Scriptures in light of cultural realities; it is the study of how the Holy Spirit works in the lives of his followers—and not just collectively but individually, personally. Though there is a tendency at times, in certain expressions of the Christian church, to disparage what is thought to be an overly individualistic, and therefore overly subjective, element to the faith,[35] the self is an important element in Christian thought and certainly so in Christian theology and spirituality.

Already in Plato (d. 347 BCE) there is a focus on the self by way of self-knowledge and self-mastery. In the dialogue *Charmides*, Socrates discusses the virtue of temperance (σωφροσύνη) with Plato's maternal uncle Charmides and Plato's maternal second cousin Critias. In general, "there is no adequate translation [of σωφροσύνη] in modern European languages." But it "means a well-developed consciousness of oneself and one's legitimate duties in relation to others . . . and in relation to one's own ambitions, social standing, and the relevant expectations as regards one's own behavior."[36] In the course of discussion, Critias argues that a person could be temperate or wise even if they were self-ignorant, but he comes to abandon this position:

> "But this," he said, "Socrates, would never happen [i.e., that a doctor could know whether he acted beneficially or harmfully when prescribing a course of treatment]. And if you think it necessary to draw this conclusion from what I admitted before, then I would rather withdraw some of my statements, and would not be ashamed to admit I had made a mistake, in preference to conceding that a man ignorant of himself could be temperate. As a matter of fact, this is pretty much what I say temperance is, to know oneself [γιγνώσκειν ἑαυτόν], and I agree with the inscription to this effect set up at Delphi. . . . I concede to you everything that was said before . . . but now I wish to give you an explanation of this definition, unless of course you already agree that temperance is to know oneself."[37]

Critias comes to realize that σωφροσύνη and self-knowledge are deeply connected, perhaps even one and the same thing. Thus, temperance, the virtue

---

34. Sheldrake, *Brief History of Spirituality*, 2.
35. Mouw, "Individualism and Christian Faith."
36. Plato, *Complete Works*, 639.
37. Plato, *Charmides* 164d–65b, in *Complete Works*, 651–52. Greek texts of all the Platonic dialogues are available online at the Perseus Digital Library, http://www.perseus.tufts.edu.

of virtues, is fully dependent on self-knowledge. Plato believes that a person can only be moral (i.e., virtuous) if they are self-knowledgeable. In the dialogue *Alcibiades*, Socrates tells the unvirtuous Athenian statesman that he lusts for power and therefore will not amount to anything unless he first pursues self-knowledge, which is the necessary foundation for all other forms of knowledge, including virtue:

> *Socrates*: Is it actually such an easy thing to know oneself? Was it some simpleton who inscribed those words on the temple wall at Delphi? Or is it difficult, and not for everybody?
> *Alcibiades*: Sometimes I think, Socrates, that anyone can do it, but then sometimes I think it's extremely difficult.
> *Socrates*: But Alcibiades, whether it's easy or not, nevertheless this is the situation we're in: if we know ourselves, then we might be able to know how to cultivate ourselves, but if we don't know ourselves, we'll never know how.
> *Alcibiades*: I agree.[38]

Moreover, for Socrates (and thus for Plato) self-knowledge is absolutely necessary for any other knowledge: "I am still unable, as the Delphic inscription orders, to know myself; and it really seems to me ridiculous to look into other things before I have understood that."[39] Thus, given that self-knowledge is the foundation of all knowledge and virtue, the self must be known and must be of importance.

This essential focus on the self as individual for virtue and knowledge's sake became important in early Christian theology as well. For example, in his *Confessions*, Augustine of Hippo says that the "human race is inquisitive about other people's lives, but negligent to correct their own." They would rather read the *Confessions*, for example, than spend any amount of time examining themselves, because Augustine's sins are more interesting than their own. Besides, even when a believer learns something about himself, he is quick to ignore it, to doubt its veracity. "But," writes Augustine, "if they were to hear about themselves from you, they could not say 'The Lord is lying.' To hear you speaking about oneself is to know oneself."[40] Consequently, he writes, "Let me confess what I know of myself. Let me confess too what I do not know of myself. For what I know of myself I know because you grant me light, and what I do not know of myself, I do not know

38. Plato, *Alcibiades* 129a, in *Complete Works*, 587. The authenticity of Plato's authorship of *Alcibiades* is still contested.

39. Plato, *Phaedrus* 230a, in *Complete Works*, 510.

40. Augustine of Hippo, *Confessions* 10.3.3 (Chadwick, 180). Latin text in Knöll, *Sancti Avreli Avgvstini Confessionvm*.

until such time as my darkness becomes 'like noonday' before your face."[41] With this desire, the *Confessions* itself becomes Augustine's introspective journey, his intentional journey into self-knowledge. He revisits his life and writes for the purpose of understanding the work of God in and around him so that he can understand himself, so that he can be formed spiritually. For Plato self-knowledge leads to knowledge and virtue, and the same is true for Augustine.

Though concepts of the self were known in Christian antiquity, the practice of self-examination was deeper and more widespread in twelfth-century Europe than at any time since the fifth century. There was a renewed commitment to the examination of the inner life and a development of modes of thought about the self. Self-knowledge was one of the dominant themes of the High Middle Ages, and self-knowledge as a path to God was taken up particularly by writers in the monastic tradition. In Byzantium, for example, twelfth-century Greek monk Peter of Damascus (fl. 1153) wrote, "To the person who knows himself is given knowledge of all things," and "he who knows himself—who knows, that is to say, that he stands midway between nobility and baseness . . . never exults or despairs."[42] Again, as in Plato and Augustine, knowledge of the self is essential for greater knowledge and proper spiritual living. A near contemporary of Peter, Nicetas Stethatos (d. ca. 1090), exhorted his readers as follows:

> Know yourself: this is true humility, the humility that teaches us to be inwardly humble and makes our heart contrite. Such humility you must cultivate and guard. For if you do not yet know yourself you cannot know what humility is, and have not yet embarked truly on the task of cultivating and guarding. To know oneself is the goal of the practice of virtues.
>
> If having achieved a state of purity, you advance to the knowledge of the essences of created beings, you will have fulfilled the injunction, "Know yourself." If, on the other hand, you have not yet attained a knowledge of the inner essences of creation and of things both divine and human, you may know what is outside and around you, but you will still be totally ignorant of your own self.[43]

41. Augustine of Hippo, *Confessions* 10.5.7 (Chadwick, 182–83), citing Isa. 58:10.

42. Peter of Damascus, *Admonition to My Own Soul*, preface, in Palmer, Sherrard, and Ware, *Philokalia*, 3:85–86. Greek text in Nicodemus of the Holy Mountain and Macarius of Corinth, Φιλοκαλία τῶν ἱερῶν νηπτικῶν, Τόμος Γ.

43. Nicetas Stethatos, *On the Inner Nature of Things and on the Purification of the Intellect: One Hundred Texts* 35–36, in Palmer, Sherrard, and Ware, *Philokalia*, 4:116. Greek text in Nicodemus of the Holy Mountain and Macarius of Corinth, eds., Φιλοκαλία τῶν ἱερῶν νηπτικῶν, Τόμος Γ.

Here it is seen that self-knowledge is the basis of humility (à la Plato's contention that self-knowledge is the basis of σωφροσύνη) and, more importantly, the basis of knowledge of created beings, which is necessary to then move to a knowledge of uncreated beings (i.e., God the Trinity). So, for Nicetas, self-knowledge is the basis of union with God, the basis of the entire Christian spiritual life: "When you know yourself you cease from all outward tasks undertaken with a view to serving God and enter into the sanctuary of God, into the noetic liturgy of the Spirit, the divine haven of dispassion and humility."[44]

At the same time, in the Western, Latin-speaking church, the self was being reintroduced by Cistercian theologians. Bernard of Clairvaux (d. 1153), in a sermon titled "Concerning Seven Steps of Confession," explains that confession "is good equipment for the soul" because "it both purifies the sinner and renders a just person more pure."[45] The first step of confession, says Bernard, is self-knowledge. Bernard even believes that the decree "Human being, know yourself" "fell from heaven."[46] Therefore, it is an essential element in confession and Christian spiritual formation. This self-knowledge consists of three parts: "that people know what they have done, what they have deserved, and what they have lost."[47] Armed with this knowledge of the self, the confessant is able to begin the long journey of restoration with God. Similarly, in the text *On Consideration*, Bernard advises Pope Eugenius III (d. 1153), himself a Cistercian monk, on the importance of self-knowledge:

> Now in order to achieve the fruit of consideration, I think you should consider four things in this order: yourself, what is below you, around you and above you. Your consideration should begin with yourself so you do not reach out to other things in vain, because you have neglected yourself. What does it profit you if you gain the whole world and lose one person—yourself? Although you know every mystery, the width of the earth, the height of the heavens, and depth of the sea; if you do not know yourself, you are like a building without a foundation; you raise not a structure but ruins. . . . Therefore, let your consideration

---

44. Nicetas Stethatos, *Inner Nature* 38, in Palmer, Sherrard, and Ware, *Philokalia*, 4:117. See also Gregory Palamas (d. 1359), who says that knowledge of oneself is greater than knowledge of science or philosophy, and that knowing oneself and knowing God are intimately connected (*Capita 150*, chap. 29).

45. Bernard of Clairvaux, *Sermones de diversis* 40.2, in *Monastic Sermons*, 202. Latin text in Leclercq and Rochais, *Sancti Bernardi Opera, Tomus VI/1*.

46. Bernard of Clairvaux, *Sermones de diversis* 40.3, in *Monastic Sermons*, 203. In the Latin Vulgate, Song of Solomon 1:7 reads, "If you know not yourself, O fairest among women, go forth." Hence, Bernard is opting to espouse a scriptural origin of the concept of self-knowledge over against Plato and/or the oracle at Delphi.

47. Bernard of Clairvaux, *Sermones de diversis* 40.3, in *Monastic Sermons*, 203.

begin and end with yourself. . . . This consideration of yourself has three divi-
sions. You should consider what you are, who you are, and what sort of man
you are: what you are in nature, who you are in person, and what sort of man
you are in character.[48]

Given that *On Consideration* is a text about the demands of the papal office
and Eugenius's need to remain grounded as pope *and* monk, Bernard's words
are meant to ensure that the pope's motivations remain authentically Christian.
Thus, Eugenius's self-knowledge is an aid in his work as pope, to make him
an effective shepherd of the flock of Jesus Christ and to keep him grounded
spiritually despite his ecclesiastical and political commitments.

In his more well-known work *On Loving God* (*De diligendo Deo*), Bernard
lays out a fairly systematic account of spiritual growth using the taxonomy
of four degrees of love. Bernard states that God is to be loved for his own
sake, not for what he does for the believer, but simply loved for who he is. The
human being is given the noble gifts of dignity, knowledge, and virtue by way
of "the higher part of his being, in his soul."[49] A person's dignity is his free
will; his knowledge is that he acknowledges this dignity but knows that it is
not of his own making; and virtue is evidenced by a believer's constant and
eager longing for God and his adherence to him once he is found. Each of
these noble gifts is dependent on the others, for "dignity without knowledge
is unprofitable, without virtue it can be an obstacle."[50] Moreover, virtue is
the fruit of dignity and knowledge. But what kind of knowledge? Again, it is
knowledge that as a human I am endowed with dignity but also the knowledge
that I am not responsible for the presence of this knowledge. To think otherwise would lead to vainglory and, ultimately, pride. Thus, the most necessary
kind of knowledge for the person being spiritually formed is self-knowledge:
"There are two facts you should know: first, what you are; secondly, that you
are not that by your own power, lest you fail to boast at all or do so in vain . . .
know yourself."[51] Thus, virtue (i.e., spiritual maturity) is dependent on one's
knowledge of self. To quote Bernard's contemporary and fellow Cistercian
Aelred of Rievaulx (d. 1167), "How great is man's knowledge when he does
not even grasp himself?"[52] In the end, not all that great, or at least not great
enough to become a truly spiritual person.

48. Bernard of Clairvaux, *On Consideration* 2.3.6–2.4.7, in *Sermons on Conversion*, 52–54.
Latin text in Leclercq and Rochais, *Sancti Bernardi Opera, Tomus III*, 393–493.
49. Bernard of Clairvaux, *On Loving God* 2.2, in *Treatises II*, 95. Latin text in Leclercq and
Rochais, *Sancti Bernardi Opera, Tomus III*, 119–54.
50. Bernard of Clairvaux, *On Loving God* 2.2, in *Treatises II*, 95.
51. Bernard of Clairvaux, *On Loving God* 2.4, in *Treatises II*, 96.
52. Aelred of Rievaulx, *Mirror of Charity* 1.5 (Connor, 95).

Related to this notion of self and self-knowledge is interiority, which brings us back to notions of the inner and outer monk. Though the New Testament has an emphasis on interiority (e.g., "But what comes out of the mouth proceeds from the heart, and this defiles a person. For out of the heart come evil thoughts, murder, adultery, sexual immorality, theft, false witness, slander. These are what defile a person" [Matt. 15:18–20]), it was in the fourth century that an interior-exterior distinction reached maturity, and no more so than in the theology of Augustine, who "is the founder of a specifically Western tradition of interiority or inwardness, embracing three interrelated concepts: inner self, inward turn, and outward signs as expressions of inner things."[53] For example, the bishop of Hippo writes in the *Confessions*, "By the Platonic books I was admonished to return into myself [*intravi in intima mea*]. With you [God] as my guide I entered into my innermost citadel";[54] and, "Through my soul I will ascend to him."[55] The way up to God (and the way out of himself) was, for Augustine, an interior movement. The Christian descends into herself in order to ascend to God.

As discussed earlier, Augustine's contemporary John Cassian, in his *Conferences*, constructs a unified spirituality wherein the monk's *telos* (final end) is the kingdom of God (or beatitude, supreme blessedness), and his *skopos* (this-worldly end) is purity of heart, a Cassinese way of speaking about Christian perfection. In his *Institutes* Cassian works this concept out as an outer versus inner distinction. He begins the *Institutes* by discussing the garb of the monk, saying that "after having exposed [the monks'] outward appearance to view we shall then be able to discuss, in logical sequence, their inner worship."[56] Moreover, when describing the monastery's horarium of nighttime prayers, Cassian says that such practical discussions are necessary because those elements of monastic life that concern the outer man come before those that concern the inner man. In Cassinese literature this means that the *Institutes* must come before the *Conferences*, the outer before the inner. Thus, for Augustine the interior-exterior distinction concerns one's spiritual ascent; it is about the spiritual life generally. With Cassian this distinction rises to the level of an institutional differentiation between cenobitic and anchoritic forms of life. Yet subsequent literature continues to move further and further away from the literal, physical monastery versus the monk's interior life and, in its place, begins to spiritualize the monastery.

53. Cary, "Interiority," 454.
54. Augustine of Hippo, *Confessions* 7.10.16 (Chadwick, 123).
55. Augustine of Hippo, *Confessions* 10.7.11 (Chadwick, 185).
56. Cassian, *Institutes* 1.1.1 (ACW 58:21).

Returning to Bernard of Clairvaux, his *Ad clericos de conversione* was likely written sometime between Lent 1139 and the early part of 1140. These sermons were first delivered in Paris to students there, at the request of Bishop Stephen. As reported by Geoffrey of Auxerre in the *Vita prima* of Bernard:

> When the holy father was traveling in the vicinity of Paris, the bishop of the city, Stephen, and all the others who were also present asked him to make a detour and come to the city, but they could not obtain their wish. Unless a serious cause prompted Bernard, he declined to attend public meetings, with some strong feelings on the matter. In the evening he had proposed to go elsewhere, but the next morning when he first spoke to the brothers, he told them to say to the bishop, "We will go to Paris as he asked." So when a great group of clergy had gathered, as they always did to hear the word of God, at once three of them were struck with compunction and turned away [*conversi*: being converted] from their inane studies to engage in true wisdom, renouncing the world and keeping close to the servant of God.[57]

"Conversion" in this context means "becoming a monk," so Bernard, at the request of the bishop, is preaching to a group of students whom he is exhorting to become monks. This is made explicit by Bernard when he exhorts his listeners to let their "profession of perfection not be found later to be a mockery and let its power now appear in the form of godliness. Let it not be an empty appearance of the celibate life [*caelibis vitae forma*], and void of truth."[58] For Bernard these students would, if they were truly learned and wise, become monks. And how would they do this? Ostensibly by leaving aside their studies and, perhaps like Bernard himself, joining a Cistercian monastery, dedicating themselves to the restrictions of the rule and placing themselves under the obedience of the abbot. It would appear, at first glance, that Bernard's suggestion is a fairly typical one and, given that it is coming from a monk, a fairly predictable one at that. Yet there's more.

It is obvious and clear that Bernard is suggesting that these men leave their studies and enter existing monasteries. Again, Geoffrey tells us that three of Bernard's student-listeners were struck with compunction and were converted to the true wisdom, which is summed up in renunciation of the world. One of these men, writes Geoffrey, "changed and afterward became a novice with great purity and devotion. . . . After many years in Clairvaux, he rested in a

57. Geoffrey of Auxerre, *Vita prima* 4.10, in William of Saint-Thierry, Arnold of Bonneval, and Geoffrey of Auxerre, *First Life*, 189.

58. Bernard of Clairvaux, *Ad clericos de conversione* 21.37, in *Sermons on Conversion*, 75. Latin text in Leclercq and Rochais, *Sancti Bernardi Opera, Tomus IV*, 69–116.

blessed end."[59] We can presume that the other two men also joined monasteries; perhaps like their confrere they too joined Clairvaux. But earlier in the *Ad clericos* Bernard laid out a vision for a different kind of monastery, not one that was in competition with the monasteries of Clairvaux and elsewhere, but one that ran parallel to them, in the inner life of the monk.

In the introduction to her translation of the *Ad clericos*, Marie-Bernard Saïd, borrowing language from Jean Leclercq, says that the text presents a psychology of conversion. Using the traditional triad of purgation, illumination, and union, Saïd thinks that paragraphs 1–11 of the *Ad clericos* describe the purgative way (the need for conversion and its obstacles), paragraphs 12–23 the illuminative way (God's consolations so that our will is turned toward conversion), and paragraphs 24–40 the unitive way (conversion and contemplation of God). Though many scholars might disagree with Saïd's assessment, it is a helpful heuristic device. At the beginning of the unitive way, Bernard sums up what he has written up to that point when he says, "All this will enable [the man who has turned away from evil] to peer though the keyhole, to look through the lattices and in sweet regard to follow the trail of that guiding ray."[60] In the remainder of this chapter the abbot of Clairvaux continues to extol the wonderful riches of this Solomonic-like garden of delight. Thus, when he begins the next paragraph, he writes, "You must not suppose this paradise of inner pleasure is some material place: you enter this garden not on foot, but by deeply-felt affections [*affectibus introitur*]."[61] Yet what exactly is this "paradise of inner pleasure"?

It would be tempting, I think, to view it as equivalent to Bernard's fourth degree of love in *On Loving God*, which is to love oneself for God's sake. That these infrequent occasions of love that only last for a moment are rapturous and deifying is clear from the text of *On Loving God*. There is parallel language between the two texts suggesting that Bernard's "paradise of inner pleasure" is akin (if not equivalent) to his fourth degree of love. But let us not forget that the *Ad clericos* is written to students to convert them to the monastic life, that is, life in a monastery that may then aid the individual monk in his ascent to the light of God. If that is the case, then this "paradise of inner pleasure" can also be viewed as a reference to an "inner monastery." Bernard says that this paradise is immaterial, and therefore it is not entered into on foot but by "deeply-felt affections." For Bernard the *affectus* is the human faculty that allows for feeling, emotion, or desire. Moreover, at times

59. Geoffrey of Auxerre, *Vita prima* 4.10, in William of Saint-Thierry, Arnold of Bonneval, and Geoffrey of Auxerre, *First Life*, 189.

60. Bernard of Clairvaux, *Ad clericos de conversione* 12.24, in *Sermons on Conversion*, 58.

61. Bernard of Clairvaux, *Ad clericos de conversione* 13.25, in *Sermons on Conversion*, 59.

in the Bernardine corpus the affect is identified with the will,[62] but a will that is tinged with sweetness.[63] So this inner monastery is entered into willingly, or affectively. Moreover, it is possible, in Bernard's thought, to be a monk outwardly while failing to be one inwardly. As he writes in his second sermon for Lent, "His tonsure remains, he has not laid aside his habit, he keeps the rule of fasting, he says the psalms at the prescribed times; but *his heart is far from me*, says the Lord."[64] Though he is still a monk outwardly, he appears to have left the inner monastery.

Yet what is only hinted at in Bernard's text is made explicit by later writings, such as *The Abbey of the Holy Ghost* and Walter Hilton's *The Mixed Life*, both discussed in chapter 2 of this book. As a result, at the time of the Reformation, someone such as Martin Luther could be suspicious of the institution of monasticism but still be in favor of monastic-like living. He could advocate for a deeply personal, interiorized Christian life that was fully connected to the life of the institutional church in such a way as to see the value of a rightly understood and correctly practiced monasticism, but not one that was understood to be more soteriologically meritorious. All baptized Christians were to be single-minded in their devotion to God, leaning fully into their universal priesthood as bequeathed to them at baptism. Like Luther, John Calvin (d. 1564) was also a supporter of monasticism when rightly practiced.[65] Moreover, he, perhaps like no other Reformation theologian, understood the importance of self-knowledge and an interiorized faith and spiritual life.

Calvin begins his magnum opus *The Institutes of the Christian Religion* with the following statement: "Nearly all wisdom we possess, that is to say, true and sound wisdom, consists of two parts: the knowledge of God and of ourselves." For "no one can look upon himself without immediately turning his thoughts to the contemplation of God."[66] Calvin believes that we, when examining ourselves, will see our own sin and, as a result, will contemplate the good things of God. At the same time, our ability to see ourselves is dependent on our seeing God: "Man never achieves a clear knowledge of himself unless he has first looked upon God's face, and then descends from contemplating him to scrutinize himself."[67] It is hard to know which comes first for Calvin:

---

62. Bernard of Clairvaux, *Sermo in ascensione domini* 3.2 and *Sermo super cantica canticorum* 42.7.

63. Bernard of Clairvaux, *Sermones de diversis* 29.1.

64. Bernard of Clairvaux, *Sermons for Lent*, 32 (italics original).

65. Peters, *Reforming the Monastery*, 38–48.

66. Calvin, *Institutes* 1.1.1 (Battles, 35). Latin text in Barth and Niesel, *Joannis Calvini opera selecta*.

67. Calvin, *Institutes* 1.1.2 (Battles, 37).

knowledge of self or knowledge of God. In the end it is impossible to say which one comes first since they are so dependent on each other. What is clear, however, is that this knowledge of God requires piety, "that reverence joined with love of God which the knowledge of his benefits induces."[68] One must have a zeal for God, not just a fear of his judgment, in order to know God rightly.[69] Further, to know God increases one's piety and desire to be in communion with God.[70] In fact, the title to Calvin's first edition of the *Institutes* was *Of the Christian Religion, an Institution, embracing nearly an entire summary of piety and what is necessary to know of the doctrine of salvation: a work most worthy to be read by all those zealous for piety.*[71] For Calvin, knowing theology (*doctrina*—that is, knowing God) is for the end of being spiritually well formed. Piety is necessary for knowledge of self and of God, and knowledge of self and of God leads to piety. Calvin also envisions that his *summa pietatis* ("summary of piety") will lead to the right reading and teaching of the Bible so as to build up each believer in the faith and to prepare the church's leaders.[72] Accordingly, Calvin's theology of self-knowledge and knowledge of God is not just for the purpose of individual spiritual formation, though it is that, but it is also for the good of the whole church.

Calvin, like Luther and other Reformers (not to mention medieval authors such as Bernard of Clairvaux), stressed both the individual and the institutional. The Christian faith could not be reduced to the individual at the expense of the institutional. Baptized Christians are to live out their life of faith in the church because they are ecclesial beings by virtue of adoption as children of God. For some this may also include living in a monastic community, whereas for many, if not most, others it will not. But that does *not* mean that affiliation with one institution (i.e., monasticism) is more salvific than membership in the other (i.e., the church). Though there is a legitimacy to thinking about monasticism as the *ecclesiola in ecclesia* (the little church within the church), it does not mean that monasticism is the *ecclesiola vera in ecclesia* (the true little church within the church).[73] There is only one church (cf. Eph. 4:4–6), and it is *the* church of Jesus Christ, whose membership is

68. Calvin, *Institutes* 1.2.1 (Battles, 39).

69. See John Calvin, *Instruction in Faith* (1537) 2.

70. See Boulton, *Life in God*.

71. Latin: *Christianae religionis institutio, totam fere pietatis summam, & quicquid est in doctrina salutis cognitu necessarium: complectens: omnibus pietatis studiosis lectu dignissimum opus.*

72. See "John Calvin to the Reader," in Calvin, *Institutes*, 4: "It has been my purpose in this labor to prepare and instruct candidates in sacred theology for the reading of the divine Word, in order that they may be able both to have easy access to it and to advance in it without stumbling."

73. Driscoll, "Monastic Community," 211–24.

composed exclusively of monks—that is, single-minded believers following the commands and demands of the gospel.

Conclusion

In the end, there is always a need in Christian spirituality for the proper spiritual formation of each baptized believer but also for the spiritual formation of the church as a whole. In John Cassian's estimation there was a split early in Christian history between those who were desirous of the demands and commands of the gospel and those who were merely asked to do the least things necessary as converts to the Christian faith. Those desirous of the demands, he tells us, went off and became the monks and nuns of the Christian church, whereas the others remained in the church. In time, those who went off and became monk and nuns comprised the spiritual elite, whereas the latter believers came to be seen as a kind of second class of Christians. It was the monks and nuns who wowed the world (and God) with their sacrificial taking of vows, becoming, in the eyes of many, those who would, in the end, be saved without doubt. They were the Christians returning a hundredfold harvest to God. Monasticism, in this version of monastic history, became a soteriological institution that was somehow better than the church itself. The church was still the ark of salvation, but it was in monastic institutions where the most spiritual persons lived and thrived.[74]

This, though, is not what it truly meant to be a monk. This was a later Christian devolution of the concept of a "monk." A "monk" was not a person who became a eunuch for the kingdom of heaven (Matt. 19:12) in a way that created a gulf between monks and everyone else. No, to be a monk was to be spiritually formed so as to live single-mindedly focused on God, living into the fullness of one's baptismal vows as priests in God's kingdom. To be a "monk" was to live into the fullness of the Christian life as laid out in the Scriptures and as it has developed in history. It was to take one's spiritual formation seriously, hoping, in the end, to be in "sweet communion" with God.[75] Only with the rise and development of the institution of monasticism (such as the Benedictines and Cistercians) was there a need to qualify the Christian

74. This is evidenced in Christian literature, for example, in Dante Alighieri's *Paradiso*. The postbiblical-era Christians who are closest to the top of Paradise (and, thus, closer to God the Trinity) are, most of the time, monastics or those in religious orders. It is also illustrative (considering only the Roman Catholic Church) that of the over ten thousand recognized saints, a mere five hundred or so were married. Many were single because they had taken vows of celibacy as monastics and members of religious orders.

75. Reuver, *Sweet Communion*.

spiritual life as one of an "interiorized monasticism." Ultimately there are those who wear the monastic habit and take monastic vows and those who do not. There is no denying that some monks and nuns live in a vowed community, under a rule. There is also no denying that many, if not most, Christian believers do *not* live in a vowed community, under a rule—at least in the sense that we think of as "monastic."[76] Nonetheless, all Christians are monks. In the paradoxical words of Martin Luther, "I am still a monk and yet not a monk."[77] But if all Christians are monks, then who are the "monks" that we call Cistercian, Benedictine, Carthusian, and so on? That is, who are the men and women who live in monasteries and abbeys around the world, often identifiable because of their unique habit and God-ordained apostolates? If all baptized believers are monks, then is there a need for monks and nuns in the traditional or exteriorized sense? Absolutely!

76. To be married, of course, is to live in vowed community of at least two people, but marriage is not monasticism, though Robert de Sorbon demonstrates that marriage and monasticism have much in common. In what I am arguing, of course, one could be a married monk inasmuch as one is married but living the Christian life in a single-minded manner.

77. Martin Luther, *The Judgment of Martin Luther on Monastic Vows* (LW 44:335).

Seven

The Vocation of Monasticism

In the Episcopal Church USA's *Book of Common Prayer*, the Holy Eucharist, after the congregation's reception of the bread and the wine, contains a prayer that is known simply as the post-Communion prayer. It reads,

> Almighty and everliving God,
> we thank you for feeding us with the spiritual food
> of the most precious Body and Blood
> of your Son our Savior Jesus Christ;
> and for assuring us in these holy mysteries
> that we are living members of the Body of your Son,
> and heirs of your eternal kingdom.
> And now, Father, send us out
> to do the work you have given us to do,
> to love and serve you
> as faithful witnesses of Christ our Lord.
> To him, to you, and to the Holy Spirit,
> be honor and glory, now and for ever. Amen.[1]

What is significant about this prayer is that it casts the Christian's primary vocation ("work") in the terms of Sacred Scripture, connecting the "mysteries of the sanctuary to the 'good works' of Christian service in the world's life (cf. Eph. ii. 10), and it relates the sacrament of the altar to the tasks of everyday life."[2] The work that God "has given us to do, to love and serve

1. *Book of Common Prayer*, 366.
2. Shepherd, *Prayer Book Commentary*, 83–84.

[him] as faithful witnesses of Christ our Lord" is simply that those gathered will now go into the world to live out the Great Commandment: "You shall love the Lord your God with all your heart and with all your soul and with all your mind. This is the great and first commandment. And a second is like it: You shall love your neighbor as yourself" (Matt. 22:37–39). The *Book of Common Prayer*'s "to love" corresponds to the first clause of Jesus's command ("love the Lord your God"), and the prayer's "serve you as faithful witnesses" corresponds to the second clause of Jesus's command ("love your neighbor as yourself"). The Christian's primary vocation or "work" that she has been given to do is love of God and neighbor.

Also in the *Book of Common Prayer*, Morning Prayer contains a concluding Prayer for Mission, which reads, "Almighty and everlasting God, by whose Spirit the whole body of your faithful people is governed and sanctified: Receive our supplications and prayers which we offer before you for all members of your holy Church, that in their vocation and ministry they may truly and devoutly serve you; through our Lord and Savior Jesus Christ. *Amen*." Here instead of "work" we have "vocation" and "ministry," and it appears that this prayer is more about the believer's daily life, in the sense that it is aware that those who pray this prayer each morning will then, most likely, make their way into the fields, factories, hospitals, or halls of business. The prayer originates in the Gelasian and Gregorian sacramentaries of the eighth century and the *Missale Gallicanum vetus* of the seventh or eighth century. In its earliest form the prayer was likely only for those in holy orders:[3] "Hear our supplications for all orders [*universis ordinibus*], that by the gift of your grace all grades [*omnibus tibi gradibus*] may faithfully serve you."[4] If that is correct, then the 1549 *Book of Common Prayer* altered it to include all members of the church: "Receive our supplications and prayers which we offer before thee for all estates of men in thy holy congregation, that every member of the same, in his vocation and ministry, may truly and godly serve thee."[5] In other words, all Christians have a vocation and ministry, not just those in holy orders.

It has been said that the greatest contribution that the Protestant Reformation made to the Christian church was the reaffirmation of the apostle Paul's doctrine of justification by faith and that the second greatest contribution was a theology of vocation. And talking about vocation was something that the Protestant Reformers did with regularity and to great effect, as will be seen below. In the Scriptures there are two primary meanings of *calling*: (1) the

3. Hatchett, *Commentary*, 127.
4. Hatchett, *Commentary*, 127. Latin text in Wilson, *Gelasian Sacramentary*, 76; see also p. 51.
5. Hatchett, *Commentary*, 127.

call to membership in the people of God (e.g., Isa. 41:8–9); and (2) particular callings by God to a special work, office, or position of responsibility within his covenant community.[6] To illustrate, the word for "church" in the New Testament is ἐκκλησία, which is derived from ἐκ (from, out of) and κλῆσις (calling). Thus, the Greek word for church literally means "calling out of" or "called-out ones." This etymology demonstrates a general call to membership in the people of God. Yet God calls some individuals out of the church (literally, out of the called-out ones) to be apostles, prophets, evangelists, shepherds, and teachers "to equip the saints for the work of ministry, for building up the body of Christ" (Eph. 4:11–12). This illustrates God's practice of calling out to a special work, office, or position of responsibility.

In God's economy "individuals have their callings within the corporate calling."[7] Further, God is the one who calls on his own initiative (see John 15:16), though his calling almost always comes through mediators. Some callings are to specialized roles in church and society, and others are to particular duties within these spheres. Douglas Schuurman sums it up well when he writes that

> the Bible has two basic meanings for vocation or calling. Each of these has two forms. The first is the one call all Christians have to become a Christian and live accordingly. Of this there is a general form, where the proclaimed word echoes the voice of creation calling all away from folly and into the wisdom that is Jesus Christ, and there is a specific form, where this call becomes existentially and personally felt. The second meaning is the diverse spheres of life in and through which Christians live out their faith in concrete ways. Of this there is a more general form, such as being a husband, wife, child, parent, citizen, preacher, etc., "in the Lord." And there is a specific form, where it refers to the actual duties each of us takes on in our concretely occupied places of responsibility "in the Lord."[8]

Below we will see how Schuurman's work builds on Reformation theologies of vocation, especially Martin Luther's.

In a similar, yet slightly different, manner, Benedictine monk Christopher Jamison writes that the "root of the Christian vocation is Christ calling people to be disciples; from the early church onwards, the response to this call has been expressed through seeking baptism and entering the life of the Church."[9]

6. Schuurman, *Vocation*, 17.
7. Schuurman, *Vocation*, 18.
8. Schuurman, *Vocation*, 40–41.
9. Jamison, *Disciples' Call*, 1.

Like Schuurman, Jamison believes that our primary calling is into the church. It is a calling to a life of discipleship.[10] Subsequently, "baptismal life leads people into many different paths of holiness, paths that Christians discover in communion with the Church through a process of discernment."[11] Jamison summarizes this as *vocation* (i.e., the call of Christ on all believers—the "call of salvation is the basic vocation"[12]) and *vocations* (a call to a specific way of life).[13] To this end Schuurman and Jamison agree about the nature of vocation. And not only do they agree with each other, but they also agree with other theologians throughout Christian history.

Theologies of Vocation in Christian History[14]

There are seven extant letters penned by the great monastic figure Anthony of Egypt (d. 356).[15] In *Letter 1* he writes that "souls, whether male or female . . . are of three kinds."[16] First, there are the Abrahamic type of Christians, that is, those who hear the call of God and go without hesitation. These individuals are ready for their call, respond immediately, and thereby easily obtain the virtues since they are already "guided by the Spirit of God."[17] Second, there are those who weigh the words of Scripture, especially those that threaten pain and punishment to the wicked but promise blessings to "those who progress" (in the Syriac version, those who "flourish in the fear of God").[18] Last, there are those who, after a life of sin, repent and enter the monastic life as a form of penance. In the words of Anthony, "They enter into the calling and attain the virtues."[19] This "calling" is to monastic life only, but it is a vocation none-

---

10. This echoes the teaching of Vatican II's *Lumen gentium* (Dogmatic Constitution on the Church): "All the faithful of Christ of whatever rank or status, are called to the fullness of the Christian life and to the perfection of charity; by this holiness as such a more human manner of living is promoted in this earthly society" (§40).

11. Jamison, *Disciples' Call*, 1.

12. Jamison, *Disciples' Call*, 3.

13. Jamison, *Disciples' Call*, 2.

14. This section is indebted to Richard Price, "Did the Early Monastic Tradition Have a Concept of Vocation?," in Jamison, *Disciples' Call*, 29–42, who in turn is indebted to Sempé, "Vocation."

15. For a study of these letters see Rubenson, *Letters of St. Antony*.

16. Rubenson, *Letters of St. Antony*, 197. They are also translated by Derwas J. Chitty in Saint Antony, *Letters of Saint Antony the Great*. The letters are extant in a number of different languages (Arabic, Coptic, Georgian, Latin, and Syriac); thus there is no one critical edition. See Rubenson, *Letters of St. Antony*, 236, for a full list of editions.

17. Rubenson, *Letters of St. Antony*, 197.

18. Rubenson, *Letters of St. Antony*, 197.

19. Rubenson, *Letters of St. Antony*, 198.

theless. This letter, which is concerned only with monastic vocations, implies that the best calling is to be a monk; but if we read between the lines, it also suggests that all monks hear a calling and that some respond immediately and willingly, some respond in the hope of avoiding sin and damnation, and some respond in penance for a life of sin. Nonetheless, in all cases the monk is called to religious life.

John Cassian (d. mid-430s), in his third conference, "On Renunciations," also says that there are three kinds of callings (*modi speciali distinctione*). The first is from God, the second is human, and the third is of necessity. The first kind of calling, as for Anthony, is the one that comes from God alone, "which spurs us on to desire eternal life and salvation and which encourages us to follow God and to adhere to his commands with a salutary compunction."[20] Exemplars of this call are Abraham and, interestingly, Anthony of Egypt. The second kind of calling occurs when the believer is "moved by the example or teachings of certain holy persons" by which she is "inflamed with a desire for salvation." This results in the believer giving herself over to the "pursuit and profession."[21] An exemplar of this is the children of Israel who were liberated from Egypt by Moses. Last, the third kind of calling "proceeds from need, when we are compelled at least involuntarily to hasten to the God whom we had disdained to follow in time of prosperity."[22] This call comes after one has pursued wealth and pleasure in the world but is then subjected to some kind of trial that threatens death or loss of these "good" things. Further, this third kind of calling can be impressed on someone when reading the Scriptures because there one can read about how the Israelites, despite being God's people, were delivered over to their enemies for the purpose of having them return obediently to the Lord.

Cassian acknowledges that the first two kinds of calling are placed on the person who makes a better beginning of their spiritual life, whereas the third kind "seems inferior and lukewarm."[23] Nonetheless, there are those who experience the third calling and live the same kind of spiritual life as those called in the first or second manner. Moreover, some who are called in the first or second way fail to fulfill their more radical callings. For Cassian, as is typical of his monastic theology, what matters is not how one begins but how one ends: "Everything, therefore, has to do with the end [*fine*]. From its perspective, whoever has been consecrated by the beginnings of even the best conversion can find himself in an inferior position because of negligence, and

20. Cassian, *Conferences* 3.4.1 (ACW 57:121).
21. Cassian, *Conferences* 3.4.2 (ACW 57:121).
22. Cassian, *Conferences* 3.4.4 (ACW 57:121).
23. Cassian, *Conferences* 3.5.1 (ACW 57:122).

whoever has been drawn by necessity to profess the title of monk can become perfect through fear of God and diligence."[24]

What Anthony and Cassian have in common is the view that there are differing motivations, different ways that people are called. Similarly, they both acknowledge that those who live the monastic life are called. People do not simply take up this life of their own initiative, though it might look this way at times, but they are responding to a divine call. Thus, in *all* cases the monk is one who is called.

For Anthony and for Cassian, and for most Christian theologians, the genesis of the call to monastic life is Jesus's command to "be perfect, as your heavenly Father is perfect" (Matt. 5:48). Added to this is the apostle Paul's understanding that the church is God's temple, and that "temple is holy" (1 Cor. 3:17); therefore all believers need to be holy, for God is holy (1 Pet. 1:16). Despite this being a universal call to holiness, Anthony and Cassian, along with so many others, took it to mean that if one were serious about being holy, one would become a monk or nun. And though there were differ-ent ways that people were called, for those who entered the monastery the end was the same: holiness and, thereby, salvation. In one sense they were advocating for everyone to become a monastic but knew that this was not going to be the case, not because God was not calling everyone to be a monk or nun, but because only those who heard God's call clearly or those who truly feared for their soul and wished to escape damnation would ultimately enter the cloister. Most Christians would risk eternal damnation; only a few would become monks. By the time of Thomas Aquinas (d. 1274) a sentiment had arisen that a calling was not even particularly necessary for one to enter religious life. Taking seriously the call to be holy as God was holy, Aquinas believed that anyone who wanted to enter religious life should be allowed to do so, despite their "calling" and fitness for such a life.

In the second part of the second part (II-II) of the *Summa Theologiae*, Aquinas addresses the topic of entrance into religious life in ten articles. In the final article he asks whether it is praiseworthy to enter religious life without taking counsel of many and previously deliberating for a long time. He responds by saying that "long deliberation and the advice of many are required in great matters of doubt . . . while advice is unnecessary in mat-ters that are certain and fixed."[25] Aquinas then considers three points about the religious life: (1) entrance into religious life is a greater good than other

24. Cassian, *Conferences* 3.5.4 (ACW 57:123).
25. Thomas Aquinas, *Summa Theologiae* II-II, Q. 189, Art. 10, in *Summa Theologica*, 4:2009. The Latin text is available online at the Corpus Thomisticum, http://www.corpusthomisticum.org/sth0000.html.

kinds of life, so choosing to live in this manner introduces no doubt; (2) those who enter religious life rely on God's power to help them stay the course, so there should be no doubt that they can, in fact, lead the life well;[26] and (3) entrants to religious life will have to choose which religious/monastic order to join, but for this they can take counsel from individuals who will not stand in their way, thereby having no doubt as to the suitability of their decision. In this way, Aquinas reasons, there will be no doubt about the goodness of religious life, a certain and fixed form of life, thus requiring no deliberation or particular calling.

In one way Aquinas can be read as saying the following: if all Christians are to be holy, and the religious life *in particular* aids in this process of holiness, then one should become a monk or religious.[27] Simply put, it is a proverbial no-brainer. This presupposes, of course, a kind of thinking that I have critiqued elsewhere in this book about the superiority of monastic life above nonmonastic lifestyles. But if one were to agree with Aquinas about the greater goodness of religious life, then Aquinas is spot on.[28] In comparison with Anthony and Cassian, what is unique in Aquinas is the absence of an explicit call to the religious life. There is a functional pragmatism in Aquinas's theology of vocation (or at least in his theology of vocation to religious life) that Anthony and Cassian would likely not have shared. It is also a perspective that did not sit well with the Protestant Reformers, especially Martin Luther.

Martin Luther on Vocation

Nearly twelve years into the Reformation, Luther preached a sermon for the nineteenth Sunday after Trinity (i.e., October 3, 1529), in which he said,

> Our foolishness consists in laying too much stress upon the show of works and when these do not glitter as something extraordinary we regard them as of no value; and poor fools that we are, we do not see that God has attached and bound this precious treasure, namely his Word, to such common works as filial obedience, external, domestic, or civil affairs, so as to include them in his order

26. Thomas does say that those with a "special obstacle" (e.g., financial indebtedness, physical handicaps or limitations) will need to give additional consideration regarding their entrance to religious life, but he says that this deliberation should not take long; that is, it should be made quickly.

27. For Thomas a person in religious life is not perfect but tending toward it: "Those who enter the state of perfection do not profess to be perfect, but to tend to perfection." *Summa Theologiae* II-II, Q. 184, Art. 5, in *Summa Theologica*, 4:1949.

28. For a defender of Aquinas's view, see R. Butler, *Religious Vocation*. For a contemporary examination of this approach, see Jamison, *Disciples' Call*, 67–84.

and command, which he wishes us to accept, the same as though he himself had appeared from heaven. What would you do if Christ himself with all the angels were visibly to descend, and command you in your home to sweep your house and wash the pans and kettles? How happy you would feel, and would not know how to act for joy, not for the work's sake, but that you knew that thereby you were serving him, who is greater than heaven and earth.[29]

Though the day-to-day drudgery of life and work could be interpreted as something that gets in the way of a greater, more noble vocation (such as priesthood or monastic life), Luther insists otherwise. Even dishwashing and child-rearing are noble, for such "mundane" tasks could, if God so chose, be commanded by Jesus or the angels. And if they were commanded by Jesus or the angels, then we would do them *as if* they were something special, simply because they would then have a godly commandment to support them. We would even be happy to do them, says Luther. On the other hand, the German Reformer sees that these tasks and responsibilities are important and divine in and of themselves. It is not a commandment that hallows them; they are hallowed because they are bound to God's Word. They are good because God says they are good: "And God saw everything that he had made, and behold, it was very good" (Gen. 1:31). Similarly, when Luther was preaching to a group of Christian rulers, he said,

> The prince should think: Christ has served me and made everything to follow him; therefore, I should also serve my neighbor, protect him and everything that belongs to him. That is why God has given me this office, and I have it that I might serve him. That would be a good prince and ruler. When a prince sees his neighbor oppressed, he should think: That concerns me! I must protect and shield my neighbor. . . . The same is true for shoemaker, tailor, scribe, or reader. If he is a Christian tailor, he will say: I make these clothes because God has bidden me do so, so that I can earn a living, so that I can help and serve my neighbor. When a Christian does not serve the other, God is not present; that is not Christian living.[30]

Christian rulers are, in one sense, no different from other Christians serving in various other occupations—all of them are to do the work that God has

---

29. Martin Luther, "Sermon for Nineteenth Sunday after Trinity" 6, quoted in Lenker, *Writings of Martin Luther*, 14:214. Luther delivered this sermon while the Marburg Colloquium was in session. It appeared in print the following year under the title "A sermon on Christian righteousness, or the forgiveness of sins, Preached at Marburg in Hesse, 1529, Martin Luther, Wittenberg, 1530."

30. Martin Luther, "Sermon in the Castle Church at Weimar," quoted in Gaiser, "What Luther *Didn't* Say," 361. This sermon was preached on October 25, 1522, the Saturday after the eighteenth Sunday after Trinity.

given them to do to the best of their ability and talent. God deserves no less from his followers, despite the perceived esteem of their profession. There were, obviously, occupations off-limits to Christians (e.g., prostitution), but in lawful occupations a believer was to do her absolute best so as to bring honor and glory to God.

By the late Middle Ages, the language of vocation or calling was often reserved for those who entered the priesthood or monastic/religious life.[31] Conversely, for Luther,

> Vocation . . . is not a term reserved for clergy. It is an all-embracing term which relates to Luther's understanding of both creation and preservation, as well as redemption. Vocation is a critical doctrine for Luther because it serves to narrate the location of the Christian in the world and its consummation. Vocation is, above all else, a consequence of the fact that *Christ's* vocation was to embrace the world on the cross so that it might come to be what it is in the will of God. Vocation, for the faithful, flows from our participation in Christ's vocation.[32]

In Luther's thought, vocation is the way in which each believer participates in the life of Jesus Christ, especially in his death. Simply put, "vocation is the place where the cross takes form."[33] This puts vocation in relationship to baptism and baptismal vows. Each person is born into a particular *Stand*, but in baptism "we understand our *Stand* differently."[34] For Christians there is a change or a modification of *Stand*. Baptized Christians and nonbaptized individuals no longer understand their *Stand* in the same way. The Christian's *Stand* is now put into the greater context of salvation and gains an eschatological perspective: "And if I thus remain in Christ, then it is certain that for His sake my vocation, my life, and my works are also acceptable to God and are precious fruits in His sight. And though I myself am still weak in the faith, and though many frailties and sinful lusts still dwell within me and always manifest themselves, this will not be reckoned against me but will

---

31. Placher, *Callings*, 6–7. This kind of thinking also characterizes Sempé's article "Vocation."

32. Jorgensen, "Crux and Vocatio," 289 (italics original).

33. Jorgensen, "Crux and Vocatio," 289. Also, "vocation is the means by which God cruciforms the faithful at the intersection of church and world."

34. Jorgensen, "Crux and Vocatio," 291. The German word *Stand* is difficult to translate but literally means "standing position," as in one's station and status in life. It can also mean "rank" or "class" and, at times, be used in terms of one's profession. Jorgensen chooses not to translate the word because he wants to juxtapose *Stand* with *Beruf* (occupation, profession, or vocation). *Stand* includes such stations as husband or wife, son or daughter, whereas *Beruf* is a believer's earthly or spiritual work. See Wingren, *Christian's Calling*, 1–10.

be forgiven, provided I do not yield to them."[35] Allen Jorgensen summarizes Luther: "Insofar as baptism ever transforms me, it transforms my *Stand* to become my *Beruf*, or *vocation*."[36] And when a baptized believer does her *Beruf* faithfully and in a cruciform manner, then "God works through [her] working" because human persons "are the means by which God does his own work."[37] Notice that for the Christian believer one's *Stand* becomes one's *Beruf*, so that one's "ordinary" life (e.g., being a mother, daughter, or wife) is now a vocation. For Luther, the baptized Christian is not waiting for God's call in order to obtain a vocation; rather, she already has a vocation *even if* she awaits further clarity on additional vocations (e.g., becoming a minister).

Luther's whole theology of vocation is built on his understanding of the two reigns, which are the church/heaven and the world.[38] These two reigns are not in tension with each other but exist, in the words of Dietrich Bonhoeffer, with-one-another (*Miteinander*), for-one-another (*Füreinander*), and over-against-one-another (*Gegeneinander*).[39] The baptized Christian lives at the intersection of these two reigns, and his vocation "belongs to this world, not to heaven; it is directed towards one's neighbor, not toward God. . . . In his vocation one is not reaching up to God, but rather [bending] oneself down toward the world."[40] And this is partially the reason why one's vocation is not salvific; that is, being a monk or priest is not more salvific, because those vocations are not for God but for the world. Concerning the reign of the church/heaven, it is not one's vocation that is important but one's faith, for it "is faith that God wants. Faith ascends to heaven."[41] Luther explicates his theology of vocation particularly well in the *Commentary on 1 Corinthians 7*, written in 1523.

Luther's comments on 1 Corinthians 7 were penned, indirectly at least, as a response to John Faber's (d. 1541) *Opus adversus nova quaedam et a christiana religione prorsus aliena dogmata Martini Lutheri* (1521; repr., 1523). In this work Faber had laid out a reasoned defense of the superiority of celibacy over marriage. Though Luther did not respond to Faber directly, Hilton Oswald suggests that Luther "was moved more than ordinarily by the effusions of Faber to study particularly 1 Corinthians 7, the chapter on which . . . the church had

35. Martin Luther, *Sermons on the Gospel of St. John*, chap. 15 (*LW* 24:221). German text in *WA* 45:465–733 and *WA* 46:1–111.

36. Jorgensen, "Crux and Vocatio," 292.

37. Jorgensen, "Crux and Vocatio," 296.

38. Luther refers to these as the *dua regna* (two kingdoms), but I am following Jorgensen's terminology. See Jorgensen, "Crux and Vocatio," 289n26.

39. Bonhoeffer, *Ethics*, 393.

40. Wingren, *Christian's Calling*, 10.

41. Wingren, *Christian's Calling*, 10.

confidently based its views concerning the preeminence of the celibate life."[42] Luther finished the work in August 1523 and dedicated it to Hans von Löser as a wedding gift, calling it a Christian *epithalamium*, a wedding song. The Dominican Conrad Kollin responded to the commentary in 1527, but Luther never bothered to reply.

From the start, Luther's biting wit is on full display. He says that many avoid marriage because it is hard work, choosing instead "free fornication." The clergy, in particular, are the object of his invective: "Our clergy have also grasped this point and have neatly committed themselves to chastity, that is, to free fornication."[43] Furthermore, says Luther, these same clergy and defenders of celibacy suggest that women were mostly created for the purpose of fornication; that is, these men would never marry a woman, but they are happy to fornicate with her to satiate their own desires. For the gift of chastity, Luther writes, cannot be instilled from without, in spite of any rules or laws legislating the behavior of men and women. Rather, chastity "is a gift from heaven and must come from within. . . . One has to have the heart for chastity."[44] In contrast, Luther believes that the state (*Stand*) of marriage is a gift to everyone, for "before God a married woman is better than a virgin."[45] But both of these lifestyles are open to Christian believers because it is not a sin to remain celibate and unmarried, assuming one has "the grace by choice and desire to live the life of a celibate."[46] If one does not have this grace and calling, then it would be better for him to be married, for marriage is also a gift from God. In fact, "marriage and virginity are equal before [God], for both are His divine gift."[47]

When it comes to the three states of life of widowhood, matrimony, and celibacy, Luther concludes that marriage, not celibacy in a monastery, is the true religious life. Luther rejects a distinction between "religious orders" and "secular orders," suggesting that, if anything, marriage is the true religious order and the so-called religious orders are actually the true secular orders.[48] Luther understands that the married life is more wholly dependent on faith

---

42. *LW* 28:ix–x. German text is in *WA* 12:92–142.

43. Martin Luther, *Commentary on 1 Corinthians 7* (*LW* 28:5).

44. Luther, *Commentary on 1 Corinthians 7*, vv. 1–2 (*LW* 28:10).

45. Luther, *Commentary on 1 Corinthians 7*, vv. 1–2 (*LW* 28:11).

46. Luther, *Commentary on 1 Corinthians 7*, vv. 1–2 (*LW* 28:11).

47. Luther, *Commentary on 1 Corinthians 7*, vv. 6–7 (*LW* 28:16).

48. This sentiment is echoed later in the sixteenth century by many Lutherans. For example, Tübingen professors Theodor Schnepf (d. 1586) and Jacob Heerbrand (d. 1600) both taught that marriage was superior to monasticism, though Heerbrand was less critical of monasticism than Schnepf was. In fact, Heerbrand presented marriage as a kind of new monasticism. See Methuen, "Preaching and the Shaping of Public Consciousness," 187–89.

than the "traditional" religious life. Those in a monastery can expect to have their material needs met by the community and by the church, whereas those outside the monastery, living a married life, will have to support their families themselves, and do so for the remainder of their lives. "Therefore," Luther concludes, "the state of marriage is by nature of a kind to teach and compel us to trust in God's hand and grace, and in the same way it forces us to believe."[49] Using Hebrews 11:1, Luther concludes that a monk has "the certainty of things at hand," whereas a married man or woman must rely on a "conviction of things not seen."[50] Furthermore, marriage affords a couple the opportunity to do good works because it gives the couple excuse and opportunity to work with their hands. Thus, marriage includes both faith and works, whereas traditional forms of religious/monastic life afford neither, according to Luther.

Again, it is important to note that Luther did *not* reject the idea that some are called to live celibate lives; he was just extremely reluctant to think that such a demanding call was common. In fact, he says that "for every chaste [i.e., celibate] person there should be more than a hundred thousand married people."[51] Marriage was not easier per se (in fact, it was harder), but it was instituted so that those who were not able to remain celibate should have a God-given way to satisfy their needs. Consequently, it was foolish for pastors, teachers, and others to "drive young people to chastity in monasteries and nunneries" when they did not have the vocation for it.[52] And this is the main point of Luther's thought: one's *Stand* was not equivalent to one's *Beruf*. Again, to be a husband, wife, son, daughter, and so on, was to describe one's *Stand*. To be a monk, however, was to describe one's *Beruf*, and in order for that vocation to be effectual, one needs both the calling and the equipping. In this case, one needs both the call to be a monk and the supernatural calling to celibacy; failure to have both would be disastrous, leading to fornication.

When *Stand* and *Beruf* are equated, says Luther, one *Beruf* then comes to be seen as superior to another because of its supposed greater virtue. That is, even a fornicating monk is seen to be engaging in a more salutary occupation simply because, it is presumed, to be in a religious order is superior to being married. This is incorrect, Luther thinks. In his own words, "Faith and the Christian life [*Christlicher Stand*] are so free in essence that they are bound to no particular order or estate of society, but they are to be found in and throughout all orders and states. Therefore you need not accept or give

---

49. Luther, *Commentary on 1 Corinthians 7*, vv. 6–7 (*LW* 28:18).
50. Luther, *Commentary on 1 Corinthians 7*, vv. 6–7 (*LW* 28:18).
51. Luther, *Commentary on 1 Corinthians 7*, vv. 6–7 (*LW* 28:28).
52. Luther, *Commentary on 1 Corinthians 7*, vv. 6–7 (*LW* 28:28).

up any particular estate in order to be saved."[53] You do not need to forsake marriage because of some delusion that you would be more easily saved as a Cistercian. On the other hand, you do not need to be married to be saved either. Soteriologically and spiritually, it is not one or the other, since faith is the main component of salvation and the spiritual life.[54] In the end, "St. Paul considers no single estate blessed except this one—the estate of being Christian."[55] Furthermore, once a person has entered into a particular form of life, they should stay there: the married should stay married, and the unmarried should not be disturbed in their consciences that they ought to marry. Luther writes, "To be a monk is nothing, and to be a layman is also nothing; to be a priest is nothing, and to be a nun is also nothing. The layman should not become a monk, and the monk should not become a layman; all of which is to say that it should not be a matter of necessity or conscience whether one is a monk or a layman. Rather each should remain as he is, provided that faith is pure and unshaken."[56] Luther is supporting the notion that whatever lifestyle supports one's faith and spiritual growth, then that is the lifestyle that one should embrace. But if faith cannot be maintained in one's chosen lifestyle, then that lifestyle should be abandoned. Luther concludes, "All outward things are optional or free before God and . . . a Christian may make use of them as he will; he may accept them or let them go."[57]

It seems that for Luther it is not as important what you do but who you are. That is, one's primary *Stand* is to be a Christian, and one's *Beruf* should be that which gives greatest attention to one's faith and the cultivation of that faith.[58] It is erroneous, at the risk of a person's eternal salvation, to suggest that one form of life is better or more salvific than another. For those who can, should. For example, if someone has the inner disposition and calling to remain celibate, then they should, assuming they do not think it salvific and superior to other forms of life; but they should also realize that they are absolutely free to marry. For those who do not have a calling to be celibate, it is ruinous to themselves and to others that they attempt to live a celibate life in a monastery, for example. They *must* marry. First and foremost, though, all baptized believers must be people of faith, for their primary standing before God is as a Christian. *Stand* and *Beruf* complement each other; they are not

---

53. Luther, *Commentary on 1 Corinthians 7*, v. 17 (*LW* 28:39).
54. See *LW* 28:39–40.
55. Luther, *Commentary on 1 Corinthians 7*, v. 17 (*LW* 28:40).
56. Luther, *Commentary on 1 Corinthians 7*, vv. 18–19 (*LW* 28:41).
57. Luther, *Commentary on 1 Corinthians 7*, v. 24 (*LW* 28:45).
58. On how calling and *Stand* came to be equated, at least in monastic history, see Holl, "Vocation (*Beruf*)," 129–31.

in competition. It is this insight of Luther, and other Protestant Reformers, that has greatly influenced later thinking about vocation.[59]

Vocation Today

By the time of the Protestant Reformation, the term *vocatio* had been commandeered by the institution of monasticism, thus making it impossible to give a "proper religious evaluation" to nonmonastic vocations.[60] During the Middle Ages guilds had developed so that those who worked in the same trades could come together and share a common life, often spiritual in nature, but this was a far cry from highly valuing the trades themselves. Rather, this could be seen more as an attempt to be quasi-monastic, in the traditional sense of late medieval monasticism, *despite* being a carpenter or a barrel maker.[61] Medieval theologians such as Berthold of Regensberg (d. 1272) acknowledged the usefulness of the "working classes" and occupations but only because they helped those in more exalted ranks reach their higher (and, thus, better) divine calling.[62] Medieval mystics, such as Meister Eckhart (d. 1328) and Johann Tauler (d. 1361), according to Karl Holl, "took the first firm step" toward an understanding of calling as vocation (*Beruf*), but the writings of these mystics were not the texts taught in the schools, thereby limiting their influence, and they were not remotely suggesting that the institution of monasticism should be altered to reflect this insight. Namely, they were not able to escape from the very soteriological system that Luther rejected so vehemently.[63]

After the Reformation, Protestant churches continued to understand vocation in the way explicated by Luther. In the Roman Catholic context, however, vocation continued to be used primarily of those who either became priests or entered monastic/religious life. This usage endured up to the time of Vatican II even (i.e., the 1960s). As stated previously, Vatican II did recognize that every Christian believer's primary calling is to holiness.[64] Beyond that, the council documents mostly talk about vocation in terms of calling to the clerical or monastic/religious life and, even more narrowly, being called to celibacy.[65] This

---

59. See, e.g., Weber, *Protestant Ethic*, though his thesis has not been universally accepted.
60. Holl, "Vocation (*Beruf*)," 136.
61. On guilds in general, see, e.g., Rosser, *Art of Solidarity*.
62. Holl, "Vocation (*Beruf*)," 138–39. See also Thomas Aquinas, *Quaestiones de quodlibet* 7, Arts. 17–18.
63. See also Holl, "Vocation (*Beruf*)," 143, where he suggests that these mystics still saw vocation in terms of suffering, which limited their ability to truly serve others.
64. See *Lumen gentium* 2.11.
65. E.g., see *Perfectae caritatis* 12; *Optatam totius* 10; and *Presbyterorum ordinis* 11.

focus on vocation as calling to clerical or monastic/religious life is further emphasized in the annual Roman Catholic "World Day of Prayer for Vocations," which the United States Conference of Catholic Bishops describes as existing

> to publically fulfill the Lord's instruction to, "Pray the Lord of the harvest to send laborers into his harvest" (Mt 9:38; Lk 10:2). As a climax to a prayer that is continually offered throughout the Church, it affirms the primacy of faith and grace in all that concerns vocations to the priesthood and to the consecrated life. While appreciating all vocations, the Church concentrates its attention this day on vocations to the *ordained ministries* (priesthood and diaconate), to the *Religious life* in all its forms (male and female, contemplative and apostolic), to *societies of apostolic life*, to *secular institutes* in their diversity of services and membership, and to the missionary life, in the particular sense of *mission "ad gentes."*[66]

This is all appropriate, of course. Christian believers surely want an assurance that their priests/pastors, monks, nuns, and religious have been called by God. Likewise, it is important that a man and woman who decide to marry have discerned that marriage is the proper vocation for them.[67] And though the Roman Catholic Church might seem to define vocation too narrowly, Protestants could likely be accused of thinking of everything as a kind of vocation by defining it too broadly. Nonetheless, when it comes to vocation, there are, I would suggest, several important principles to note that are common to both Roman Catholic and Protestant theologies.

First, vocation involves good intention and a willingness to use all that is in one's power to carry out that intention. Perhaps another way to say this is that vocation is never entered into lightly, or unadvisedly, while waiting for something better to come along. In the sagacious words of theologian Hans Urs von Balthasar (d. 1988), "Vocation requisitions the entire life of a human being, and demands a correspondingly whole answer, and that the 'once and for all' of the surrender belongs to the fundamental form of the life of everyone who has been called."[68] There is no half or partial marriage—it is

---

66. "World Day of Prayer for Vocations," United States Conference of Catholic Bishops, http://www.usccb.org/beliefs-and-teachings/vocations/world-day-of-prayer-for-vocations.cfm (accessed November 25, 2017). There is an acknowledgment of many vocations, but it is the clerical and monastic/religious life that receives the attention.

67. Luther rejects the notion that marriage is a particular vocation (*Beruf*) in the way that being a church minister is a vocation, for example. He thinks of it rather as a *Stand* that then becomes one's *Beruf* in light of the work of Jesus Christ on the cross. However, even Pope Francis, for example, has referred to marriage as a vocation (in his address to World Youth Day Volunteers given in Brazil on July 28, 2013), and this is becoming common in theologies of marriage and family life.

68. Balthasar, "Vocation," 119.

"all in" and (ideally) indissoluble. Similarly, in the religious life, a "perpetuation of 'temporary vows' is theologically nonsensical, and allows the act of definitively giving oneself away never to take place."[69] In biblical language this is Jesus's command to "Let what you say be simply 'Yes' or 'No'; anything more than this comes from evil" (Matt. 5:37; cf. James 5:12b). If one is called to be married and is married, then one needs to be married wholeheartedly, with all the attendant difficulties and joys. If one enters religious life, then one needs to be wholly devoted to the rule, life, and apostolate(s) of the community or congregation. If one's vocation involves the taking of solemn vows (e.g., marriage, monastic life, and holy orders), then those vows need to be honored.[70] Luther talks about the "inner life of faith in the heart,"[71] and the most noble vocations are those that drive, impel, and force a person "to the most inward, highest spiritual state, to faith."[72] A true vocation is based on faith and therefore will be pursued faithfully, with all one's heart.

Second, there should be no impediments to performing one's vocation fully. These impediments could be spiritual, moral, legal, and so on. If a man is already married, then he is unable to enter into another marriage sacramentally (as well as legally).[73] In the Roman Catholic Church, if a man has taken priestly vows, he cannot enter into marriage vows without first being dispensed from his priestly vows and laicized. In many Christian traditions divorce disqualifies one from entering the priesthood or becoming a pastor. In the Anglican tradition, the man and the woman, as part of the marriage rite, are asked pointedly whether they know of any reason why they may not be united in marriage lawfully. If so, they must confess it, and the priest will determine whether he can continue performing the ceremony. Similarly, at the ordination of a priest (in the Anglican tradition) the bishop asks the ordinand's presenters: "Has he been selected in accordance with the canons of this Church? And do you believe his manner of life to be suitable to the exercise of this ministry?"[74] In other words, is he legally fit to be a priest, and

69. Balthasar, "Vocation," 119.

70. Reformation theologians would insist that only vows made freely and to God are licit and thereby worthy of keeping. For Luther that would not include lifelong monastic/religious vows, which he believed were not always made freely (e.g., because the person making them either was forced to do it by parents, teachers, or the fear of damnation, or was under the delusion that their vow taking was salvifically meritorious) and were ultimately not made to God but to the pope. See Luther, *The Judgment of Martin Luther on Monastic Vows* (LW 44:336–55).

71. Luther, *Commentary on 1 Corinthians 7*, vv. 6–7 (LW 28:17).

72. Luther, *Commentary on 1 Corinthians 7*, vv. 6–7 (LW 28:19).

73. I am making a general statement here, laying no claim to any particular Christian tradition's canon law.

74. *Book of Common Prayer*, 526.

is he personally (i.e., emotionally, physically, spiritually, ethically, etc.) fit to be a priest? To answer "no" would be to say that there is an impediment to his vocation.

The lack of impediments to the proper and full exercise of one's vocation is closely related to Ignatius of Loyola's conviction that "every vocation from God is something pure, stainless, and without mingling of the flesh or any other disordered affection."[75] Balthasar, citing this text, concludes that a vocation "is not questionable, merely possible, and therefore tormented, but rather, at the moment of the human being's definitive assent to it, it is 'one hundred percent,' and therefore calming and joyful."[76] These might seem like overly optimistic views on the surety of a person's discernment of vocation because it is (likely) universally true that despite the depth of one's conviction vis-à-vis vocation, there will be moments of doubt. As Luther acknowledges in his *Commentary on 1 Corinthians 7*, marriage is at times burdensome and difficult, causing some to want "out." But a pure and stainless vocation to marriage would preclude these burdens and difficulties from becoming justifications for seeking a divorce. In sum, "God wants a joyful giver, even when the gift perhaps increasingly becomes a cross."[77]

Third, discernment of vocation requires proper self-knowledge. In the previous chapter I showed how important self-knowledge and introspection are in Christian spirituality, and they are no less important in discernment of vocation. There is a general consensus in the modern Christian church that baptized believers are, in essence, self-determining members of society and the church. To say it differently, at some point in the early modern period (though some like to pin it on the Reformation) Western society in particular took a hard turn toward the self, in the sense of self-autonomy and even self-indulgence.[78] The rise of Freudian psychology with its understanding of the tripartite psyche, combined with the rise of democratic systems of government, inevitably led (and not always in bad ways) to the sense that the "I," as self, was of utmost importance. New and sometimes innovative justifications for civic society and civic duty were put forward, but gone were the days when someone primarily understood herself in reference to an intricate and sometimes sophisticated set of relationships.[79] Contributing to this was the rise of

75. Ignatius of Loyola, *Spiritual Exercises* 172 (Ganss, 162). See also Jamison, *Disciples' Call*, 85–93.

76. Balthasar, "Vocation," 127.

77. Balthasar, "Vocation," 127.

78. See the chapter "A Brief History of Individualism" in Urbinati, *Tyranny of the Moderns*, 49–69.

79. E.g., Cicero's "I am a Roman citizen!" (*civis romanus sum*). See Cicero, *In Verrem* 2.5.162.

the profit economy in the Middle Ages.[80] No longer did an individual need to remain close to home because that was the source of his food and well-being. With the profit economy (and the resurgence of portable currency) a person could leave home, could say goodbye to his community and strike out on his own, obtaining all he needed to survive by purchasing and selling. This was a particularly appealing option for those children born after a number of other siblings who, because of the paucity of resources, would not benefit from an inheritance of land on which to sustain themselves or their own families. All of this, along with many other factors, created a situation in which a person became independent to the point of self-autonomy and, worse, self-indulgence.

Biblically, emphasis is always on community, though not to the rejection of the individual.[81] Theologically, even the soteriological doctrine of election is communal in nature.[82] As noted by Balthasar, any Christian doctrine of vocation is rooted in the gospel since our calling as Christians—which, as we have seen, is our first and foremost calling—is an invitation to participate with God as full members of his creation. God invites and we respond. This calling is, in the first instance, a trinitarian one since we are invited to participate in the life of the Trinity, and only secondarily is it connected to the church. It is vertical before it is horizontal in that our vocation to be Christian believers comes before our individual vocations to life within the world and the church.[83] God's unique election (i.e., soteriological calling) of individuals is rooted in his plan for the world: "When God's universal plan for the world, for its creation and for its redemption, thus definitively moves into view, it becomes impossible to interpret the doctrine of election in the Old and New Covenants, with their clear preference for one individual vis-à-vis others, other than as a moment within this universal plan."[84] God's calling is always for the sake of others. He called Israel for the sake of the gentiles (Rom. 11), and the Christian church, as the "called-out ones," is also for the sake of the world. This means that each individual calling, in the modern sense of vocation, is also for the sake of others: "Every personal call within the Church [means] . . . to be called for the sake of those who . . . are not called."[85] Jesus Christ, as

80. Little, *Religious Poverty*.

81. This community is both with the Trinity and with other members of God's church. See, e.g., 1 John 1:3, 6–7.

82. Even the most impassioned Calvinist statement on an individual believer's election (the epitome, for some, of soteriological individualism) remains rooted in the concept of community, despite often being understood otherwise by both supporters and detractors of the Genevan Reformer. See Calvin, *Institutes* 3.24.1–5.

83. Balthasar, "Vocation," 112.

84. Balthasar, "Vocation," 113.

85. Balthasar, "Vocation," 113.

the one called to die for the sins of the world, is the icon of Christian calling. At the same time as believers respond to this universal call for the sake of others, we must also acknowledge that all vocation is "primarily personal, in order—from a personal assent to God—to be able to be used functionally."[86] And Christian believers are not called simply to fulfill particular roles in the church, but their callings have merit in and of themselves apart from their ecclesiastical usefulness.[87] Abraham was called (cf. Gen. 12) before there was a corporate "Israel" to be called into, and the nation of Israel is dependent on Abraham's call—had Abraham not responded positively to God's call, he would not have been the father of God's chosen people. Thus, Abraham's call was for Israel, for the sake of others.

So despite a modern emphasis on the individual in which the "I" or the "me" is more important than anyone and anything else, Christian theology posits that the "I" and the "me" only exist in relationship to others, and my very existence is for the sake of others. It is true that I may be called to a particular vocation (e.g., a priest or professor), but that vocation is for others, and it is not even my primary calling, which is to be a Christian in relationship to God the Trinity and the good world that he created. The nuts and bolts of how one discerns this "secondary" vocation (vocations, with an *s*, in Jamison's terminology) vary, though it is certainly some combination of the recognition of one's gifting, the needs of the world and how one's gifts may address those needs, and the pneumatological work of God in which the Holy Spirit writes God's will on one's heart and mind. All humans have a *Stand* and a *Beruf*, to use Luther's terms. This truth orients baptized Christian believers toward the church and the world and creates the possibility to pursue one's interests and giftedness wholeheartedly. Assuming one's choice of vocation (in the sense of a job or career) does not lead to sin or run contrary to the moral fabric of God's world, Christians may do whatever they want to do in life. And for some this means living in monastic communities.

Conclusion

In Philip Gröning's 2005 movie *Die große Stille* (released in English as *Into Great Silence*), the viewer is introduced to two novices hoping to live out their lives and their vocations as Carthusian monks of the Grande Chartreuse in France. As the film progresses, only one of those novices continues

---

86. Balthasar, "Vocation," 114.

87. In other words, ecclesial vocations (e.g., to priesthood or monastic life) are not more important than being called to be a lawyer or a retail clerk.

to make an appearance. It could be that Gröning chose to focus on only one of them, or it could be that the other novice was unsuccessful, that is, that he left the monastery when it became clear to him and the community that he did not have a vocation for Carthusian monastic life. Similarly, Nancy Klein Maguire's *An Infinity of Little Hours: Five Young Men and Their Trial of Faith in the Western World's Most Austere Monastic Order* tells the story of five Carthusian novices who entered the charterhouse of Parkminster, England, in 1960. Not all of them made it to final profession. Granted, becoming a Carthusian may be one of the most difficult things to do given the order's austerity, but the reality is that not everyone succeeds in their monastic vocation, even if they feel they have one and even if this calling is tentatively affirmed by others. The same is true, of course, outside the monastery. There is a phenomenon, at least in North America, in which many individuals decide midcareer and midlife to change professions, and sometimes quite radically. In fact, some suggest there is an "existential necessity" for this midlife change.[88] There are many reasons for this, to be sure, such as boredom, anxiety, the prospect of financial gain, a significant life event (such as divorce), being dismissed by one company and unable to find another job in the same field, and so on. But surely another reason for this is the realization that one has been in the wrong vocation. Despite my limited experience, I have met more than one monk who came to the monastery later in life, after a career in business and/or being widowed, for example. These later-in-life vocations to monasticism and priesthood used to be rather rare but are becoming more and more common.

Young people today often make decisions without a sense of vocation. Their decision-making faculties are fairly subjective. It is not uncommon in my profession as a university professor of undergraduates to have quite a few seniors come to me for the express purpose of talking about their future. Many of the conversations begin like this: "I am graduating in a few months, and I don't know what I am going to do." Having had this experience enough times over the years to develop a "strategy" for this conversation, I often respond with, "Well, what led you to major in _____?" Unfortunately the answer I am often given is "It seemed interesting" or, worse, "This was really what my parents wanted me to do." Now, one's choice of university major as an eighteen-year-old does not need to then dictate one's career choice at the age of twenty-two or later. But it would seem that these two choices would be naturally and necessarily connected to each other. The adage "Major in whatever you want because you can always do whatever you want later" seems

88. Strenger and Ruttenberg, "Existential Necessity."

outdated. The reality is that there may be few jobs to be had directly out of university, and the ones that are available may not match the qualifications received in one's chosen field of study.

What seems, at least to me, to be a better way of navigating life would be to immerse oneself in the difficult process of vocational discernment and to do so as early and as intentionally as possible. Martin Luther chastises teachers who (erroneously) sway impressionable students toward the monastic life without knowing whether they have a genuine vocation to such a life.[89] That is foolish and will lead only to frustration and failure. The discernment of vocation will be difficult and may not be without its share of false starts and tangents.[90] But if believers have a "secondary" vocation (*Beruf*) beyond their general vocation of being Christians (*Stand*), then they need the structures to live out these vocations. Because vocations are divine, there are any number of vocations that a person could be called to do that would please God. To assist us, God has given us the Holy Spirit, holy persons, and practical wisdom to discern which of these vocations we should pursue and when we should pursue them. If, as a result of this discernment, a woman or man determines that becoming an enclosed monk or nun (as compared to an interiorized monk) is their calling, then they need the structures to live out that calling. Accordingly, in order for them to live in this manner, there need to be monasteries. Hence, institutional monasticism is necessary.

Cistercian monk Thomas Merton (d. 1968) once wrote, "A man knows when he has found his vocation when he stops thinking about how to live and begins to live."[91] An interesting quote considering Merton himself spent seasons of his life somewhat tortured about his own monastic calling. Not only did he wrestle with the very meaning of monasticism, but he also felt deeply that much of what was passing for monasticism was not a deep, true monasticism and was not meaningful for the modern era. Further, he was not always convinced that he should be a Trappist. In the mid-1950s he attempted to move from his abbey of Gethsemani in Kentucky to the Italian monastery of Camaldoli, which he idealized as a place of monastic peace. Ultimately he did not leave Gethsemani but instead discovered his vocation as a hermit, so his superior allowed him to move into a hermitage near the monastery. The moral of the story, if you will, is that those called to the monastic life need a place in which to live out their divine calling. And that means monastic structures

89. Luther, *1 Corinthians 7*, vv. 8b–9 (*LW* 28:21–31).

90. I once took a "vocational aptitude test" that told me I should drive tractor-trailers simply because I liked to travel and enjoyed being alone. As noble a profession as that may be, I cannot imagine enjoying such a vocation on the sole basis of those two character qualities.

91. Merton, *Thoughts in Solitude*, 84.

and institutionalized monasticism need to exist. Interiorized monasticism is not enough, though all Christians are to be interiorized monks.

Though the how and the why of monasticism's genesis is complex, and though the church misunderstood the purpose of monasticism when it assigned it salvific merit, and though the reasons for the continuation of monasticism are multifaceted, it seems reasonable to me to see the need for monasticism as intimately connected to the work that God is doing in the lives of particular people vis-à-vis vocation—people whom God is calling to be the next monks and nuns, people who will need a place to live out their calling. Institutional monasticism is as necessary today as it has always been, not because it is historical and therefore should be maintained or because it is the fast track to salvation, but because God keeps calling people to this unique vocation. Monasticism exists for vocation's sake, and because vocation is from God, monasticism exists for God's sake.

EPILOGUE

In December 2016 the Benedictine monks of Conception Abbey in the United States posted an article on their website titled "5 Ways to Live Like a Monk in the World."[1] The five suggested ways are to (1) cultivate silence, (2) be faithful to daily prayer, (3) form authentic community, (4) make time for *lectio divina*,[2] and (5) practice humility. In one sense these practices are just good Christian practices; that is, there is nothing particularly monastic about them. Jesus models silence when he goes away from the crowds and his disciples to pray (e.g., Luke 5:16). The Acts of the Apostles depicts the ideal Christian church as one in which its members will be in deep communion with one another ("All who believed were together and had all things in common" [Acts 2:44]) and will join together to meditate on and devote themselves to the apostles' teaching (Acts 2:42). Moreover, Christians have always taught that humility is a *sine qua non* of holiness and proper spiritual living because it, among the virtues, is so distinctly christological (e.g., Phil. 2:1–11). Nevertheless, because the article was posted by a monastery, one can surmise that these five things—silence, prayer, community, *lectio divina*, and humility—"make" monasticism (at least according to the monks of Conception Abbey). Yet each of these can and should be done by every baptized Christian believer. And this reinforces the point that I have been making throughout much of this book: all monks are Christians and all Christians are monks, though most monks do not live in a monastery proper but live monastically interiorly.

1. Fr. Paul Sheller, "5 Ways to Live Like a Monk in the World," Conception Abbey, December 14, 2016, https://www.conceptionabbey.org/5-ways-live-like-monk-world.
2. *Lectio divina* (divine reading) is a slow, contemplative praying of the Christian Scriptures that enables the Word of God to become a means of union with God. See M. Casey, *Sacred Reading*; and Wilhoit and Howard, *Discovering Lectio Divina*.

Yet this can sound reductionistic (though I hope the contents of this book demonstrate otherwise), and, perhaps worse, this can sound deconstructive or even destructive, issuing forth, à la sixteenth-century England, in a dissolution of the monasteries. However, I am no iconoclast. What I hope to have shown in this book is that I am not advocating or defending a deconstructive project that seeks to strip historic monasticism of its meaning and relevance. Rather, my theology of monasticism is a constructive one, attempting to forge a theology of monasticism and spirituality that is applicable to the entire Christian church—Protestant, Roman Catholic, and Eastern Orthodox. Consequently, the theology of monasticism that I have put forth is done in a spirit of humility, not in competition with but as a complement to other theologies of monasticism and the spiritual life, especially those born from confessional perspectives (e.g., Roman Catholic and Eastern Orthodox theologies of monasticism).

It is very common for Protestants, especially those in the "free church" tradition (e.g., Baptists and Presbyterians), to be accused of being ahistorical (or even antihistorical), suggesting that these churches and their members are oblivious or antagonistic to the historical development of the Christian church.[3] Though this accusation is not always without merit, it is frequently exaggerated. It is true, however, that monasticism has often been maligned by Protestants[4] despite Martin Luther's and John Calvin's measured assessments of the institution.[5] And this deleterious perspective of monasticism has impoverished Protestant spiritual life and practice. In its place has arisen other means of spiritual formation, such as Christian camps and conferences, parachurch ministries, and pseudo-monastic intentional communities (e.g., the erroneously named "New Monasticism").[6] However, there is now more momentum than perhaps ever among Protestants (with the possible exception of nineteenth-century Anglicanism) for the reintroduction of institutional monasticism. For example, the Anglican Church in North America is actively in discussion with particular Roman Catholic monastic/religious communities about the possibility of Anglican aspirants to the monastic life to receive their initial formation in these communities, with the understanding that these women and men will not become Roman Catholic monastics.[7] In light of this kind of movement, there is a need for a historically and theologically

3. See D. Williams, *Retrieving the Tradition*, and D. Williams, *Free Church*.
4. See, e.g., Kollar, "'Punch' and the Nuns."
5. Peters, *Reforming the Monastery*, 19–48.
6. See Rutba House, *School(s) for Conversion*, and Wilson-Hartgrove, *New Monasticism*.
7. There is historical precedence for this kind of Roman Catholic-Anglican monastic assistance. See Anson, *Benedictines of Caldey*.

grounded Protestant theology of monasticism, and this book is an attempt to provide that historical and theological foundation.

All the while, however, I have also been motivated to offer a theology of monasticism that is consistent with monasticism's presence in Roman Catholicism and Eastern Orthodoxy and that is not in conflict with their respective theological commitments. In other words, what I am putting forward is an ecumenical theology of monasticism.[8] I have noticed over the years that often a person's definition or understanding of monasticism is influenced by their own commitments, not only theological but practical as well. This is true, for example, of Protestantism's New Monastic movement, which is really an exercise in communal living, something more akin to Dorothy Day's Catholic Worker Movement.[9] These folks adopt the communal living structures of historic monasticism (e.g., having belongings in common and common prayer), but they fixate more on "doing" social justice than on personal transformation and union with God *by way of* living in community.[10] And this focus on spiritual progress and union with God is historic monasticism's *telos*: "The goal of monastic life . . . is to be united to God by Grace, to be 'divinized,' all of his fervor is directed toward cleansing his heart of the passions and making it a bright throne and chamber where the Holy Trinity might dwell."[11] But monks and nuns, those living the daily nuts-and-bolts routine of monastic life, sometimes also present monasticism in terms that are more practical than theological. That seems to be true in the "5 Ways to Live Like a Monk in the World" from Conception Abbey. By *doing* these things, you will be like a monk. But in the words of Louis Bouyer, "What really distinguishes monks *qua* monks is not an external function. . . . The meaning of monastic

8. I am using "ecumenical" here in the best sense of the word, that is, as something that strives to bring about the kind of unity prayed for by Jesus to his heavenly Father in John 17. This is a unity rooted in the oneness of God's being ("We believe in one God"), the integrity and consistency of God's truth (e.g., Rom. 1), and the work of the Holy Spirit in Christian believers and the church (e.g., bringing Jewish and gentile believers together as one people of God [see, e.g., Rom. 9–11]).

9. Day, *Loaves and Fishes*.

10. This is *not* to say that social justice is not a monastic concern, but it is historically not an essential condition of monasticism. For example, it is true that in the fourth century care of the nonmonastic sick and assistance to Christian pilgrims were part of the warp and woof of Basilian monasticism. See in general Constantelos, *Byzantine Philanthropy*, esp. chap. 7. However, apart from welcoming guests as if they were Christ himself, the *Rule of Benedict*, perhaps history's most influential monastic rule, has little to say about how monks are to assist those in need. It is not silent, but it offers little concrete guidance.

11. Metropolitan Cyprian of Oropos and Fili, *Monastic Life*, 18–19. This, as Metropolitan Cyprian acknowledges, is the goal, of course, of all Christian believers, but it is the particular goal of the monastic.

life will be found in a reality which is fundamentally interior."[12] Likewise, "the search, the true search, in which the whole of one's being is engaged, not for some thing but for some One: the search for God—that is the beginning and end of monasticism."[13] Outward practices are merely aids to the greater end of union with God. Accordingly, monasticism cannot be reduced to its external forms, which also means that its historical external forms are exactly that—historical.[14]

What I have offered here is a theology of monasticism that attempts to rise above unnecessary ecclesiastical entanglements and the particular historical ways in which institutional monasticism manifests itself (e.g., as Benedictine, Cistercian, or Athonite) to get to the historical and theological heart of the God-given gift of monasticism. I have tried, hopefully successfully, to peel back the extraneous layers of monastic historicism and theological "hagiography" so that the institution can be seen in a fresh light, as a movement intimately connected to the day-in and day-out working of the Christian church and to all Christian believers. I have tried to show that there are not monks (a kind of spiritual elite) and then all other baptized Christian disciples (the lesser-sanctified hoi polloi). I have tried to show instead that the baptismal priest-hood of all believers means that there are monks and then there are . . . well, more monks. In the words of Fyodor Dostoevsky, by way of Father Zosima, "For monks are not a different sort of men, but only such as all men on earth ought also to be."[15] Some monks live in monasteries, adopting a distinctive dress or lifestyle and taking vows, while other interiorized monks live in the *saeculum*, wearing suits like Alyosha while fulfilling their God-given *Stand* and living wholly into their God-given vocations (*Beruf*). All the while both types of monks are working out their own salvation with fear and trembling (Phil. 2:12). All of these monks (i.e., all baptized Christians), *as monks*, must be pursuing God single-mindedly, navigating the challenges and successes of the Christian spiritual life in brick-and-mortar monasteries and/or in the "world" all the same.

It is true, though, that those called to institutionalized monasticism are living out the commands and demands of the gospel as fully and integrally as possible.[16] In the words of Bouyer, "What distinguishes the monk from the

12. Bouyer, *Meaning of the Monastic Life*, 5.
13. Bouyer, *Meaning of the Monastic Life*, 8.
14. Peifer, *Monastic Spirituality*, 25: "In every form of religious life a distinction must be made between the basic ideology, the theory according to which the various means of perfection are harmoniously organized in pursuit of the goal, and the institutions, which are the concrete implementation of this theory in particular structures."
15. Dostoevsky, *Brothers Karamazov*, 164.
16. This is Paul Evdokimov's "eschatological maximalism." *Ages of the Spiritual Life*, 233.

Christian who is not such, is that he binds himself not only to the principle of renunciation (everybody is bound to this by baptism), but to its effective reality, a reality as immediate as possible."[17] The apostle Paul was simply right when he said the "unmarried man is anxious about the things of the Lord, how to please the Lord. But the married man is anxious about worldly things, how to please his wife, and his interests are divided. And the unmarried or betrothed woman is anxious about the things of the Lord, how to be holy in body and spirit. But the married woman is anxious about worldly things, how to please her husband" (1 Cor. 7:32–34). Thus, institutional monasticism provides for those who have the gift and calling to be enclosed monks so that they can be "anxious about the things of the Lord." At the same time, interiorized monks will continue to grow spiritually in spite of having divided interests. For, in God's divine plan and because of his ongoing providential care, this is the way it is supposed to be. Again in the words of the apostle Paul, all of this is for our "own benefit" (1 Cor. 7:35). Institutional monastic life and interiorized monastic life are simply two sides of the same coin—and that coin is the baptized Christian life. Both are necessary, and both give glory to God.

---

17. Bouyer, *Meaning of the Monastic Life*, 46–47.

BIBLIOGRAPHY

Adam, Alfred. "Grundbegriffe des Mönchtums in sprachlicher Sicht." *Zeitschrift für Kirchengeschichte* 65 (1953/54): 209–39.

Addison, James Thayer. *The Medieval Missionary: A Study of the Conversion of Northern Europe AD 500–1300*. New York: International Missionary Council, 1936.

Aelred of Rievaulx. *Mirror of Charity*. Translated by Elizabeth Connor. Kalamazoo, MI: Cistercian Publications, 1990.

Alfeyev, Hilarion. *St. Symeon the New Theologian and Orthodox Tradition*. Oxford: Oxford University Press, 2000.

Anizor, Uche, and Hank Voss. *Representing Christ: A Vision for the Priesthood of All Believers*. Downers Grove, IL: IVP Academic, 2016.

Anson, Peter F. *The Benedictines of Caldey: The Story of the Anglican Benedictines of Caldey and Their Submission to the Catholic Church*. London: Burns, Oates & Washbourne, 1940.

Antony, Saint. *The Letters of Saint Antony the Great*. Translated by Derwas J. Chitty. Oxford: SLG, 1975.

Athanasius. *The Life of Antony and the Letter to Marcellinus*. Translated by Robert C. Gregg. Classics of Western Spirituality. New York: Paulist Press, 1980.

Augustine. *The City of God against the Pagans*. Translated and edited by R. W. Dyson. Cambridge: Cambridge University Press, 1998.

———. *Confessions*. Translated by Henry Chadwick. Oxford: Oxford University Press, 1991.

———. *Expositions of the Psalms 121–150*. Translated by Maria Boulding. The Works of Saint Augustine: A Translation for the 21st Century 3/20. Hyde Park, NY: New City Press, 2004.

————. *Marriage and Virginity: The Excellence of Marriage, Holy Virginity, The Excellence of Widowhood, Adulterous Marriages, Continence.* Translated by Ray Kearney. The Works of Saint Augustine: A Translation for the 21st Century 1/9. Hyde Park, NY: New City Press, 1999.

Balthasar, Hans Urs von. "Vocation." *Communio: International Catholic Review* 37 (2010): 111–28.

Bardy, G. "Apatheia." In *Dictionnaire de Spiritualité, Tome I,* 727–46. Paris: Beauchesne, 1937.

Barnes, Timothy D. *Constantine and Eusebius.* Cambridge, MA: Harvard University Press, 1981.

Barth, Peter, and Wilhelm Niesel, eds. *Joannis Calvini opera selecta.* Munich: C. Kaiser, 1926–59.

Basil, Saint. *Ascetical Works.* Translated by M. Monica Wagner. Fathers of the Church 9. Washington, DC: Catholic University of America Press, 1962.

Bede. *A History of the English Church and People.* Translated by Leo Sherley-Price. Harmondsworth, UK: Penguin Books, 1968.

Behr, John. *Asceticism and Anthropology in Irenaeus and Clement.* Oxford: Oxford University Press, 2000.

Bell, David N. *Understanding Rancé: The Spirituality of the Abbot of La Trappe in Context.* Kalamazoo, MI: Cistercian Publications, 2005.

Bériou, Nicole. "Robert de Sorbon." In *Dictionnaire de Spiritualité, Tome XIII,* 816–24. Paris: Beauchesne, 1987.

Bériou Nicole, and David L. d'Avray. "Henry of Provins, O. P.'s Comparison of the Dominican and Franciscan Orders with the 'Order' of Matrimony." In *Modern Questions about Medieval Sermons: Essays on Marriage, Death, History and Sanctity*, edited by Nicole Bériou and David L. d'Avray, 71–75. Spoleto: Centro italiano de studi sull'alto medioevo; Florence: S.I.S.M.E.L., 1994.

Bernard of Clairvaux. *Monastic Sermons.* Translated by Daniel Griggs. Collegeville, MN: Cistercian Publications, 2016.

————. *Sermons for Lent and the Easter Season.* Translated by Irene Edmonds. Collegeville, MN: Cistercian Publications, 2013.

————. *Sermons on Conversion: On Conversion, A Sermon to Clerics and Lenten Sermons on the Psalm "He Who Dwells."* Translated by Marie-Bernard Saïd. Kalamazoo, MI: Cistercian Publications, 1981.

————. *Treatises II: The Steps of Humility and Pride/On Loving God.* Translated by Robert Walton. Kalamazoo, MI: Cistercian Publications, 1980.

Besserman, Lawrence. *Sacred and Secular in Medieval and Early Modern Cultures: New Essays.* New York: Palgrave Macmillan, 2006.

Blake, N. F., ed. *Middle English Religious Prose.* London: E. Arnold, 1972.

Bloesch, Donald G. *Centers of Christian Renewal*. Philadelphia: United Church Press, 1964.

Boffey, Julia. "The Charter of the Abbey of the Holy Ghost and Its Role in Manuscript Anthologies." *The Yearbook of English Studies* 33 (2003): 120–30.

Bonhoeffer, Dietrich. *Ethics*. Translated by Ilse Tödt et al. Minneapolis: Fortress, 2005.

Bonner, Gerald. "Libido and Concupiscentia in St. Augustine." Studia Patristica 6 (1962): 303–14.

The Book of Common Prayer. New York: Seabury Press, 1979.

Boulton, Matthew Myer. *Life in God: John Calvin, Practical Formation, and the Future of Protestant Theology*. Grand Rapids: Eerdmans, 2011.

Bouquet, Martin, ed. *Recueil des historiens des Gaules et de la France, Tome 20*. Paris: Imprimerie Royale, 1840.

Bouyer, Louis. *The Meaning of the Monastic Life*. London: Burns & Oates, 1955.

Brady, G. "Apatheia." In *Dicionnaire de Spiritualité, Tome I*, edited by Marcel Viller et al., 727–46. Paris: Beauchesne, 1937.

Brock, Sebastian P. "Die Übersetzungen des Alten Testaments ins Griechische." In *Theologische Realenzyklopädie*, vol. 6, *Bibel—Böhmen und Mähren*, edited by Gerhard Krause and Gerhard Müller, 163–72. Berlin: Walter de Gruyter, 1980.

Bumazhnov, D. F. "Some Further Observations Concerning the Early History of the Term ΜΟΝΑΧΟΣ (Monk)." In Studia Patristica 45 (2010): 21–26.

Burnell, Peter. "Concupiscence." In *Augustine through the Centuries: An Encyclopedia*, edited by Allan D. Fitzgerald, 224–27. Grand Rapids: Eerdmans, 1999.

Burr, David. *The Spiritual Franciscans: From Protest to Persecution in the Century after Saint Francis*. University Park: Pennsylvania State University Press, 2001.

Butler, Cuthbert. *The Lausiac History of Palladius*. Cambridge: Cambridge University Press, 1898.

———. *Western Mysticism: The Teaching of SS. Augustine, Gregory and Bernard on Contemplation and the Contemplative Life*. 2nd ed. London: E. P. Dutton, 1926.

Butler, Richard. *Religious Vocation: An Unnecessary Vocation*. Chicago: H. Regnery, 1961.

Cahill, Thomas. *How the Irish Saved Civilization: The Untold Story of Ireland's Heroic Role from the Fall of Rome to the Rise of Medieval Europe*. New York: Nan A. Talese, 1995.

Calvin, John. *Institutes of the Christian Religion*. Edited by John T. McNeill. Translated by Ford Lewis Battles. Philadelphia: Westminster, 1960.

Cameron, Michael. "*Enarrationes in Psalmos*." In *Augustine through the Centuries: An Encyclopedia*, edited by Allan D. Fitzgerald, 290–96. Grand Rapids: Eerdmans, 1999.

Caner, Daniel F. *Wandering, Begging Monks: Spiritual Authority and the Promotion of Monasticism in Late Antiquity*. Berkeley: University of California Press, 2002.

———. "'Not of This World': The Invention of Monasticism." In *A Companion to Late Antiquity*, edited by Philip Rousseau, 588–600. Oxford: Wiley-Blackwell, 2009.

Cantor, Norman F. "The Crisis of Western Monasticism, 1050–1130." *American Historical Review* 66 (1960): 47–67.

Cary, Phillip. "Interiority." In *Augustine through the Centuries: An Encyclopedia*, edited by Allan D. Fitzgerald, 454–56. Grand Rapids: Eerdmans, 1999.

Casey, Michael. *Sacred Reading: The Art of* Lectio Divina. Liguori, MO: Liguori/ Triumph, 1995.

Casey, Robert P. "Clement of Alexandria and the Beginnings of Christian Platonism." *Harvard Theological Review* 18 (1925): 39–101.

———. "Early Russian Monasticism." *Orientalia Christiana Periodica* 19 (1953): 372–423.

Cassian, John. *The Conferences*. Translated by Boniface Ramsey. Ancient Christian Writers 57. New York: Newman, 1997.

———. *The Institutes*. Translated by Boniface Ramsey. Ancient Christian Writers 58. New York: Newman, 2000.

Catherine of Siena. *The Dialogue*. Translated by Suzanne Noffke. Classics of Western Spirituality. New York: Paulist Press, 1980.

Chadwick, Henry. "The Ascetic Ideal in the History of the Church." In *Monks, Hermits and the Ascetic Tradition*, edited by W. J. Sheils, 1–23. Oxford: Basil Blackwell, 1985.

Chambon, Félix. *Robert de Sorbon: De consciencia et De tribus dietis*. Paris: Alphonse Picard et Fils, 1902.

Choat, Malcolm. "The Development and Usage of Terms for 'Monk' in Late Antique Egypt." *Jahrbuch für Antike und Christentum* 45 (2002): 5–23.

Cholij, Roman. *Theodore the Stoudite: The Ordering of Holiness*. Oxford: Oxford University Press, 2002.

Clark, James G., ed. *The Religious Orders in Pre-Reformation England*. Woodbridge, UK: Boydell, 2002.

Clark, J. P. H., and C. Taylor, eds. *Walter Hilton's Latin Writings*. 2 vols. Salzburg: Institut für Anglistik und Amerikanistik, 1987.

Clement of Alexandria. *Christ the Educator*. Translated by Simon P. Wood. Fathers of the Church 23. Washington, DC: Catholic University of America Press, 1954.

Coakley, Sarah, and Charles M. Stang, eds. *Re-Thinking Dionysius the Areopagite*. Chichester, UK: Wiley-Blackwell, 2009.

Cohn, Norman. *The Pursuit of the Millennium: Revolutionary Millenarians and Mystical Anarchists of the Middle Ages*. Rev. and expanded ed. New York: Oxford University Press, 1970.

Congar, Yves M. J. *Lay People in the Church*. Rev. ed. Translated by Donald Attwater. Westminster, MD: Christian Classics, 1965.

Consacro, D. Peter. "The Author of the Abbey of the Holy Ghost: A Popularizer of the Mixed Life." *Fourteenth Century English Mystical Writers Newsletter* 2 (1976): 15–20.

———. "A Critical Edition of *The Abbey of the Holy Ghost* from All Known Extant English Manuscripts with Introduction, Notes and Glossary." PhD diss., Fordham University, 1971.

Constable, Giles. *The Abbey of Cluny: A Collection of Essays to Mark the Eleven-Hundredth Anniversary of Its Foundation*. Berlin: Lit Verlag, 2010.

———. *Three Studies in Medieval Religious and Social Thought: The Interpretation of Mary and Martha, The Ideal of the Imitation of Christ, The Orders of Society*. Cambridge: Cambridge University Press, 1995.

Constable, Giles, and B. Smith, eds. and trans. *Libellus de diversis ordinibus et professionibus qui sunt in Aecclesia*. Oxford: Clarendon, 1972.

Constantelos, Demetrios J. *Byzantine Philanthropy and Social Welfare*. New Brunswick, NJ: Rutgers University Press, 1968.

Cyril of Scythopolis. *Lives of the Monks of Palestine*. Translated by R. M. Price. Kalamazoo, MI: Cistercian Publications, 1991.

Dabin, Paul. *Le sacerdoce royal des fidèles dans la tradition ancienne et modern*. Paris: Desclée, De Brouwer, 1950.

Dagron, Gilbert. "La Vie ancienne de saint Marcel l'Acémète." *Analecta Bollandiana* 86, nos. 1–2 (1968): 271–321.

Damian, Theodor. "The Desert as a Place of the World's Transformation according to Eastern Asceticism." In *Monastic Tradition in Eastern Christianity and the Outside World: A Call for Dialogue*, edited by Ines Angeli Murzaku, 55–66. Leuven: Peeters, 2013.

Dante Alighieri. *The Inferno*. Translated by Anthony Esolen. New York: Modern Library, 2002.

Darrouzès, Jean, ed. *Syméon le Nouveau Théologien: Traités théologiques et éthiques* [4–15]. Paris: Cerf, 1967.

Dawson, Christopher, ed. *Mission to Asia: Narratives and Letters of the Franciscan Missionaries in Mongolia and China in the Thirteenth and Fourteenth Centuries*. New York: Harper & Row, 1966.

Day, Dorothy. *Loaves and Fishes*. Maryknoll, NY: Orbis Books, 1963.

Diekstra, Frans N. M. "Robert de Sorbon on Men, Women and Marriage: The Testimony of His *De Matrimonio* and Other Works." In *People and Texts: Relationships in Medieval Literature: Studies Presented to Erik Kooper*, edited by Thea Summerfield and Keith Busby, 67–85. Amsterdam: Rodopi, 2007.

———. "Robert de Sorbon's *Cum repetes (De modo audiendi confessiones et interrogandi)*." *Recherches de théologie et philosophie médiévales* 66 (1999): 79–153.

———. "Robert de Sorbon's *De consciencia*: Truncated Text and Full Text." *Recherches de théologie et philosophie médiévales* 70 (2003): 22–117.

———. "Robert de Sorbon's *Qui vult vere confiteri* (ca. 1260–74) and Its French Versions." *Recherches de théologie et philosophie médiévales* 60 (1993): 215–72.

Donkin, R. A. "Cistercian Sheep-Farming and Wool-Sales in the Thirteenth Century." *Agricultural History Review* 6 (1958): 2–8.

Dostoevsky, Fyodor. *The Brothers Karamazov*. Translated by Richard Pevear and Larissa Volokhonsky. New York: Farrar, Straus & Giroux, 1990.

Driscoll, Martha E. "The Monastic Community: Ecclesiola in Ecclesia." *Cistercian Studies Quarterly* 38 (2003): 211–24.

Dubuisson, Daniel. "L'Irlande et la théorie médiévale des 'trois orders.'" *Revue de l'histoire des religions* 188 (1975): 35–63.

Duby, Georges. *The Three Orders: Feudal Society Imagined*. Translated by Arthur Goldhammer. Chicago: University of Chicago Press, 1980.

Dunn, Marilyn. *The Emergence of Monasticism: From the Desert Fathers to the Early Middle Ages*. Oxford: Blackwell, 2000.

Dysinger, Luke. "Asceticism and Mystical Theology." In *The Oxford Handbook of Mystical Theology*, edited by Edward Howells and Mark McIntosh. Oxford: Oxford University Press, forthcoming.

Eastwood, Cyril. *The Priesthood of All Believers: An Examination of the Doctrine from the Reformation to the Present Day*. Minneapolis: Augsburg, 1962.

———. *The Royal Priesthood of the Faithful: An Investigation of the Doctrine from Biblical Times to the Reformation*. Minneapolis: Augsburg, 1963.

Elisabeth of Schönau. *The Complete Works*. Translated by Anne L. Clark. New York: Paulist Press, 2000.

Elliott, John H. *The Elect and the Holy: An Exegetical Examination of 1 Peter 2:4-10 and the Phrase "Baseleion Hierateuma."* Leiden: Brill, 1966.

———. *1 Peter: A New Translation with Introduction and Commentary*. The Anchor Bible. New York: Doubleday, 2000.

Enders, Ludwig. *Luther und Emser: Ihre Streitschriften aus dem Jahre 1521*. 2 vols. Halle: Max Niemeyer, 1890–92.

Eusebius. *The Ecclesiastical History*. Vol. 1. Translated by Kirsopp Lake. Loeb Classical Library 153. Cambridge, MA: Harvard University Press, 1926.

Evdokimov, Paul. *Ages of the Spiritual Life*. Crestwood, NY: St. Vladimir's Seminary Press, 1998.

———. "Le monachisme intériorisé." In *Le millénaire du Mont Athos 963–1963: Études et mélanges I*, 331–52. Chevetogne: Éditions de Chevetogne, 1963–64.

———. *The Sacrament of Love: The Nuptial Mystery in the Light of the Orthodox Tradition*. Crestwood, NY: St. Vladimir's Seminary Press, 1985.

Fagerberg, David W. "Liturgical Asceticism: Enlarging Our Grammar of Liturgy." *Pro Ecclesia* 13 (2004): 202–14.

———. *On Liturgical Asceticism.* Washington, DC: Catholic University of America Press, 2013.

———. *Theologia Prima: What Is Liturgical Theology?* 2nd ed. Chicago: Hillenbrand, 2004.

Finn, Richard. *Asceticism in the Graeco-Roman World.* Cambridge: Cambridge University Press, 2009.

Foucault, Michel. *The Use of Pleasure.* Translated by Robert Hurley. New York: Vintage Books, 1985.

Fraade, Steven D. "Ascetical Aspects of Ancient Judaism." In *Jewish Spirituality: From the Bible through the Middle Ages*, edited by Arthur Green, 253–88. New York: Crossroad, 1986.

Francis of Assisi and Clare of Assisi. *Francis and Clare: The Complete Works.* Translated by Regis J. Armstrong and Ignatius C. Brady. Classics of Western Spirituality. New York: Paulist Press, 1982.

Frank, Karl Suso. *Angelikos Bios: Begriffsanalytische und begriffsgeschichtliche Untersuchung zum "engelgleichen Leben" im frühen Mönchtum.* Münster im Westfalen: Aschendorff, 1964.

Frend, W. H. C. "The *Cellae* of the African Circumcellions." *Journal of Theological Studies* 3 (1952): 87–89.

———. "Circumcellions and Monks." *Journal of Theological Studies* 20 (1969): 542–49.

Fry, Timothy, ed. *RB 1980: The Rule of St. Benedict in Latin and English with Notes.* Collegeville, MN: Liturgical Press, 1981.

Gabriel, Astrik L. *The Paris Studium: Robert of Sorbonne and His Legacy.* Frankfurt am Main: Verlag Josef Knecht, 1992.

Gaiser, Frederick J. "What Luther *Didn't* Say about Vocation." *Word & World* 25, no. 4 (2005): 359–61.

Gippius, Anna. *Sviatoi Tikhon Zadonskii: episkop Voronezhskii i vseia Rossii chudotvorets.* Paris: YMCA Press, 1927.

Glorieux, P. *Aux origines de la Sorbonne I: Robert de Sorbon.* Paris: J. Vrin, 1966.

Goehring, James E. *Ascetics, Society, and the Desert: Studies in Early Egyptian Monasticism.* Harrisburg, PA: Trinity Press International, 1999.

Golitzin, Alexander. *Mystagogy: A Monastic Reading of Dionysius Areopagita.* Edited by Bogdan G. Bucur. Collegeville, MN: Liturgical Press, 2013.

Goodrich, Richard J. *Contextualizing Cassian: Aristocrats, Asceticism, and Reformation in Fifth-Century Gaul.* Oxford: Oxford University Press, 2007.

Gori, Franco, ed. *Augustinus: Enarrationes in Psalmos 119–133*. Corpus Scriptorum Ecclesiasticorum Latinorum 95.3. Vienna: Verlag der österreichischen Akademie der Wissenschaften, 2001.

Gorodetzky, Nadejda. *St. Tikhon of Zadonsk*. Crestwood, NY: St. Vladimir's Seminary Press, 1976.

Griffith, Sidney H. "Asceticism in the Church of Syria: The Hermeneutics of Early Syrian Monasticism." In *Asceticism*, edited by Vincent L. Wimbush and Richard Valantasis, 220–45. Oxford: Oxford University Press, 1998.

Griggs, Daniel K. "Religious Experience in Symeon the New Theologian's Hymns." PhD diss., University of Leeds, 1999.

Guibert, J. de. "La notion d'ascèse, d'ascétisme." In *Dictionnaire de Spiritualité, Tome I*, 936–38. Paris: Beauchesne, 1937.

Guillaumont, Antoine. *Aux origines du monachisme chrétien: Pour une phénoménologie du monachisme*. Bégrolles en Mauges: Abbaye de Bellefontaine, 1979.

Hallinger, Kassius, ed. *Corpus Consuetudinum Monasticarum, Tomus I: Initia Consuetudinis Benedictinae*. Siegburg: Verlag Franz Schmitt, 1963.

Hanron, Margaret Mary. "Evolution of the Teaching on Commitment by Monastic Vow: Cluny to the End of the 19th Century." *Cistercian Studies* 12 (1977): 41–65.

Hatchett, Marion J. *Commentary on the American Prayer Book*. New York: Seabury Press, 1980.

Hatlie, Peter. *The Monks and Monasteries of Constantinople, ca. 350–850*. Cambridge: Cambridge University Press, 2007.

Hauréau, Jean Barthélemy. *Notices et extraits de quelques manuscrits Latins de la Bibliothèque Nationale, Tome I*. Paris: C. Klincksieck, 1890.

Hausherr, Irénée, ed. *Un grand mystique byzantine: Vie de Syméon le Nouveau Théologien*. Translated by Gabriel Horn. Rome: Pont. Institutum Orientalium Studiorum, 1928.

Heil, Günter, and Adolf Martin Ritter, eds. *Corpus Dionysiacum*. Vol. 2, *Pseudo-Dionysius Areopagita. De Coelesti Hierarchia, De Ecclesiastica Hierarchia, De Mystica Theologia, Epistulae*. Berlin: Walter de Gruyter, 1991.

Heimbach, Gustavus Ernestus, ed. *Authenticum: Novellarum constitutionum Iustiniani, Versio vulgata, Pars prior*. Leipzig, 1851.

Heppell, Muriel, trans. *The "Paterik" of the Kievan Caves Monastery*. Cambridge, MA: Harvard University Press, 1989.

Heussi, Karl. *Der Ursprung des Mönchtums*. Tübingen: Mohr, 1936.

Holl, Karl. "The History of the Word Vocation (*Beruf*)." *Review and Expositor* 55 (1958): 126–54.

Hunt, Hannah. "The Monk as Mourner: Gendered Eastern Christian Self-Identity in the Seventh Century." *Journal of Medieval Monastic Studies* 2 (2013): 19–37.

Hunter, David G. "Augustinian Pessimism? A New Look at Augustine's Teaching on Sex, Marriage and Celibacy." *Augustinian Studies* 25 (1994): 153–77.

———, trans. *A Comparison between a King and a Monk / Against the Opponents of the Monastic Life: Two Treatises by John Chrysostom.* Lewiston, NY: Edwin Mellen, 1988.

———. *Marriage, Celibacy, and Heresy in Ancient Christianity: The Jovinianist Controversy.* Oxford: Oxford University Press, 2007.

Ignatius of Loyola. *Spiritual Exercises and Selected Works.* Edited by George E. Ganss. Classics of Western Spirituality. New York: Paulist Press, 1991.

Jamison, Christopher, ed. *The Disciples' Call: Theologies of Vocation from Scripture to the Present Day.* London: Bloomsbury, 2013.

Jerome. *The Letters of St. Jerome.* Vol. 1. Translated by Charles Christopher Mierow. Ancient Christian Writers 33. New York: Newman, 1963.

Joest, Christoph. "Once Again: On the Origin of Christian Monasticism: Recent Historical and Exegetical Insights and a New Proposal with an Ecumenical Perspective." *American Benedictine Review* 61 (2010): 158–82.

John Chrysostom. *A Comparison between a King and a Monk / Against the Opponents of the Monastic Life: Two Treatises by John Chrysostom.* Translated by David G. Hunter. Lewiston, NY: Edwin Mellen, 1988.

John Climacus. *The Ladder of Ascent.* Translated by Colm Luibheid and Norman Russell. Classics of Western Spirituality. New York: Paulist Press, 1982.

Jorgensen, Allen. "Crux and Vocatio." *Scottish Journal of Theology* 62 (2009): 282–98.

Judge, E. A. "The Earliest Use of *Monachos* for 'Monk' (P. Coll. Youtie 77) and the Origins of Monasticism." *Jahrbuch für Antike und Christentum* 20 (1977): 73–89.

Kaelber, Lutz. *Schools of Asceticism: Ideology and Organization in Medieval Religious Communities.* University Park: Pennsylvania State University Press, 1998.

Kardong, Terrence G. *Benedict's Rule: A Translation and Commentary.* Collegeville, MN: Liturgical Press, 1996.

———. *The Life of St. Benedict by Gregory the Great: Translation and Commentary.* Collegeville, MN: Liturgical Press, 2009.

———. *Pillars of Community: Four Rules of Pre-Benedictine Monastic Life.* Collegeville, MN: Liturgical Press, 2010.

Kavanagh, Aidan. "Eastern Influences on the Rule of Saint Benedict." In *Monasticism and the Arts,* edited by Timothy Verdon, 53–62. Syracuse: Syracuse University Press, 1984.

Keating, James, ed. *Liturgy and Priestly Formation: Sharing the Life of Christ.* Omaha: IPF Publications, 2017.

Kenworthy, Scott M. *The Heart of Russia: Trinity-Sergius, Monasticism, and Society after 1825.* Washington, DC: Woodrow Wilson Center Press; New York: Oxford University Press, 2010.

Knöll, Pius, ed. *Sancti Avreli Avgvstini Confessionvm libri tredecim*. Vienna: F. Tempsky, 1896.

Koder, Johannes, ed. *Syméon le Nouveau Théologien: Hymnes 1–15*. Translated by Joseph Paramelle. Paris: Cerf, 1969.

———. *Syméon le Nouveau Théologien: Hymnes 16–40*. Translated by Louis Neyrand. Paris: Cerf, 1971.

Kollar, Rene. "'Punch' and the Nuns: Anti-Catholicism and Satire in Mid-Nineteenth Century England." *Downside Review* 160 (2012): 1–26.

Kooper, Erik. "Loving the Unequal Equal: Medieval Theologians and Marital Affection." In *The Olde Daunce: Love, Friendship, Sex, and Marriage in the Medieval World*, edited by Robert R. Edwards and Stephen Spector, 44–56. Albany: State University of New York Press, 1991.

Krailsheimer, A. J. *Rancé and the Trappist Legacy*. Kalamazoo, MI: Cistercian Publications, 1985.

Krivochéine, Basile, ed. *Syméon le Nouveau Théologien: Catéchèses 6–22*. Translated by Joseph Paramelle. Paris: Cerf, 1964.

Lake, Kirsopp, trans. *Eusebius: The Ecclesiastical History*. Vol. 1. Loeb Classical Library 153. Cambridge, MA: Harvard University Press, 1926.

Lavenant, René. "La lettre à Patricius d'Édesse de Philoxène de Mabboug. Édition critique du texte syriaque et traduction française." In *Patrologia Orientalis 30*, edited by François Graffin, 721–894. Paris: Firmin-Didot, 1963.

Lawless, George. *Augustine of Hippo and His Monastic Rule*. Oxford: Clarendon, 1987.

Leclercq, Jean. "Monasticism and Angelism." *Downside Review* 85 (1967): 127–37.

Leclercq, Jean, and H. M. Rochais, eds. *Sancti Bernardi Opera, Tomus III*. Rome: Editiones Cistercienses, 1963.

———. *Sancti Bernardi Opera, Tomus IV*. Rome: Editiones Cistercienses, 1966.

———. *Sancti Bernardi Opera, Tomus VI/1*. Rome: Editiones Cistercienses, 1970.

Leech, Kenneth. *Soul Friend: Spiritual Direction in the Modern World*. Harrisburg, PA: Morehouse, 2001.

Lehto, Adam. *The Demonstrations of Aphrahat, the Persian Sage*. Piscataway, NJ: Gorgias, 2010.

Lenker, John Nicholas, ed. *The Precious and Sacred Writings of Martin Luther*. Vol. 14. Minneapolis: Lutherans in All Lands, 1905.

Leyser, Conrad. *Authority and Asceticism from Augustine to Gregory the Great*. Oxford: Clarendon, 2000.

Little, Lester K. *Religious Poverty and the Profit Economy in Medieval Europe*. Ithaca, NY: Cornell University Press, 1978.

Louth, Andrew. *Denys the Areopagite*. Wilton, CT: Morehouse-Barlow, 1989.

———. *Introducing Eastern Orthodox Theology*. Downers Grove, IL: IVP Academic, 2013.

———. *Modern Orthodox Thinkers: From the* Philokalia *to the Present*. Downers Grove, IL: IVP Academic, 2015.

Luckman, Harriet A., and Linda Kulzer, eds. *Purity of Heart in Early Ascetic and Monastic Literature*. Collegeville, MN: Liturgical Press, 1999.

Lupton, J. H. *A Life of John Colet, D.D.* London: George Bell and Sons, 1909.

Luther, Martin. *The Christian in Society I*. Edited by James Atkinson. Vol. 44 of *Luther's Works*. Philadelphia: Fortress, 1966.

———. *Church and Ministry I*. Edited by Eric W. Gritsch. Vol. 39 of *Luther's Works*. Philadelphia: Fortress, 1970.

———. *Church and Ministry II*. Edited by Conrad Bergendoff. Vol. 40 of *Luther's Works*. Philadelphia: Muhlenberg, 1958.

———. *Commentaries on 1 Corinthians 7, 1 Corinthians 15, Lectures on 1 Timothy*. Edited by Hilton C. Oswald. Vol. 28 of *Luther's Works*. St. Louis: Concordia, 1973.

———. *Sermons on the Gospel of St. John, Chapters 14–16*. Edited by Jaroslav Pelikan. Vol. 24 of *Luther's Works*. St. Louis: Concordia, 1961.

———. *Treatise on Good Works*. Translated by Scott H. Hendrix. Minneapolis: Fortress, 2012.

———. *Word and Sacrament II*. Edited by Abdel Ross Wentz. Vol. 36 of *Luther's Works*. Philadelphia: Muhlenberg, 1959.

———. *Word and Sacrament III*. Edited by Robert H. Fischer. Vol. 37 of *Luther's Works*. Philadelphia: Muhlenberg, 1961.

Maguire, Nancy Klein. *An Infinity of Little Hours: Five Young Men and Their Trial of Faith in the Western World's Most Austere Monastic Order*. New York: Public Affairs, 2006.

Malone, Edward E. *The Monk and the Martyr: The Monk as the Successor of the Martyr*. Washington, DC: Catholic University of America Press, 1950.

Markus, Robert A. "Donatus, Donatism." In *Augustine through the Centuries: An Encyclopedia*, edited by Allan D. Fitzgerald, 284–87. Grand Rapids: Eerdmans, 1999.

Marrier, Martin, and André Duchesne, eds. *Bibliotheca Cluniacensis*. Paris, 1614.

Marriott, G. L. *Macarii Anecdota: Seven Unpublished Homilies of Macarius*. Cambridge, MA: Harvard University Press, 1918.

Martin, John Rupert. *The Illustration of the Heavenly Ladder of John Climacus*. Princeton: Princeton University Press, 1954.

Maximus the Confessor. *Selected Writings*. Translated by George C. Berthold. Classics of Western Spirituality. New York: Paulist Press, 1985.

McCreesh, T. "Heart." In *Collegeville Pastoral Dictionary of Biblical Theology*, edited by Carroll Stuhlmueller, 422–23. Collegeville, MN: Liturgical Press, 1995.

McGuckin, John. "The Notion of Luminous Vision in 11th Century Byzantium: Interpreting the Biblical and Theological Paradigms of St. Symeon the New Theologian." In *Work and Worship at the Theotokos Evergetis*, edited by Margaret Mullett, 90–123. Belfast: Queens University Press, 1997.

————. "Symeon the New Theologian's *Hymns of Divine Eros*: A Neglected Masterpiece of the Christian Mystical Tradition." *Spiritus* 5 (2005): 182–202.

McKenna, John H. *The Eucharistic Epiclesis: A Detailed History from the Patristic to the Modern Era*. 2nd ed. Chicago: Hillenbrand, 2009.

McNeill, John T., and Helena M. Gamer. *Medieval Handbooks of Penance: A Translation of the Principal* Libri poenitentiales *and Selections from Related Documents*. New York: Columbia University Press, 1990.

Merton, Thomas. *Thoughts in Solitude*. New York: Farrar, Straus & Giroux, 1958.

Methuen, Charlotte. "Preaching and the Shaping of Public Consciousness in Late Sixteenth-Century Tübingen: Martin Crusius' *Corona Anni*." *Zeitschrift für Kirchengeschichte* 123 (2012): 173–93.

Metropolitan Cyprian of Oropos and Fili. *The Monastic Life: A Most Beneficial Dialogue between an Orthodox Monk and a Contemporary Theologian*. Etna, CA: Center for Traditionalist Orthodox Studies, 1988.

Minnich, Nelson H. "The Priesthood of All Believers at the Council of Trent." *Jurist* 67 (2007): 341–63.

Morard, Françoise-E. "Monachos, Moine: Histoire du terme grec jusqu'au 4ᵉ siècle." *Freiburger Zeitschrift für Philosophie und Theologie* 20 (1973): 332–411.

Moreschini, Claudio, and Enrico Norelli. *Early Christian Greek and Latin Literature: A Literary History*. 2 vols. Translated by Matthew J. O'Connell. Peabody, MA: Hendrickson, 2005.

Mouw, Richard J. "Individualism and Christian Faith." *Theology Today* 38 (1982): 450–57.

Mudge, Bede Thomas. "Monastic Spirituality in Anglicanism." *Review for Religious* 37 (1978): 505–15.

Murray, Robert. *Symbols of Church and Kingdom: A Study in Early Syriac Tradition*. Rev. ed. London: T&T Clark, 2006.

Muthiah, Robert A. *The Priesthood of All Believers in the Twenty-First Century: Living Faithfully as the Whole People of God in a Postmodern Context*. Eugene, OR: Pickwick, 2009.

Nagel, Norman. "Luther and the Priesthood of All Believers." *Concordia Theological Quarterly* 61 (1997): 277–98.

Nicodemus of the Holy Mountain and Macarius of Corinth, eds. Φιλοκαλία τῶν ἱερῶν νηπτικῶν, Τόμος Γ. Athens: Astir, 1991.

Nietzsche, Friedrich. *On the Genealogy of Morals and Ecce Homo*. Edited by Walter Kaufmann. New York: Vintage Books, 1967.

Oakley, Francis. *The Conciliarist Tradition: Constitutionalism in the Catholic Church 1300–1870*. Oxford: Oxford University Press, 2003.

O'Day, Rosemary. *The Professions in Early Modern England 1450–1800: Servants of the Commonweal*. New York: Routledge, 2000.

Oexle, Otto Gerharde. "Tria genera hominum. Zur Geschichte eines Deutungsschemas der sozialen Wirklichkeit in Antike und Mittelalter." In *Institutionen, Kultur und Gesellschaft im Mittelalter, Festschrift für Josef Flechenstein zu seinem 65. Geburtstag*, edited by Lutz Fenske, Werner Rösener, and Thomas Zotz, 483–500. Sigmaringen: Jan Thorbecke, 1984.

Otten, Willemien. "Augustine on Marriage, Monasticism, and the Community of the Church." *Theological Studies* 59 (1998): 385–405.

Palladius. *The Lausiac History*. Translated by Robert T. Meyer. Westminster, MD: Newman, 1965.

———. *Palladius: Dialogue on the Life of St. John Chrysostom*. Translated and edited by Robert T. Meyer. Mahwah, NJ: Paulist Press, 1985.

Palmer, G. E. H., Philip Sherrard, and Kallistos Ware, trans. and ed. *The Philokalia: The Complete Text*. Vol. 3. London: Faber and Faber, 1984.

———. *The Philokalia: The Complete Text*. Vol. 4. London: Faber and Faber, 1995.

Panikkar, Raimon. *Blessed Simplicity: The Monk as Universal Archetype*. New York: Seabury Press, 1982.

———. "Christians and So-Called 'Non-Christians.'" *Cross Currents* 22 (1972): 281–308.

———. *Mysticism and Spirituality: Spirituality, The Way of Life*. Vol. 1.2 of *Opera Omnia*. Edited by Milena Carrara Pavan. Maryknoll, NY: Orbis Books, 2014.

Pauley, John-Bede. "The Implication of Monastic Qualities on the Pastoral Provision for the 'Anglican Use.'" *Antiphon* 10 (2006): 261–76.

Peifer, Claude J. *Monastic Spirituality*. New York: Sheed and Ward, 1966.

Percival, John. "Villas and Monasteries in Later Roman Gaul." *Journal of Ecclesiastical History* 48 (1997): 1–21.

Peters, Greg. "Coenobitism." In *The Oxford Dictionary of the Middle Ages*, edited by Robert E. Bjork, vol. 2, *C–J*, 418. Oxford: Oxford University Press, 2010.

———. "Monastic Orders." In *Encyclopedia of Christian Civilization*, edited by G. T. Kurian, 3:1551–55. Oxford: Wiley-Blackwell, 2011.

———. "Monasticism." In *Zondervan Dictionary of Christian Spirituality*, edited by Glen G. Scorgie, 618–20. Grand Rapids: Zondervan, 2011.

———. "Monasticism: Instrument of the Holy Spirit in the Renewal, Revival and Revitalization of Today's Church." In *The Holy Spirit and the Christian Life*, edited by Wolfgang Vondey, 41–57. New York: Palgrave Macmillan, 2014.

———. *Reforming the Monastery: Protestant Theologies of the Religious Life*. Eugene, OR: Cascade Books, 2014.

―――. *The Story of Monasticism: Retrieving an Ancient Tradition for Contemporary Spirituality*. Grand Rapids: Baker Academic, 2015.

Petschenig, Michael, and Gottfried Kreuz, eds. *Collationes XIIII*. Vienna: Verlag der Österreichischen Akademie der Wissenschaften, 2004.

―――, eds. *De Institutis Coenobiorum / De Incarnatione contra Nestorium*. Vienna: Verlag der Österreichischen Akademie der Wissenschaften, 2004.

Phan, Cho Dinh. "Evdokimov and the Monk Within." *Sobornost* 3 (1981): 53–61.

―――. "Mariage, monachisme et eschatalogie: Contribution de Paul Evdokimov à la spiritualité Chrétienne." *Ephemerides Liturgicae* 93 (1979): 352–80.

Philo of Alexandria. *The Contemplative Life; The Giants; and, Selections*. Translated by David Winston. Classics of Western Spirituality. New York: Paulist Press, 1981.

―――. *Philo*. Vol. 9, *Every Good Man Is Free. On the Contemplative Life. On the Eternity of the World. Against Flaccus. Apology for the Jews. On Providence*. Translated by F. H. Colson. Loeb Classical Library 363. Cambridge, MA: Harvard University Press, 1954.

Placher, William C., ed. *Callings: Twenty Centuries of Christian Wisdom on Vocation*. Grand Rapids: Eerdmans, 2005.

Plato. *Complete Works*. Edited by John M. Cooper. Indianapolis: Hackett, 1997.

Plekon, Michael. "'Interiorized Monasticism': A Reconsideration of Paul Evdokimov on the Spiritual Life." *American Benedictine Review* 48 (1997): 227–53.

―――. "Monasticism in the Marketplace, the Monastery, the World, and Within: An Eastern Church Perspective." *Cistercian Studies Quarterly* 34, no. 3 (1999): 339–68.

―――. "Paul Evdokimov, a Theologian within and beyond the Church and the World." *Modern Theology* 12 (1996): 85–107.

Posnock, Ross. *Renunciation: Acts of Abandonment by Writers, Philosophers, and Artists*. Cambridge, MA: Harvard University Press, 2016.

Postles, Dave. "Augustinian Canons." In *Encyclopedia of Monasticism*, edited by William M. Johnston, vol. 1, *A–L*, 101–3. Chicago: Fitzroy Dearborn, 2000.

Pseudo-Dionysius. *The Complete Works*. Translated by Colm Luibheid. Classics of Western Spirituality. New York: Paulist Press, 1987.

Ramsey, Ann W. "Flagellation and the French Counter-Reformation: Asceticism, Social Discipline, and the Evolution of a Penitential Culture." In *Asceticism*, edited by Vincent L. Wimbush and Richard Valantasis, 576–87. Oxford: Oxford University Press, 1998.

Relations de la mort de quelques Religieux de l'Abbaye de la Trappe. Nouvelle edition, augmentée de plusieurs vies qui n'avoient pas encore paru, avec une description abrégée de cette abbaye. Paris: G. Desprez, 1755.

Reuver, Arie de. *Sweet Communion: Trajectories of Spirituality from the Middle Ages through the Further Reformation*. Grand Rapids: Baker Academic, 2007.

Robinson, I. S. "Church and Papacy." In *The Cambridge History of Medieval Political Thought c. 350–c. 1450*, edited by J. H. Burns, 252–305. Cambridge: Cambridge University Press, 1988.

Roques, René. "Éléments pour une théologie de l'état monastique selon Denys l'Aréopagite." In *Théologie de la vie monastique: Études sur la Tradition patristique*, 283–314. Paris: Aubier, 1961.

Rorem, Paul. *Biblical and Liturgical Symbols within the Pseudo-Dionysian Synthesis.* Toronto: Pontifical Institute for Mediaeval Studies, 1984.

———. *Pseudo-Dionysius: A Commentary on the Texts and an Introduction to Their Influence.* New York: Oxford University Press, 1993.

Rosser, Gervase. *The Art of Solidarity in the Middle Ages: Guilds in England 1250–1550.* Oxford: Oxford University Press, 2015.

Rubenson, Samuel. *The Letters of St. Antony: Monasticism and the Making of a Saint.* Minneapolis: Fortress, 1995.

Rutba House, The, ed. *School(s) for Conversion: 12 Marks of a New Monasticism.* Eugene, OR: Cascade, 2005.

Schmemann, Alexander. "The Mission of Orthodoxy." Accessed March 9, 2018. http://www.peterandpaul.net/schmemann-missionoforthodoxy.

Schürer, Emil. *The History of the Jewish People in the Age of Jesus Christ (175 B.C.–A.D. 135).* Vol. 2. Edinburgh: T&T Clark, 1979.

Schuurman, Douglas J. *Vocation: Discerning Our Callings in Life.* Grand Rapids: Eerdmans, 2004.

Sedgefield, Walter John. *King Alfred's Version of the Consolations of Boethius.* Oxford: Clarendon, 1900.

Sempé, L. "Vocation." In *Dictionnaire de Théologie Catholique, Tome Quinzième, Deuxième Partie: Trinité - Zwinglianisme*, edited by A. Vacant et al., 3148–81. Paris: Librairie Letouzey et Ané, 1950.

Sheldrake, Philip. *A Brief History of Spirituality.* Malden, MA: Blackwell, 2007.

Shepherd, Massey Hamilton. *The Oxford American Prayer Book Commentary.* New York: Oxford University Press, 1950.

Sheridan, Mark. "Early Egyptian Monasticism: Ideals and Reality, or, The Shaping of the Monastic Ideal." *Journal of the Canadian Society for Coptic Studies* 7 (2015): 9–24.

Silvas, Anna M. *The Asketikon of St Basil the Great.* Oxford: Oxford University Press, 2005.

Smith, James K. A. *Desiring the Kingdom: Worship, Worldview, and Cultural Formation.* Grand Rapids: Baker Academic, 2009.

———. *You Are What You Love: The Spiritual Power of Habit.* Grand Rapids: Brazos, 2016.

Smither, Edward L. *Missionary Monks: An Introduction to the History and Theology of Missionary Monasticism*. Eugene, OR: Cascade Books, 2016.

Sorg, Rembert. *Holy Work: Towards a Benedictine Theology of Manual Labor*. St. Louis: Pio Decimo, 1953.

Stählin, Otto, ed. *Clemens Alexandrinus, Erster Band: Protrepticus und Paedagogus*. Leipzig: J. C. Hinrichs'sche Buchhandlung, 1905.

Stewart, Columba. *Cassian the Monk*. Oxford: Oxford University Press, 1998.

———. "The Origins and Fate of Monasticism." *Spiritus* 10 (2010): 257–64.

Stoop, E. de, ed. "Vie d'Alexandre l'Acémète." In *Patrologia Orientalis*, Tomus Sextus, edited by R. Graffin and F. Nau, 645–705. Paris: Firmin-Didot, 1911.

Strenger, Carlo, and Arie Ruttenberg. "The Existential Necessity of Midlife Change." *Harvard Business Review* 86, no. 2 (February 2008): 83–90.

Suchla, Beata Regina. *Corpus Dionysiacum*. Vol. 1, *Pseudo-Dionysius Areopagita. De Divinis Nominibus*. Berlin: Walter de Gruyter, 1990.

Swanson, Robert N. "Apostolic Successors: Priests and Priesthood, Bishops, and Episcopacy in Medieval Western Europe." In *A Companion to Priesthood and Holy Orders in the Middle Ages*, edited by Greg Peters and C. Colt Anderson, 4–42. Leiden: Brill, 2016.

———, trans. *Catholic England: Faith, Religion and Observance before the Reformation*. Manchester: Manchester University Press, 1993.

———. *Religion and Devotion in Europe, c. 1215–c. 1515*. Cambridge: Cambridge University Press, 1995.

Symeon the New Theologian. *The Discourses*. Translated by C. J. deCatanzaro. Classics of Western Spirituality. New York: Paulist Press, 1980.

———. *Divine Eros: Hymns of St. Symeon the New Theologian*. Translated by Daniel K. Griggs. Crestwood, NY: St. Vladimir's Seminary Press, 2010.

———. *Hymns of Divine Love*. Translated by George A. Maloney. Denville, NJ: Dimension Books, n.d.

———. *On the Mystical Life: The Ethical Discourses*. Vol. 1, *The Church and the Last Things*. Translated by Alexander Golitzin. Crestwood, NY: St. Vladimir's Seminary Press, 1995.

Tabacco, Giovanni, ed. *Petri Damiani: Vita Beati Romualdi*. Rome, 1957.

Taft, Robert. *The Liturgy of the Hours in East and West: The Origins of the Divine Office and Its Meaning for Today*. 2nd rev. ed. Collegeville, MN: Liturgical Press, 1993.

Talbot, Alice-Mary, and Robert F. Taft. "Akoimetoi, Monastery of." In *Oxford Dictionary of Byzantium*, edited by Alexaner P. Kazhdan and Alice-Marie Talbot, 1:46. New York: Oxford University Press, 1991.

Tanner, Norman P., ed. *Decrees of the Ecumenical Councils*. 2 vols. Washington, DC: Georgetown University Press, 1990.

Tetz, Martin. "Eine asketische Ermunterung zur Standhaftigkeit aus der Zeit der maximinischen Verfolgung (311/313)." *Zeitschrift für die Neutestamentliche Wissenschaft* 81 (1990): 79–102.

Thomas, Hugh M. *The Secular Clergy in England, 1066–1216.* Oxford: Oxford University Press, 2014.

Thomas à Kempis. *The Imitation of Christ.* Translated by Leo Sherley-Price. London: Penguin Books, 1952.

Thomas Aquinas. *Summa Theologica.* Translated by Fathers of the English Dominican Province. 5 vols. Westminster, MD: Christian Classics, 1948.

Tinnefeld, Franz. "Praepositus." In *Brill's New Pauly: Encyclopedia of the Ancient World,* edited by Hubert Cancik and Helmuth Schneider, 11:767. Leiden: Brill, 2007.

Turner, H. J. M. *St. Symeon the New Theologian and Spiritual Fatherhood.* Leiden: Brill, 1990.

Urbinati, Nadia. *The Tyranny of the Moderns.* New Haven: Yale University Press, 2015.

Veilleux, Armand. *La liturgie dans le cénobitisme pachômien au quatrième siècle.* Rome: Pontificium Institutum S. Anselmi / I.B.C. Libreria Herder, 1968.

———, trans. *Pachomian Koinonia.* Vol. 2, *Pachomian Chronicles and Rules.* Kalamazoo, MI: Cistercian Publications, 1981.

Venarde, Bruce L., trans. *Robert of Arbrissel: A Medieval Religious Life.* Washington, DC: Catholic University of America Press, 2003.

Verger, J. "R. de Sorbon." In *Lexikon des Mittelalters VII: Planudes bis Stadt (Rus'),* edited by Robert Auty et al., 911–12. Munich: Lexma Verlag, 1995.

Verheijen, Luc. "L'*Enarratio in Psalmum* 132 de saint Augustin et sa conception du monachisme." In *Forma futuri: studi in onore del cardinale Michele Pellegrino,* 806–17. Torino: Bottega d'Erasmo, 1975.

———. *Saint Augustine's Monasticism in the Light of Acts 4:32–35.* Villanova, PA: Villanova University Press, 1979.

Vermes, Geza. *Post-Biblical Jewish Studies.* Leiden: Brill, 1975.

Vivian, Tim, Kim Vivian, and Jeffrey Burton Russell, trans. *The Life of the Jura Fathers: The Life and Rule of the Holy Fathers Romanus, Lupicinus, and Eugendus, Abbots of the Monasteries in the Jura Mountains.* With the assistance of Charles Cummings. Kalamazoo, MI: Cistercian Publications, 1999.

Vogüé, Adalbert de. *La règle de Saint Benoît, Tome V: Commentaire historique et critique (Parties IV-VI).* Paris: Cerf, 1971.

———. "Monachisme et Église dans la pensée de Cassien." In *Théologie de la vie monastique: Études sur la Tradition patristique,* 213-40. Paris: Aubier, 1961.

Vööbus, Arthur. *History of Asceticism in the Syrian Orient: A Contribution to the History of Culture in the Near East.* 2 vols. Louvain: Secrétariat du CorpusSCO, 1958–60.

———. "The Origin of Monasticism in Mesopotamia." *Church History* 20 (1951): 27–37.

Waddell, Helen, trans. *The Desert Fathers*. Ann Arbor, MI: Ann Arbor Paperbacks, 1957.

Ward, Benedicta, trans. *The Sayings of the Desert Fathers: The Alphabetical Collection*. Kalamazoo, MI: Cistercian Publications, 1975.

Ware, Kallistos [Timothy]. "The Monk and the Married Christian: Some Comparisons in Early Monastic Sources." *Eastern Churches Review* 6 (1974): 72–83.

———. *The Orthodox Church*. New ed. London: Penguin Books, 1993.

———. "The Spiritual Father in Orthodox Christianity." *Cross Currents* (1974): 296–313.

———. "The Way of the Ascetics: Negative or Affirmative?" In *Asceticism*, edited by Vincent L. Wimbush and Richard Valantasis, 3–15. Oxford: Oxford University Press, 1998.

Watson, Richard, ed. *A Biblical and Theological Dictionary: Explanatory of the History, Manners, and Customs of the Jews, and Neighbouring Nations*. New York: B. Waugh and T. Mason, 1832.

Watt, Archibald. *The Priesthood of All Believers*. Edinburgh: The Saint Andrew Press, 1960.

Weber, Max. *The Protestant Ethic and the Spirit of Capitalism*. Oxford: Oxford University Press, 2011.

Whitelock, D., M. Brett, and C. N. L. Brooke, eds. *Councils and Synods with Other Documents Relating to the English Church*, vol. 1, *A.D. 871–1204*. Oxford: Clarendon, 1981.

Wilhoit, James C., and Evan B. Howard. *Discovering Lectio Divina: Bringing Scripture into Ordinary Life*. Downers Grove, IL: IVP Books, 2012.

William of Saint-Thierry, Arnold of Bonneval, and Geoffrey of Auxerre. *The First Life of Bernard of Clairvaux*. Translated by Hilary Costello. Athens, OH: Cistercian Publications; Collegeville, MN: Liturgical Press, 2015.

Williams, D. H., ed. *The Free Church and the Early Church: Bridging the Historical and Theological Divide*. Grand Rapids: Eerdmans, 2002.

———. *Retrieving the Tradition and Renewing Evangelicalism: A Primer for Suspicious Protestants*. Grand Rapids: Eerdmans, 1999.

Williams, Megan Hale. *The Monk and the Book: Jerome and the Making of Christian Scholarship*. Chicago: University of Chicago Press, 2006.

Wilson, H. A., ed. *The Gelasian Sacramentary: Liber sacramentorum Romanae ecclesia*. Oxford: Clarendon, 1894.

———. *The Gregorian Sacramentary under Charles the Great*. London: Harrison and Sons, 1915.

Wilson-Hartgrove, Jonathan. *New Monasticism: What It Has to Say to Today's Church*. Grand Rapids: Brazos, 2008.

Wimbush, Vincent L., and Richard Valantasis, eds. *Asceticism*. Oxford: Oxford University Press, 1998.

Windeatt, Barry, ed. *English Mystics of the Middle Ages*. Cambridge: Cambridge University Press, 1994.

Wingren, Gustaf. *The Christian's Calling: Luther on Vocation*. Edinburgh: Oliver and Boyd, 1957.

Winston, David, trans. *Philo of Alexandria: The Contemplative Life; The Giants; and, Selections*. Classics of Western Spirituality. New York: Paulist Press, 1981.

Worp, K. A. "Marginalia on Published Documents." *Zeitschrift für Papyrologie und Epigraphik* 78 (1989): 133–38.

Yarnell, Malcolm B., III. *Royal Priesthood in the English Reformation*. Oxford: Oxford University Press, 2013.

Zakar, Polycarpe. *Histoire de la stricte observance de l'ordre cistercien depuis ses débuts au généralat du cardinal de Richelieu (1606–1635)*. Roma: Editiones Cistercienses, 1966.

Zenkovsky, Serge A., ed. *Medieval Russia: Epics, Chronicles, and Tales*. New York: Meridian, 1974.

Ziolkowski, Margaret. *Hagiography and Modern Russian Literature*. Princeton: Princeton University Press, 1988.

INDEX